Three Visionary Screenplays

Three Visionary Screenplays

Bruce Joel Rubin

Sticking Place Books
New York

Also by Bruce Joel Rubin
It's Only a Movie

© Sticking Place Books 2024
Cover image by Bruce Joel Rubin

www.brucejoelrubin.com
www.stickingplacebooks.com

All rights reserved.
No part of this book may be reproduced, stored in or introduced into a retrieval system, or transmitted, in any form or by any means (electronic, mechanical, photocopying, recording or otherwise) without the written permission of the publishers, except in the case of brief quotations embodied in critical articles or reviews.

ISBN 978-1-942782-57-5

CONTENTS

Foreword by Joseph Maddrey   vii

Introduction   xi

Quasar   1

Teratoma   133

Secrets of the Astral Plane   323

Foreword

by Joseph Maddrey

Bruce Joel Rubin is best known as the Oscar-winning screenwriter of the blockbuster romance *Ghost* (1990), the mind-bending horror film *Jacob's Ladder* (1990), and the sci-fi cult classic *Brainstorm* (1983). If he had written only those three films and no others, he would have secured a place in film history.

Bruce's personal journey began in earnest in the summer of 1965 with a massive overdose of LSD. Until then, he had been a film student at NYU with big ambitions but one problem: he didn't have a story to tell. A chemically-induced trip through Jung's collective unconscious transformed him, providing an expanded sense of "reality" and sending him on an exploration of spiritual teachings from across the world and throughout history. It also gave him a story to tell – or, rather, a series of stories with a common theme.

For fifty years, Bruce's work has explored metaphysics and mystical ideas with a seriousness that is rare in Hollywood. For every script produced, he wrote several that didn't make it to the silver screen. Now, three of those lost stories – each one a counterpart, in a way, to Bruce's three most famous works, and the mythic journey behind them – have a chance to shine.

Quasar, *Teratoma* and *Secrets of the Astral Plane* can be read as spiritual twins of *Brainstorm*, *Jacob's Ladder* and *Ghost*, respectively. Taken together, these six stories reflect an evolving perspective on the mysteries of life, death and rebirth, as well as American culture and cinema in the 1970s and 1980s.

Quasar, co-written in 1970 with experimental filmmaker David Bienstock, is in many ways a successor to Stanley Kubrick's *2001: A Space Odyssey*, which raised the bar for science fiction cinema. Like Kubrick, Rubin and Bienstock wanted to do more than entertain; they wanted to make a film that would awaken audiences to an expanded reality.

The script follows a scientist named Stuart Townley, whose discovery of a quasi-stellar object alters his consciousness. Convinced that he has witnessed "the moment of creation itself," the Big Bang, he embarks on a journey into a deeper understanding of time, mind and the meaning of human life. The story ends with a premonition that the entire culture is about to be transformed in the same way. *Quasar* could have been an epic paean to the '60s, but by the time it was written, the decade was over.

Bruce spent the next several years writing and developing *The George Dunlap Tape*, a screenplay about a scientist who invents an empathy machine that enables one person to share another's thoughts, feelings and experiences – even death. This script also fell by the wayside. Channeling the darker spirit of the late '70s, several new writers turned *George Dunlap* into *Brainstorm*, while Bruce explored different demons in a new pair of scripts.

In 1977, he made a vow to write a full script during one week alone in a hotel room. The result was *Teratoma*, a body horror film about a viral outbreak that heralds something much stranger. To reveal more of the story would dilute the impact of a first reading. Suffice to say that *Teratoma* is as harrowing and provocative as the early films of David Cronenberg, but with a metaphysical twist that only Bruce Rubin could have conceived. Horror fans might perceive similarities to several contemporary films – *The Crazies* (1973), *It's Alive* (1974), *Shivers* (1975), *God Told Me To* (1976), *Eraserhead* (1977), *Invasion of the Body Snatchers* (1978), even *Alien* (1979) – but there has never been a film quite like *Teratoma*.

Bruce followed up with an even more audacious horror script about one man's journey through hell (or, more accurately, the Tibetan Bardo of Becoming). In the early 1980s, many Hollywood insiders regarded *Jacob's Ladder* as one of the best unproduced screenplays around. At that time, nobody wanted to take a chance on filming it.

In 1982, Bruce returned to the creative well, drawing on experiences he had in the wake of his LSD trip to produce *Secrets of the Astral Plane*, about a young man who suffers a traumatic injury that awakens an ability to project his disembodied spirit around the world. While struggling to understand his new power without alienating the woman he loves, he finds himself at the center of a secret war between Soviet spies and a ragtag team of American psychics. It's a script that speaks to the romantic and often zany cinema of the early 1980s, reminiscent of films like *WarGames* and *Dreamscape*.

Unfortunately, *Secrets of the Astral Plane* remained secret. Hollywood executives probably thought a story about psychics and astral travel was too esoteric to be commercially viable. At least, that's the reaction Bruce received when he pitched his next movie idea: a love story between a ghost and a woman who doesn't believe in ghosts. It wasn't until 1990 that *Ghost* finally made it to the big screen. After that, Bruce's screenwriting career took off and he didn't look back.

Until now…

Introduction

by Bruce Joel Rubin

In 1965, when I was 23 years old, I mistakenly took a massive overdose of pure LSD from a bottle making its way to Timothy Leary from its creator, Albert Hoffman, in Sandoz Laboratories, Switzerland. Needless to say, my life was radically changed.

Everything I knew up to that moment was dramatically altered by an expansive awareness that couldn't be explained in any conceptual reality I had known up to that moment. The experience was timeless, although it seemed to last billions of years. In the end I was certain that I was dead. And then my oceanic unborn self felt suddenly impregnated by an unseen force, and without explanation my long forgotten body rematerialized, molecule by molecule, along with the room I had been lying in. I was back.

I began roaring with laughter and asked out loud why I had been brought back to life. To my amazement, a Voice answered as if the entirety of space was speaking to me. "To tell people what you saw," it said. Those were my marching orders. There was one core problem: I had no idea what I had seen. I had somehow touched the Infinite, but I was clueless.

Gradually I began to find words for what had happened to me, often defined in spiritual realms as a mystical experience. I still had no idea how to contextualize or even understand it, so I began a journey lasting a year and a half, hitchhiking around the world, trying to find a teacher or guru who might help me grasp the ungraspable. I did eventually find that teacher, but only after I returned to America.

As I began to intuit the massive and infinite depth of what I had seen, I started to experience an enormous sense of obligation to share that vision with others, still with little idea of actually how to do it. I had gone to film school at New York University and had become a film editor at NBC News in New York City and then a film curator at the Whitney Museum of American Art, where I co-ran a program called The

New American Filmmakers Series with a dear friend, David Bienstock, who had created the series. David knew I wanted to be a screenwriter but that I was struggling to find my voice, so he offered to help. I had come up with the idea for a film I called *Quasar*, about an astronomer who discovers what he thinks is a massive black hole and then comes to realize that he has in fact found the original Big Bang itself, the very creation of the universe. The story is an attempt to see how his discovery anticipates a total transformation of the human race as his mind/body experience undergoes much of what I had witnessed on LSD.

    David and I worked hard on the script during our time at the Whitney. It was a steep learning curve for me. In truth, neither of us knew much about storytelling and screenwriting. Over two years and many failed drafts, we arrived at a version of the script that we felt was presentable. When Ingo Preminger, fresh from producing *M*A*S*H*, wanted to buy a two-year option on it, we were elated. Naively, I said he could have it for only three months. During that period, he had time to show *Quasar* to only one studio, Warner Bros., which turned it down because they didn't understand the ending. David and I offered to do a rewrite, but Warners' response was a fatal blow. We were innocent and unable to get anyone else interested, so the script went onto a shelf, where it has sat for fifty years. When I read it again recently, I was surprised to see how relevant the story is today, its unproduceable ending more impactful and enduring than I had imagined. Does it need work? Sure. But it contains the seeds of a remarkable movie that suggests the drama of many of my produced movies that followed.

    A few years later, when I was living in an ashram with my wife and young son in Bloomington, Indiana, and working a full-time job, I had a desperate need to jump-start my screenwriting career. I decided to take a week, lock myself in a hotel room, put the TV in the closet, and not leave until I had a finished script sitting beside me. I had read something in the newspaper about a strange form of cancer called a "teratoma," a bizarre tumor that mimics body parts – fingernails and eyeballs – and grows inside the human body. Somehow I thought there was a horror film in that. My wife and son brought meals to the room and I worked day and night. In the end, the horror aspect evolved into something shockingly unexpected, and I couldn't type fast enough. Somehow, I walked out of that room eleven days later with *Teratoma*. Scary as it was, it turned out not to be a horror film, and the fact that it somehow transcended genres made it hard to sell. It joined *Quasar* on my bookshelf. Not long ago, I read *Teratoma* for the first time in decades. With its sense of a pandemic universe, I was bowled over by its prescience. I wonder if the time for this story hasn't finally arrived.

I wrote *Secrets of the Astral Plane* before *Ghost*, and in many ways it paved the road for the film that won me an Oscar. For several years after my LSD journey, I had a series of episodes known as "astral projections." I had never heard of them before. Finding myself lying paralyzed in my bed, my body would begin shaking. I was suddenly propelled out of my body and began floating above it. I didn't know such things were possible. At first it was terrifying, but eventually I was able to tell when it was about to happen and I gradually relaxed into the experience. I learned how to hover, float and fly around the room. I even learned how to fly out the window (it didn't need to be open) and soar over Manhattan. One night I decided to fly toward the moon and arrived faster than I could imagine. In seconds I was flying through the universe. The Earth and the Moon dwindled into a massive galactic vision and I lost sight of my home planet. At that moment of terror, I shot back into my body and sat up, panting uncontrollably.

I somehow managed to resist ever taking another astral flight after that. I did once attend a class of astral projectors, a bizarre group of people. I found them all confused, unable to put their experiences into context, and many with god complexes who wanted to take control of the universe. *Secrets of the Astral Plane* is about a small group, a kind of *Dirty Dozen* of gifted psychics, on a mission to save the world. A number of Hollywood executives embraced the script, but no one was willing to shell out the vast budget that such an effects-laden film required.

There are, as you can imagine, many unproduced screenplays on my shelves, along with a collection of scripts that were filmed and made it into theaters worldwide. The stories in this book are a look into the early stages of what might have followed. I think they are entertaining, inspiring, terrifying and fun. And who knows… one day they may even show up in a theater near you.

Bruce Joel Rubin
Red Hook, New York
May 2023

In each case,
these scripts have been reproduced
as originally formatted.

Quasar

David Bienstock
and
Bruce Rubin

People are standing in lines. They are waiting in department stores and restaurants, at bus stops and supermarkets, in front of movie theaters. Everyone seems quiet and complacent, hardly aware of being on line. The lines grow. There is a sense of anxiety in the waiting. The lines move slowly past cashiers and ticket takers. They are kept moving. The texture of the lines changes. The people seem more distracted, older and sadder. There appears to be nothing but these lines and nowhere else for anyone to be. The lines now go beyond the commonplace merging into one continuous stream of people. Like a column of insects they move slowly onward, their eyes glazed and unseeing. The line travels through a dark and narrow passageway that suddenly expands into a giant, sunlit corridor with vast granite walls towering on either side. A massive black opening appears far in the distance at what seems to be the end of the corridor. It grows more fearsome and menacing as we approach it. One by one the people in front of the line are taken through a dark archway into the base of the gigantic structure. It is obvious that what they see on the other side is completely traumatic. Some scream and cry like children. The sense of terror grows more intense as the viewer approaches the opening. The woman directly in front of us turns around to scream, but it is a soundless cry. It is her turn and she enters. The fear finally breaks from her throat. The camera stares into blackness. Suddenly we too are moved through the opening. What we see is complicated in its construction and terrifying in its effect. Two women are joined together with nooses around their necks. There is a loud gasp as they see each other. Lying before them is a great abyss. Stretching across it into the blackness are two thin tightrope wires. Between the wires and running parallel to them is a long stiff pole. The women are made to walk across the wires on either side of the pole. It is obvious that if one of them should lose her balance, both would fall and be hung. They step cautiously onto the wires. They stare madly, ferociously at each other as they inch their way across. It is impossible to tell if the tightrope ever ends. One of the women rocks to her left. The other tries to counterbalance but slips, and the two bodies fall crashing into one another, their necks broken. As the camera peers dizzyingly down we realize that the abyss is an unending vortex of countless tightropes and victims, above and below, with bodies walking, falling and hanging. The line ends in a paranoid vision of inescapable death.

Stuart Townley, in his middle forties, is lying in bed. His eyes are wide open and very still. His face is pale. Slowly his gaze begins to move around the room. He glances at the empty pillow beside him. He stares at it for a moment and then sits up. He seems lost in thought. He looks over at the clock. It is ten after four. Slowly he gets out of bed and walks to the window. He raises the dark shade and his image nearly disappears in the intensity of the late afternoon sunlight. The alarm rings but Stuart doesn't hear it. There are footsteps and a door opening. The alarm stops. Stuart suddenly turns around and sees his wife. There is a tender concern on her face.

>   ELLEN
>   (*Speaking softly.*)
> Another dream? (*He nods his head.*) As bad
> as before?

>   STUART
> Worse. They're not even like dreams
> anymore. They're almost real, Ellen.

>   ELLEN
>   (*Concerned, as she walks over
>   to Stuart and hugs him.*)
> Why don't we go away Stuart? Joan said we
> could use their cottage whenever we wanted
> to. I think you need the rest.

>   STUART
> I know I need it... But how?

>   ELLEN
> Maybe if things slow down?

>   STUART
> Maybe. (*There is a long pause.*)

>   ELLEN
> Stuart... (*She looks at him tenderly.*)

Stuart smiles softly and embraces her. They kiss for a moment and then gently separate. Ellen begins to unbutton Stuart's pajamas.

ELLEN
I think a cold shower will do wonders for your head.

STUART
You do, do you?

ELLEN
And there'll be a cup of hot coffee waiting when you get out.

STUART
I'll probably need ten of them to thaw me out.

ELLEN
All you want. But hurry.

He walks to the bathroom and turns on the shower.

Stuart is sitting in the breakfast nook of a comfortable suburban kitchen. Ellen pours him a glass of orange juice as he reaches for the morning newspaper. There is a quizzical expression on his face as he stares at the front page. He turns quickly to the second section and looks at it with the same confusion. He begins leafing quickly through the pages.

STUART
Ellen, this is yesterday's paper.

ELLEN
(*Absentmindedly.*)
Oh, I'm sorry. (*She goes to look for the morning paper, then remembers.*) Oh Stuart... (*Her tone is mildly joking.*) How about reading that one again?

STUART
Ellen, what happened to the paper?

ELLEN
We needed it for the sit-in… (*Stuart looks at her.*) At the supermarket. I told you.

STUART
You had to take my paper?

ELLEN
Caroline forgot hers. We had to sit on something.

STUART
(*Exasperated.*)
Ellen!

ELLEN
I'm sorry, but it was important. Besides, we won. They took all the grapes off the shelf.

STUART
Damn it Ellen, how can I eat breakfast without the newspaper?

ELLEN
It's been done.

STUART
Very funny. Is there anything else I can read?

ELLEN
Yes, in fact. It came this morning. From Mickey.

STUART
You're kidding. A letter? (*He reads it silently.*) That's it? (*He looks for another page. He reads aloud.*) "Dear Mommy and Daddy. I got poison ivy on my legs. Please

send me $5 for a leather kit. Love Mickey."
Brilliant.

ELLEN
Well, what do you expect? (*Stuart doesn't answer and continues eating. Ellen comes over to him.*) Nervous?

STUART
No.

ELLEN
(*Looking up at the clock.*)
Hey, you better hurry. (*He looks at his watch and quickly sips down his coffee.*) Think we'll ever get a chance to spend some time together?

STUART
I'll try and get home early.

ELLEN
Before or after the sun comes up?

STUART
Don't be cynical.

ELLEN
Who? Me? What time's the interview? Six?

STUART
Six-fifteen.

Stuart leaves to put on a tie and suit jacket. Ellen finishes cleaning the table.

ELLEN
(*Calling out.*)
Oh Stu, I forgot. The television is really getting worse.

> STUART
> Well, call the repair man and have him come over tomorrow morning. And if he decides he has to fix it, get an estimate first.

> ELLEN
> (*Looking pleased.*)
> O.K. Wait, Stuart!

> STUART
> What? I'm late.

> ELLEN
> Wear a bright tie – it's in color.

> STUART
> (*Smiling.*)
> Thanks.

Stuart leaves his home in a relatively plush suburb of Los Angeles and begins driving to Television City in Hollywood. All the dreariness of Southern California gas station culture is evident as he speeds past flashy old ladies in chartreuse jax slacks and advertisements for $289 burials in Forest Lawn. His car moves from tree-lined streets into flat, four-lane avenues and onto the vast network of freeways. Evening rush hour traffic has slowed to a crawl and Stuart grows increasingly impatient. He stares at the people trapped in their cars around him. To his left, barely moving, is a long military convoy looking strangely out of place. The men sitting in the backs of the trucks seem hot and restless. The cars inch forward. Stuart turns on his radio for a traffic report and hears of an accident ahead with cars tied up for miles. There is a slight static hum on the radio and Stuart turns it off. He glances at his watch and exits at the first ramp he comes to. Cut to Stuart pulling quickly into the TV studio parking lot and hurrying to the door. Gerald Cooper, a Hugh Downs-type newscaster, is waiting for him in the reception area.

> COOPER
> Dr. Townley.

                    STUART
             Mr. Cooper. (*They shake hands.*) I hope I'm
             not late.

                    COOPER
             Not really. We have about ten minutes. We
             start taping as soon as the six o'clock report
             goes off the air.

They walk down a long hall and toward the color studios. We cut to
the control room, where the engineers are scanning the master control
panel and various TV monitors. The six o'clock news is in progress. The
actual news broadcast is intercut with shots of the engineers and Stuart
talking with Gerald Cooper preparing for the interview. Even when our
attention is pulled away from it, the news program is constantly in the
background.

                    STUART
             (*Pulling on a cigarette.*)
             It doesn't matter how many times I've gone
             through this, I still get nervous.

COOPER	
I'll tell you something. So do I (*They enter the control room. The engineers are arguing about something technical and the sound is up very loud.*) I think we better go in here. (*He points to the studio. Stuart makes a motion for him to wait a second so he can catch a piece of the news. He hears about Israel's projected testing plans. Cooper nudges him after the report is finished and they go into the studio. We see the cameras and newscaster as the show continues. Cooper speaks in a whisper.*) That reminds me... When we spoke the other day	Israel announced today plans for a series of tests involving the use of atomic explosives in the atmosphere. The series will consist of several devices of the three-megaton capacity, which will test Israel's defensive systems. Russia and the United States immediately denounced the series calling it totally alien to the interests of humanity. Dr. Thomas Hardingwood-Jones of the World Health Organization in an interview in Paris said, "The blasts will only further pollute an already dangerous atmosphere." Said Dr. Hardingwood-Jones, "The level of toleration for human beings and perhaps life itself is close to saturation."

you compared the force of this thing to so many hydrogen bombs. (*Stuart nods.*) Well, that's exactly the kind of description that's helpful. The audience can understand that amount of energy. Like TNT, they know what you're talking about.

STUART
Of course it's much more powerful than that.

COOPER
I realize that, but we have to be careful not to get too technical. Then we'll go into more personal things like (*he pretends he is interviewing*): how does it feel to be the one who discovered it?

STUART
(*Smiling and acting as if he is on the air.*)
Judging by the publicity I've been getting, I'd say it discovered me. (*Cooper laughs.*)

COOPER
And then: has anything new developed since we last spoke with each other?

STUART
Not unusual enough to mention. Just a great deal of analysis with nothing confirmed.

In the Caribbean, the sea squall which turned into Hurricane Blanche ripped through Jamaica last night leaving in its wake twenty-seven known dead, hundreds missing and thousands homeless. Damage is estimated at over $75 million with both the death toll and the cost rising. Blanche is expected to hit the mainland tomorrow.

The nation's longest dock strike has gone into its second month. Owners of the major fleet lines still continue to refuse to meet with Union officials. Special legislation is being prepared by a group of senators to remedy the situation. But opponents have threatened any new bill with a filibuster.

India is going to have more intensive food problems, said Krishna Karandanti. Dr. Karandanti, who heads the Commission for the Population Crisis in India, said that unless a way is found to encourage a more workable birth control program and unless there can be discovered in the next two years a method for tripling the present food production, India will become a sea of hungry and dying people. India's food supply recently suffered a crippling setback when a severe drought left its largest wheat-producing provinces barren.

              COOPER   Sometimes we forget how lucky
     (*Slowly nodding his head.*)   we are. That's it for now. See you
     Fine. It's going to go very well. later for the eleven o'clock report.

                                        ANNOUNCER
                                        This has been your six o'clock
                                        report with Allen Hunter. Stay
                                        tuned for the weather, which
                                        follows immediately.

                                        2ND ANNOUNCER
                                        This is KLMW, Channel 1, Los
                                        Angeles.

                                        VOICE IN STUDIO
                                        Kill the monitor. (*The news ends
                                        and the commercials are timed in.*)

The newscaster leaves the set and says a quick hello to Gerald Cooper. The cameras are being repositioned for Stuart's taping. In the control room the director is giving instructions for camera angles. They seem to be ready. Stuart and Cooper are sitting in a traditional interview set-up. An order is given for the tape to roll.

                                        VOICE
                         Tape segment for *TV Journal*. Air time 8
                         P.M., Saturday, August 15th.

Gerald Cooper looks at the camera. A hand gives a signal to him and he begins.

                                        COOPER
                         In the last two weeks astronomers
                         around the world have been debating
                         the significance of a new astronomical
                         discovery. Tonight we are talking with Dr.
                         Stuart Townley, head astronomer at the Mt.
                         Palomar and Mt. Wilson observatories, the
                         man who first discovered this phenomenon
                         – a giant quasar. Dr. Townley, to begin with,
                         what exactly is a quasar?

STUART
Well, that's part of the problem – we don't really know what these "quasars" are. At first we thought they were stars, or star-like, so we called them quasi-stellar objects. But we've learned only recently that they can't be stars. They are objects very far from our own galaxy, incredibly powerful and unusually small for the vast energy they contain. It is this fact which leads us to believe that their energy must be so intensely concentrated as to be an entirely new phenomenon – perhaps even a new form of energy. Their discovery has caused both astronomers and physicists to re-evaluate, in many ways, our present concepts of the universe.

COOPER
What is so special about this new quasar?

STUART
First of all, we're not even sure it is a quasar. It does seem to have many of the same properties of other quasars, but on a much grander scale.

COOPER
Have you actually seen it?

STUART
No. It's too far away to sight visually. But we are monitoring its radio wave emissions.

Cooper seems to get confused for a few seconds, as if he had momentarily lost the sense of progression in his questions. Sensing the brief awkwardness, he motions to the cameras.

COOPER
Cut the tape. Let's try that again.

Stuart is driving up a long winding road. High at the top is a great silver dome, the Mt. Palomar Observatory. Stuart enters the secretarial area of his office. Iris, his secretary, looks up from her typing and greets him.

> IRIS
> Oh, you're here, Dr. Townley. They've been trying to reach you for an hour. You'd better call Dr. Klein right away.

> STUART
> Thanks Iris. Get him on the phone. I'll take it inside.

Stuart goes into his office. It is spacious and well appointed. Hanging on the walls are various university degrees and autographed photographs of the astronauts. Stuart sits at his desk and begins opening his mail. There is a buzz and he pushes down the intercom button.

> MILTON'S VOICE
> Stuart, this is Milton. We've been waiting for you.

> STUART
> I had that interview. What's up?

> MILTON'S VOICE
> Can you come up to the observatory right away? We're picking up a frequency change on that new quasar. We think you ought to check it out.

> STUART
> Are you taping it?

> MILTON'S VOICE
> Yes.

> STUART
> O.K. I'll be right over.

Stuart goes to the observatory. The room is immense. The great telescope it houses completely dwarfs the five men in astronomers coats standing at its base.

>STUART
>Good evening. (*They exchange greetings.*)

>MILTON
>Look at this, Stuart. (*He hands Stuart some sheets which he glances over quickly.*) Strange, isn't it?

>STUART
>(*Tapping the folder nervously with his finger.*)
>Phil, what's the record on rocket launches? NASA hasn't done something without telling us?

>PHIL
>No, nothing. NASA, Vandenberg are clear.

>STUART
>Skip, what do the computers say about satellite noise?

>SKIP
>Negative. We put a trace on everything up there.

>MILTON
>Didn't Yerkes put out a notice of solar flares?

>SKIP
>It wouldn't make any difference. The computers would filter that out.

MILTON
(*Hesitantly.*)
Stuart... we may have a visual. None of us could make it out but Elliot swears he sees something.

STUART
That isn't possible.

ELLIOT
It's faint, but there seems to be a luminous build up. It was hard to tell. I checked in the spectrascope but the only reading was white. I can't imagine that I was just seeing things. I put on every prism we had and there was no breakdown.

STUART
(*Very dubious.*)
Elliot are you sure you...

ELLIOT
Stuart, I know that I saw something.

STUART
When? When was the sighting?

ELLIOT
About an hour ago.

PAUL
We tried to take some plates but we didn't get anything.

STUART
(*Addressing Paul.*)
And what did you see?

                    PAUL
              (*Shrugging his shoulders.*)
         Nothing, really.

                   STUART
         Let me take a look.

The massive dome begins to separate. The telescope and the entire sighting platform rotate until the viewing lens is projecting into the audience. Stuart, wearing high-powered earphones, leans slowly into the eyepiece. The sudden vision of space is overwhelming. Millions of stars fill the screen as the telescoping image glides swiftly through them. Galaxies, nebulae and giant star clusters, beautiful and awesome, appear and disappear. An unusually bright light forms in the distance, growing larger as the telescope draws closer. A high-pitched series of radiowave pulses is barely discernible but begins to grow louder as the light comes more completely into view. Unexpectedly, they merge into one high pitched note like a ringing in the ears: powerful, almost above the range of hearing.

                   STUART
         Something's happening. Was this your
         center?

                   ELLIOT
         Dead on.

The sound, a massive electronic hum, grows stronger and stronger like a great generator. The light begins to pulsate as it grows brighter. Within a few moments it reaches a blinding intensity and breaks into a swirl of sensuous colors which shoot out into space, speeding towards Stuart and entering his eyes. Stuart is transfixed. His head becomes translucent, then transparent as the strange light-energy from the quasar flows like neon through his veins. The sound continues to roar like a rocket in his ears. Stuart's head is transformed into a landscape of energy flashes. It is as if we are seeing an incalculable number of nerve synapses releasing their energy simultaneously. The flashes sparkle in Stuart's mind like a galaxy of twinkling stars and the universe in Stuart's head appears no different from the universe in the telescope. Slowly we pull out of this vision of space and are back in the observatory.

Stuart takes off the earphones and turns with a look of dazed confusion. He recognizes his colleges but he stares blankly between them. The confusion is contagious.

      MILTON
  What happened? What did you see?

      STUART
  (*He does not answer for several moments. When he speaks his voice is low and uncertain. He talks slowly and with effort.*) I'm not sure... Elliot may be right. (*He pauses uncomfortably. The fact that he is hiding something extraordinary makes his attempt to conceal it painful. It is almost as if he refuses to believe what happened.*)

      ELLIOT
You see. I knew it – barely noticeable. It's a shame the plates didn't turn out.

      STUART
  Milton, take a look... Tell me what you see.

      PHIL
  Do you think we really have something?

      STUART
Let me check those computer sheets. (*Paul hands them to him and he stares at them intensely, almost as if he is trying to avoid the gaze of the men standing around him. Milton finishes looking through the telescope.*) Well, what did you see?

      MILTON
  I don't see anything unusual.

STUART
(*Nervously.*)
Are you sure?

MILTON
Yes, I'm sure.

STUART
Skip, give us a playback from the time I began listening.

SKIP
Right.

The tape is played back. There is a low fixed pulsation. Stuart tensely anticipates the frequency change but it does not reoccur. He puts his hand to his head as if he has a headache. The tape continues for a moment and is then turned off.

SKIP
That's it.

STUART
(*Disturbed.*)
Elliot, describe your sighting.

ELLIOT
(*Bewildered.*)
But I already told you. (*He realizes Stuart wants an answer.*) A luminous build up – very faint – probably the same thing you saw.

STUART
That's all?

ELLIOT
That's all. (*He shrugs his shoulders as though he wishes he could provide more but can't.*)

MILTON
(*Looking at Stuart.*)
Are you feeling all right?

STUART
(*Irritated.*)
I want a monitor on this thing. Have the lab check that spectrascope. Paul, try and get some photographs. Milton, we should get a hold of Jodrell Bank and ask them to put their dish on it. In fact, let's ask Australia if they could put some time in too. We'll compare findings next week.

The group begins to break up. They seem confused by Stuart's sudden rush of orders. Milton and Stuart walk toward the exit.

MILTON
Are you certain all this excitement is necessary?

STUART
No. (*Milton looks at him questioningly.*) I'm not certain of anything.

There is the sound of a door slamming. Ellen is sitting in the living room with some friends. She gets up quickly.

ELLEN
Excuse me a second. (*She runs to the front hallway and sees Stuart.*) Stuart! What are you doing home?

STUART
I wasn't feeling well… a headache. I couldn't work…

ELLEN
(*Hugging him.*)
What's wrong?

STUART
Nothing – just tired, I guess.

A voice calls from the living room.

RITA
Ellen, who is it?

STUART
(*Whispering.*)
Who's that?

ELLEN
Rita. We're rehearsing. (*She calls back.*) It's just Stuart. (*Softly.*) Can I get you something?

STUART
No. I just have to relax.

ELLEN
(*Looking gently and affectionately at him.*)
Do you want me to tell them to go?

STUART
No, no. It's all right. I'll go upstairs.

ELLEN
We're almost done anyway.

STUART
That's O.K. I just have to rest for a while. (*He starts to walk upstairs.*)

ELLEN
(*A bit worried.*)
Did the interview go all right?

STUART
Fine.

Stuart goes into the bedroom. He seems uncomfortable. He goes to the bathroom and takes some aspirin out of the medicine cabinet and swallows them with a glass of water. He walks over to a reading chair near the bed and sits down. He seems distracted. He picks up a book, opens it to the bookmark, and begins to read. We follow his eyes across the page. After scanning a paragraph or two they stop moving and he just stares at the book. After a few moments he closes it. He stands up and goes over to the bed. He unbuttons his shirt, unbuckles his pants, takes off his shoes and lies down. He can hear Ellen and her friends downstairs. Their conversation seems overly animated and somehow theatrical. Stuart closes his eyes as if attempting to fall asleep. He lies still for several moments and begins drifting off. Then suddenly his eyes open. He is afraid.

There is a sudden cut to the sound of a door buzzing. Stuart is standing in a doctor's office waiting room. He pushes against the buzzing door but it doesn't open.

NURSE
Pull.

Stuart pulls the door and it opens easily. Down the hall he sees Dr. Leo Dalton. They are old friends. Leo motions for him to come into his office. They shake hands warmly.

DALTON
What's up, Stu? You sounded worried on the phone. (*He motions for Stuart to sit down.*)

STUART
(*Taking out a cigarette and lighting it.*)
I don't know, Leo. I don't know how to explain.

DALTON
What's wrong?

STUART
I'm seeing things. Illusions, hallucinations.

I've been having nightmares regularly... terrifying ones. I'm almost afraid to go to sleep. Last night, while bringing in something with the telescope – I don't know how to describe it – it was so unlike anything I've ever experienced before. (*He stops, recalling the experience. The silence continues until Dalton interrupts.*)

DALTON

Was there any dizziness, blacking out?

STUART

No... not exactly... Just a horrifying sense of disintegrating... coming apart... but that's not it either. A feeling of being electrocuted, maybe. I've never felt anything like it before.

DALTON

You never had any injuries to your head, back or spine, have you?

STUART

No, nothing of the sort. It sounds like delusions, I know. I thought I should have a check-up.

DALTON

It could be simply that you're overworked and need a rest. Let's take a look. (*He rises and walks over to a door.*) You'd be surprised what fatigue can do to a person's mind. (*He opens the door and steps into the next room.*) Strip down to your shorts and get up on the table. We'll run you through some tests. I'll be right back.

Dalton leaves the room looking seriously concerned about his friend. Stuart strips to his shorts. He touches his forehead lightly to see if he has a fever, but can't quite tell. He goes over to the doctor's table and lies down. Stuart's attention comes to rest on the light directly above him. Rings start to form around it, halos, softly glowing. Stuart hears the sound of the door opening and suddenly the light dims to an ugly, greenish tint. We hear someone entering and coming over to the table. The doctor and a nurse appear, their heads blocking out the light as they lean over Stuart, looking down on him.

                    NURSE
      We have no idea how it happened, doctor.
      There seems to have been no apparent cause
      of death.

                    DALTON
      Well, that's what this autopsy is for – to find
      out. (*He reaches for a glimmering scalpel
      and holds it directly above Stuart.*) I think
      we should make the initial incision just
      under the heart. It's most probable there was
      a malfunction in the pulmonary artery.

Dalton places the scalpel under Stuart's heart. He squints his eyes professionally as he is about to make the incision. As he leans forward there is a rapid series of pointed knives, daggers, bayonets and other objects which pierce Stuart's skin in a rush of morbid and horrifying death fantasies. Stuart screams and the screen goes black. In the distance two stars can be seen speeding toward us. As they approach they seem like two small portholes with light streaming through them. As they get closer and become larger we can see a man's face in each of them as if reflected in a rippling pool of water. The two portholes begin to overlap and then fuse into one as they fill the whole screen. We see Dalton staring directly at us. He looks intense and somewhat menacing. We realize that we are back in the doctor's office. Stuart, gasping madly for breath, shoots upright, screaming.

                    STUART
      LEO WHAT ARE YOU DOING? WHAT
      ARE YOU DOING? (*Stuart is hysterical.
      Dalton is frightened and confused.*)

> DALTON
> What do you mean, what am I doing? Relax!
> Relax! I'm taking your blood pressure.
> What's wrong with you?

> STUART
> WHAT'S WRONG? WHAT'S WRONG?

He tries to get a hold of himself and stares suspiciously around the office. The overhead light still seems to have a slight greenish tint. The camera pans across the ceiling and walls, down to the face of the nurse looking at him very carefully. Then Stuart's attention moves over to Dr. Dalton, who is standing beside her. There is a long, uneasy silence as Dalton scans Stuart's face. He looks concerned, yet oddly sinister as well.

> DALTON
> Are you all right, Stuart? Tell me what happened.

Stuart does not answer but stares at Dalton's face. He does not seem sure that it is over. We see Dalton signal with his eyes to the nurse standing beside him. Stuart turns to her and sees a syringe being filled.

> DALTON
> (*Quietly, yet suspiciously.*)
> It's just a tranquilizer, Stuart. It's all right.

Stuart looks frantically at Dalton and then back to the nurse. His eyes search madly for the syringe but she is empty-handed. He suddenly sees Dalton coming at him but before he can recoil the doctor injects the serum into his arm and he begins to relax almost immediately.

> DALTON
> (*Waiting for signs of the tranquilizer's effect.*)
> What happened Stuart? (*Stuart looks up at him. He seems very relaxed but does not respond. Dalton seems uncomfortable.*)
> Here, let's take this thing off your arm. (*He removes the blood pressure tape.*) Do you

think you can put on your clothes? (*Stuart nods slowly.*)

Dalton is sitting back at his desk. Stuart is sitting opposite him.

> **DALTON**
> Can you describe what happened?

> **STUART**
> (*Defensively.*)
> I don't know what to tell you.

> **DALTON**
> Was it like the observatory?

> **STUART**
> In a way.

> **DALTON**
> Were you being electrocuted?

> **STUART**
> No. It wasn't like that.

> **DALTON**
> What was it like?

> **STUART**
> (*Looking straight at Leo almost as if he was challenging him.*)
> Like I was dead. You were operating on me.

Dalton looks at Stuart, maintaining his professional composure. Stuart keeps staring at him. Dalton, beginning to grow uncomfortable, starts spinning through his address file. He writes an address on a piece of paper.

> **DALTON**
> Listen, Stuart. I'm going to recommend you see someone who's more equipped to handle this.

STUART
(*Looking at the paper.*)
A psychiatrist?

DALTON
That's right. He's one of the best and he's a friend.

STUART
I know, but...

DALTON
Stuart, you just scared the hell out of me. What went on just now, your being upset and this hallucination or vision... this isn't the normal Stuart Townley. There's nothing physically wrong with you. Let's call it a little preventive medicine. He'll probably prescribe a couple of weeks unwinding somewhere.

STUART
Maybe you're right. I'll think it over.

DALTON
I'm giving you professional advice.

STUART
I know you are.

DALTON
(*Giving Stuart a box of pills he
has dug up from his desk.*)
Take these to relax. One every four hours. But if you don't need them, don't take them.

STUART
More tranquilizers?

DALTON
(*Nods.*)
I don't think you'll be able to get home alone. I'm going to have Martha drive you.

STUART
I'm all right now.

DALTON
You've got a drug in you and according to the law I'm not allowed to let you drive.

STUART
Leo, it's just ten minutes.

DALTON
I'm serious. Martha can take you. No driving.

STUART
I'll take a bus.

DALTON
Stuart.... I think you should rest awhile. There's a couch in the next room.

STUART
I'm O.K. Besides, I want some fresh air.

Stuart leaves Dalton's office and walks through the waiting room. There are five people now sitting on the chairs, and each of them silently looks up at him as he passes. Out on the street the sounds of the cars and other surrounding noises seem louder than usual. The street is particularly crowded. Faces rush past him quickly. Everyone seems distant, vaguely macabre, almost caricatures of themselves. An odd looking man steps out from a doorway as Stuart passes him and the man seems to follow him. Stuart senses the man's gaze behind him and his footsteps keeping pace with his. He reaches the bus stop and gets on line. The man behind him walks past. Stuart is relieved, not quite sure what his nervousness was all about. He looks down the line of people standing in front of him. They are reminiscent of the people in his dream of the night before. Stuart tenses again, and a feeling of utter confusion and hopelessness enters his eyes.

Stuart arrives home. He calls for Ellen but there is no answer. The house is very still and lifeless, magnifying Stuart's sense of loneliness and isolation. He walks into the kitchen and opens the refrigerator door. There is hardly anything inside it, just yogurt and some leftovers. Stuart stares at the barren shelves. His face grows increasingly upset. His eyes seem on the verge of tears. He tries to quell the sudden surge of emotion, wiping his hands over his eyes and closing the refrigerator door. A car is heard coming up the driveway. We can hear Ellen coming into the house. She walks into the kitchen carrying a bag of groceries and is surprised to see Stuart standing there.

> ELLEN
> Stu! I didn't see your car... (*Stuart is noticeably upset.*) What happened? (*Stuart doesn't know what to answer.*) Not an accident?

> STUART
> (*Quickly, almost under his breath.*) No, no. It's at the garage. I'm just having it looked at.

> ELLEN
> (*Putting the groceries down.*) The brakes again? (*Stuart nods. Ellen begins putting the groceries away.*) Stu, you won't believe this. They put the grapes back on the shelf. Isn't that incredible? After we sat there for three hours yesterday. I swear it's the last time I shop at that store. (*She walks over to the refrigerator with a container of milk and kisses Stuart as she passes.*) Do you think I'm right?

> STUART
> About what?

ELLEN
Not shopping there anymore.

STUART
(*Coldly.*)
Sure.

ELLEN
Hungry? Want a sandwich?

STUART
I'm not hungry.

Ellen shrugs and continues putting the groceries away. She seems angry. She stops suddenly and bangs a package of meat on the counter.

ELLEN
You know, they just can't get away with that. I'm going to call Caroline. (*She walks toward the phone. It starts to ring just as she is about to pick it up. She looks surprised.*) Hello... Yes... (*Her mood changes rapidly. Her face grows serious and concerned. She looks over at Stuart and notices that he is staring at her. She looks away.*)

STUART
Who is that? (*She doesn't answer but motions for him to wait a minute.*) Is that Dalton?

ELLEN
Yes, I understand... Right... Right... Thanks Leo. Bye. (*She hangs up. She looks at Stuart and he turns away. She walks over to him. Her tone is soft and tender.*) Are you all right? (*Stuart doesn't answer.*) Why didn't you tell me?

STUART
(*Feeling guilty and sorry for himself.*)
What am I supposed to do? Wear a sign?

ELLEN
What's happening? I don't understand.
(*Stuart doesn't answer. Ellen speaks sharply.*) Why don't you ever say anything?

STUART
(Angrily)
Say what?

He stands up and goes into the living room. Ellen follows him. He goes toward the window and begins to pace back and forth in front of it. Ellen watches silently, bewildered by his outburst.

ELLEN
Stuart, what's going on?

STUART
I can't explain it. I don't know what to tell you... What did Dalton say?

ELLEN
That you were emotionally upset. He wants you to see a psychiatrist.

STUART
(*Angrily, irrationally.*)
I don't need a psychiatrist. Leo just said that.

ELLEN
What do you mean he just said it?

Stuart can't answer. He paces nervously around the room.

STUART
I think I'm going insane.

ELLEN
Because of the dreams?

STUART
It's much more than that.

ELLEN
Can you tell me?

STUART
They're not just dreams, Ellen. They're happening all the time.

ELLEN
Is it happening now?

STUART
No. Last night, in the observatory. In Leo's office. It was like being pulled into another world.

ELLEN
What do you mean?

STUART
I can't describe it. I've tried.

ELLEN
Is there anything you haven't said?

STUART
Like what?

ELLEN
Oh, I don't know. (*She hesitates and then says nothing.*) Is there anything I can do?

STUART
I don't think so.

ELLEN
Want to go for a walk or something?

STUART
(*He shakes his head*)
I have to work it out myself.

ELLEN
I'll call Joan and tell her we're not coming.

STUART
Wait a while. We'll see how I feel.

Stuart and Ellen are sitting at a table in the dining room of Joan and Harry Robinson. Fred and Dorothy Shultz are with them. The meal is half over. Stuart is paying minimal attention to the conversation and eating with what appears to be deep concentration.

FRED
I wired in at least seven articles and they only printed three.

HARRY
That's because our celebrity here has been taking all your space.

FRED
I guess I should be writing articles about you. (*He muses.*) An exposé. "The Secret Nightlife of Stuart Townley." I hear you've been spending a lot of time up in the observatory, Stu.

STUART
(*Looking up, smiling mechanically.*)
Yep, just me and my telescope. (*Joan giggles.*)

FRED
What have you been looking at? Stars or starlets? I bet you can see clear into the girl's dorm at USC with that thing.

STUART
(*With a locker room reflex.*)
You don't think I took up astronomy for nothing? (*He winks and continues eating.*)

HARRY
Hey, Stu, I read about those astronomers in England.

STUART
You mean the "distant civilization" group?

FRED
Right. The "signals." What do you think?

STUART
I think they're... unprofessional.

FRED
No possibility?

STUART
Sure, there's always a possibility. But this is just wild speculation. We don't have enough to go on.

FRED
Are you making any guesses?

STUART
No. Not for the public anyway.

FRED
In private?

STUART
(*Mockingly, as if being interviewed.*)
Is the tape rolling? (*He clears his throat.*)

DOROTHY
(*Laughing.*)
Don't let him get to you, Stu. He interviews me all the time too.

HARRY
(*Looking at his watch.*)
Hey, we better hurry. Stu's interview will be on in a few minutes.

The guests walk into the living room. Everyone seems full and satisfied. Harry goes over to turn on the set.

JOAN
Harry, you might have some trouble with the reception. I noticed I was getting that buzzing this afternoon.

HARRY
You've been telling me that for days, but I still don't hear anything.

ELLEN
Are you getting that humming sound too?

JOAN
Yes, we're getting a very faint buzz, but lately it seems to be getting louder.

ELLEN
Same with us. It's weird. Must be in the atmosphere.

HARRY
Would anyone want a brandy? Stu, an after-dinner drink?

STUART
No thanks.

HARRY
Fred?

FRED
Sure, if it's no problem.

HARRY
No problem. (*Calling out.*) Girls, I'm serving after-dinner drinks.

JOAN
(*Calling back.*)
Make it something sweet.

ELLEN
(*Calling back.*)
Make that two.

DOROTHY
(*Calling back.*)
Make that three.

HARRY
Witness the only consensus of their minds in history.

Harry goes over to the bar to get the drinks. The women are talking and laughing. Stuart is sitting directly opposite the television, which is on very low in the background. He is quietly observing everyone's movements. He watches the women and, for an instant, imagines he sees them getting older. In a few moments they seem to age forty years, and then revert back to their original appearance. All of this occurs very rapidly. He begins to realize that everyone in the room is enveloped in an aura of dim, fuzzy light which surrounds them as they move. Their actions become very slow and mechanical, like puppets. Their voices are almost indistinguishable from each other, and strangely, but subtly, electronic. Occasionally they look over at Stuart and then back at each other as if they are talking about him. Stuart seems curious, not quite certain that all this is happening. He nervously reaches for a cigarette and realizes that it is taking him an inordinately long time to lift it to his mouth. He lights the match in extreme slow motion and seems barely able to raise it upward as it travels through an infinity of space before reaching the tip of his cigarette. The flame catches the tobacco strands and paper as air is sucked through. Stuart is about to shake the match when it suddenly goes out. He looks up and sees Harry, far above him, smiling, Stuart seems transfixed by the whiff of smoke from the smoldering match head and his own exhalation as it swirls slowly and sensuously through the air. Harry calls Stuart's name, as if from far away. He motions to Stuart, directing his attention to the television. Although it is the interview tape recorded earlier, Stuart's image appears vaguely different. His face seems very powerful, almost otherworldly, as it stares intently from the television. The tone of his voice is strange, although it is unmistakably his own.

> TV
> We are now entering the final moments in a phase-one time freeze. This is a pre-molecular time warp involving biological and psychological functions.

All eyes are fixed on the TV. Harry turns his head toward Stuart, and speaks to him softly, but it is Stuart's own voice which comes from Harry's mouth.

> HARRY
> Stuart, don't try to hold on. There is nothing to fear. Just relax.

> TV
> Linear time progression has slowed to one unit per horizontal movement. Biological functions are stabilizing. Subject's brain count too rapid for vertical time transition. Heart flow seven over twenty. Decrease by five.

The television screen suddenly shifts to an image of Stuart sitting in the Robinsons' living room. It shows Stuart's face and body from many different angles, as if it were studying him clinically. His image momentarily breaks up into rapidly changing schematic lines and movements, synchronized with the narrator's voice describing his bodily functions. Dorothy and Ellen smile at Stuart and his voice seems to come from each of them.

DOROTHY AND ELLEN
Stuart, you must relax. Do not be afraid, there is nothing to fear.

TV
You are about to experience an instant out of your normal time consciousness. All men will have this experience in time. Resistance to the flow will bring pain and confusion. The fear will dissolve if you will it to. Pulse decreasing to two over twenty. Horizontal time movement constant. Mental phase active. Begin vertical time.

There is some intermittent static on the television and a vertical bar begins to pass across the screen. It moves slowly at first, but increases frequency until it forms an hypnotic strobe-like flicker. Unexpectedly a horizontal line rises through the entire living room and Stuart realizes that everything and everybody around him is a gigantic televised image. The rapidly scanning electron which forms the television image begins to slow down. It is as if, by a deceleration of time, we are suddenly able to see the actual electronic process which goes into forming each televised image. The breakdown continues and the entire living room disappears. Only one single electron remains in the center of the movie screen. This dot transforms itself into a very detailed IBM-like digital recording of all number and alphabet systems since the beginning of time: hieroglyphics, Chinese characters, etc. The screen is deluged with symbols which mold themselves quickly into new and different shapes in a constant flux of movement. The Roman letter section seems to contain beginnings and endings of words and phrases reminiscent of biblical passages. But their rate of change is so fast that we cannot decipher anything definite. As if exhausted by the flood of symbols, the dot re-emerges and multiplies itself until the entire screen is filled with small dots. A picture starts to emerge from this grid pattern similar to a newspaper photograph reproduced by a half-tone process. Recognizable images, people and events appear and disappear meteorically on the matrix of dots. A rapid kaleidoscopic view of world history is revealed. It is as if we are viewing in a few moments the entire evolution of the human race as it is recorded in one man's vast conscious and unconscious storehouse of accumulated knowledge and experience. The diversity, scope and emotional impact of the images is overwhelming. As we approach the twentieth century scenes of a very personal nature to Stuart, including some we have seen in the film, are evoked.

> TV
> These are the imprints of your mind, your
> own thought forms. Let them go. You
> created them and you can dissolve them.
> They will repeat themselves forever if you
> allow them to control you. Go beyond
> them. Go to the next stage. Do not be afraid.
> There is no death. Only the imprints die.
> Let them go. Allow yourself to experience
> the primal energy. Merge with it.

As the voice on the TV speaks, the pictures begin to slow down and become less defined, as if the mental process which was forming them had begun to malfunction. The white dots start to form an intense white light, bleaching out most of the other dots and making the flow of images less perceptible as its brightness increases. The light becomes almost unbearably bright in its blinding intensity, as if some new and strange form of energy were suddenly exploding before our eyes – beautiful yet frightening in its fantastic strength.

> TV
> Merge with the light. Allow your mind and
> thoughts to dissolve.

There is a strong tension between the narrative voice instructing Stuart to let go, and the pictures which begin to appear again. It is as if Stuart's mind cannot contain the light's energy, and out of fear it returns to the somewhat familiar landscape of flowing images. A scene of Stuart talking with Ellen appears in the rush of moving pictures. Suddenly, however, the movie frame seems to dislodge from the screen and behind it we can see a long progression of similar images, each frame a moment back in time, stretching into infinity. It is as if we have stepped out of the present and can observe the past and future simultaneously. We can see any point and moment along the line of action or watch the entire transmission at once. A new scene appears as a sequence of thought originates somewhere in the far reaches of the mind and advances toward the audience. We see the Robinson's dinner party beginning. Everyone is around the dinner table talking. The TV is turned on, the broadcast, the TV turned off, everyone saying goodnight, Stuart and Ellen get into their car. It all happens at an astonishing speed. Suddenly the camera races past the image closest to us, moving alongside the train of preceding pictures, as if Stuart's conscious mind was desperately seeking a grasp on time and reality. We stop on an image of Harry walking over to the television, reaching for a knob, and turning it off. The stream of thought-images rushes furiously back into the confines of the Robinson's TV set and solidifies into a little white dot as the set goes off. Stuart is back at the dinner party, but seems totally unaware of the people around him and what they are saying.

      HARRY
  It's really strange. I can't imagine what the
  noise is.

      JOAN
  It feels like someone's drilling a hole in my
  brain.

      ELLEN
  (*Directing the conversation to Stuart
  and throwing her arms around him.*)
  You were really great! Now you're a
  celebrity!

      FRED
  It was very interesting, Stuart.

      DOROTHY
  You really look good on television.

Stuart is noticeably uncomfortable. It is not clear exactly what he is feeling, but he is obviously distant from the general conversation.

                        JOAN
          Is something wrong, Stuart?

                        HARRY
          Nothing's wrong with Stuart. Some people
          just never get used to seeing themselves on
          TV.

Stuart and Ellen are driving home. Stuart is at the wheel. His mind seems to be working feverishly. Ellen is obviously unaware of what has happened to him, and has apparently had a very enjoyable evening with her friends.

                        ELLEN
          I still don't understand why Joan can't make
          a decent roast beef. You'd think that after all
          these years she'd begin to get the knack. Her
          salads are good though, don't you think?
          (*Stuart doesn't answer.*) You're awfully
          quiet. (*He still doesn't answer.*) Are you
          thinking about what happened today?

                        STUART
          It's hard not to... Listen, Ellen... (*There is a
          long pause.*)

                        ELLEN
          What?

                        STUART
          What went on back there?

                        ELLEN
          Back where? At Joan and Harry's?

                        STUART
          Yes.

                        ELLEN
          I don't know what you mean.

STUART
With the television. What happened to the television?

ELLEN
You were there. Why are you asking me? (*He doesn't answer.*) Did something happen again? But how could it?

STUART
Just tell me what happened.

ELLEN
What happened? Nothing happened. We just watched your interview. (*Stuart seems lost in thought.*) Stuart?

STUART
Ellen, something incredible is going on and I don't understand for the life of me what it is.

ELLEN
What do you mean?

STUART
I don't know how to describe it... but we weren't watching the same television show.

ELLEN
I don't understand.

STUART
Neither do I. (*Stuart is quiet for a few moments, as if trying to piece things together.*) Ellen, did you notice anything unusual during the broadcast? Was anyone acting strangely?

ELLEN
No... not that I can remember. Except that buzzing sound seemed to annoy Harry a lot.

STUART
What sound?

ELLEN
You know... that humming sound.

Stuart and Ellen are entering the front door of their home. Stuart is obviously excited and goes immediately to the telephone. He begins dialing.

ELLEN
Who are you calling?

STUART
Frank Press.

ELLEN
But it's two in the morning in New York.

STUART
(*Waving her off.*)
Shh. Frank? Stuart. Fine, we're all fine. Not exactly. Listen, did you watch television at all tonight? No, this isn't a survey. No. I'm not fishing for compliments... Well, thanks. (*Ellen smiles.*) Listen, this is serious. Are you picking up any interference or buzzing, like a ringing in your ears? No? (*Stuart is surprised and disappointed.*) What about Ruth? Oh really? Would you mind waking her?

ELLEN
Stuart!

STUART
Really, Frank, it's important.

ELLEN
Stuart, you're being ridiculous.

STUART
(*He pauses for a moment and then grimaces as Ruth gets on the phone.*) Now is that any way for a lady to talk? No, I have to ask you some important... She's fine. No, nothing's wrong... I'm glad you liked it. Listen Ruth, I just wanted to know if you happened to notice a sort of strange humming sound coming from the television lately... Really? Right... Right... No, you're not the only one. That's what we thought too but a lot of people seem to be hearing it... I know, Frank told me he didn't. Uh-huh... Uh-huh... It's nothing to worry about. I was just confirming a suspicion. Just go back to bed... O.K. maybe for Christmas. Say good-bye to Frank. Bye... Whew!

ELLEN
They must think you're crazy.

STUART
Ellen, it's happening over the entire country.

ELLEN
It's probably just atmospheric disturbance. (*Stuart shakes his head as he dials the observatory.*) Now where are you calling? Bombay? (*The camera holds on Ellen's face as Stuart talks in the background. She is tense and suspicious.*)

STUART
Paul? Stuart. How are the plates coming. Uh-huh. Well, keep trying. Paul, what's the latest meteorological report on atmospheric disturbances, magnetic storms, solar flares? (*He motions with his finger for Ellen to come close to the phone.*) Go ahead Paul...

Uh-huh. Not at all. Right. That's what I thought. Thanks. Have a good night. (*He hangs up.*) Ellen, listen. I don't know what it's all about yet but there's a connection... between the sound and the quasar.

ELLEN
Stuart, I'm not concerned about the sound or the quasar.

STUART
(*Looking at Ellen, surprised by her response.*)
But Ellen, don't you see...

ELLEN
(*Upset.*)
Stuart, let's go to bed. You've gone through a lot today.

STUART
But Ellen...

She looks at her husband for a moment, until the worry and fear on her face begin to upset him. Then she turns quickly to go upstairs. Stuart just stands there as she leaves, his excitement and confidence deeply shaken.

Stuart is in a psychiatrist's office, sitting in a thick leather chair.

DR. ROWAN
These repetitive death dreams you describe, have they happened before?

STUART
No. They started just a few weeks ago.

ROWAN
What about nightmares?

STUART
I never had them. Not bad ones anyway.

ROWAN
And these (*searching for the word*) "experiences" you had yesterday… Can you remember ever having felt such things before? In your childhood maybe?

STUART
(*Thinking for a few moments.*)
No. Not really. But there is something familiar about them, in a strange way. Like having been somewhere before…

ROWAN
(*Reflecting momentarily.*)
I spoke with Leo Dalton yesterday.

STUART
He called you?

ROWAN
Yes. And he described your reaction in his office as "panicked."

STUART
I think that's a suitable description.

ROWAN
And yet, talking to you now I don't detect any trace of it.

STUART
Is that unusual?

ROWAN
Not necessarily. But how do you account for the change?

STUART
I don't know if I can. It's just that the experience watching the TV last night was more awesome than frightening. I felt in touch with something so much greater than myself. And yet, it was part of me – of my own mind. It was trying to reveal something.

ROWAN
What was it revealing?

STUART
I don't know. Last night... (*He thinks for a moment.*) It's strange how I can't remember it... There was this feeling, but it was more than that... a light – it was going to absorb me... and I wanted to let it happen but I couldn't. I didn't think I'd ever come back.

ROWAN
(*Thinking for a moment before asking.*)
Dr. Townley, would you consider yourself a religious man?

STUART
(*Surprised by the question.*)
No. Not very. When I was young, maybe.

ROWAN
(*Nodding his head.*)
You know some people with strong religious backgrounds, and sometimes even people with none at all, talk of seeing lights and other things similar to what you describe. (*Stuart appears very interested in what Rowan is saying.*) In psychiatric terms there is really very little to distinguish the visions of mystics from those of schizophrenics. Of course, I don't mean to

imply that you are either, but only that there are well-documented clinical explanations for the events you've been talking about. If you are interested in searching for the answers, I think I can help you.

STUART
(*Attentive.*)
How serious do you think this is?

ROMAN
Frankly, Dr. Townley, these visions, these hallucinations, are not the symptoms of a healthy mind. I think it would be to your advantage to try and understand what's causing them.

STUART
What does that involve?

ROMAN
Analysis, to begin with. And should these experiences reoccur, perhaps more intensive help.

STUART
(*Noticeably upset.*)
What about the quasar? Don't you think it's possible... ?

ROMAN
(*Interrupting him.*)
No, I don't think the cause of these hallucinations will be found in outer space. These disturbances are purely psychological. They exist in your mind and it is the mind we must explore.

STUART
But what do you think is causing them?

ROWAN
It would be foolish for me to say anything at this point.

STUART
Foolish or not, I have a right to know.

ROWAN
(*Thinking for a moment.*)
Judging from the things you've told me today, I'd say that there is a deeply rooted unconscious fear in you that is just beginning to emerge. You can't really accept it yet, so it manifests mainly in dreams and hallucinations. They seem to be happening "outside" you, but these are just strong projections of the inner fear.

STUART
A fear of what?

ROWAN
A fear of death.

STUART
(*Not quite satisfied.*)
But isn't everyone afraid of death?

ROWAN
To some degree, yes. But when this fear begins to dominate your dreams and even your waking reality – something's wrong.

STUART
But you said before that other people had experiences similar to mine. Mystics or religious people.

ROWAN
And schizophrenics. Most of them were probably just that. A deep psychological disorder can make a person, almost any person, believe he is seeing or hearing things which aren't really there.

STUART
So they're not real. I'm just "hallucinating" these things.

ROWAN
Yes. (*Stuart looks annoyed and unconvinced.*) But if you begin analysis we could search out the reasons for these experiences and then hopefully be able to resolve the problem areas.

STUART
(*A little hostile.*)
How long will that take? A year? Five years?

ROWAN
Maybe sooner.

STUART
I can't wait that long.

Stuart is sitting at a table in a drug store. We see him from the outside looking in. The passing traffic is reflected in the glass. He is not eating – just looking pensively out onto the street. A waitress brings him a cup of coffee which he doesn't touch. He sits for a while as the chaotic street imagery floods over him. Stuart pays at the cashier and walks slowly down the block. He pauses before a downtown bookstore and looks at the window display of bestsellers. He goes into the store and speaks with a salesman. They talk for a moment and then the salesman walks him casually to the door. He points to a building down the street. Stuart thanks him.

Stuart is wandering down the aisles of a Los Angeles occult bookshop. He is surprised by the vast number of books and stops often to leaf through the volumes which attract him. Following him, constantly looking over his shoulder, is an elderly woman of European background, probably Jewish. She is the proprietor of the shop, intelligent, charming, and in love with all aspects of the occult. Her running commentary is guided by the books Stuart chooses to look at and some she quickly and excitedly leads him to.

          MRS. GRASTOK
      (Speaking clearly but with
  a rapid, machine-gun fire delivery.)
The Christian mystics, the Yogis in India, the Kabalists... they have all explored the mysterious powers of the mind. The occult sciences are more developed than you may think.

Stuart opens some books and glances at pictures of ascetics and wisemen, yogis twisted into various positions, pictures of wondrous visions and charts and diagrams of strange origin.

          MRS. GRASTOK
Most people don't believe in these powers because they've never experienced them. But when they do... (*She smiles.*) Whole new worlds open up to them – if they aren't afraid. (*She is about to continue but Stuart interrupts.*)

          STUART
But why do these things happen?

          MRS. GRASTOK
They only happen when you're ready. Most people have to work for it. Praying, meditating, fasting, yoga. There are so many ways. Even some drugs can show you, but only a glimpse. It's different for everyone. In time, everyone will know. That is the

goal of evolution. It takes many lifetimes.
(*She hesitates, looking at Stuart.*) Oh, I can
see this is all still new to you. I can tell by
your look. But you understand what I'm
talking about. I know. It's in your eyes. And
it will come. It's all so strange at first. You
must give up so much, so many old ideas,
about everything. But new insights will take
their place. It will feel very natural after a
while. (*She smiles again.*) Or should I say
"supernatural?" (*She pulls him by the hand
like a child.*) Come, let me give you some
books. They will help you for now.

A large black cat jumps onto a shelf in front of Stuart. It sensuously sticks out its tongue and licks Stuart's face.

MRS. GASTOK
He likes you. That's a good sign. (*She hands
Stuart a book.*) Here. The *Bhagavad Gita*.
It's Hindu. Very clear. Especially when you
realize it's all true. (*She leans over to a far
shelf.*) Oh, you'll love this. (*She hands him*
The Tibetan Book of the Dead.) Tibetans
understand so much. It tells you how to die
scientifically – the afterlife, step by step. It's
all right here. Of course they don't mean real
death, just the ego, but it's the same thing.
Take it. Jung wrote the introduction. He knew
so much more than Freud. Are you Jewish?

STUART
No.

MRS. GRASTOK
That's all right. (*She reaches for the
Kabbalah.*) It's complicated, but it's good.
(*She takes it down and then reaches far over
to another shelf and manages to grasp* The
Bible.) And here. Read this again.

Stuart clutches the growing pile of books in both arms and nearly trips over two young hippies sitting on the floor reading. Mrs. Grastok smiles and shrugs her shoulders apologetically. They both walk toward the counter as she continues piling books into Stuart's arms.

>   MRS. GRASTOK
> Read these... (*She tallies the cost.*) And if
> you have any questions, I'm here all the
> time. (*She leans over the counter, as if to say
> something more confidentially.*) But you
> shouldn't have to ask me. You have all the
> answers inside already. Believe me... Trust
> yourself. And listen, you shouldn't talk too
> much. They won't understand anyway.

Stuart laughs and gives her a knowing look, half serious and half indulgently, as he pays her and leaves the store.

Stuart pulls into his driveway and notices a strange car already parked there. He backs into the street and leaves his car at the curb. As he walks to the porch and up the steps the front door begins to open and he sees his wife standing there. She seems very anxious.

>   ELLEN
> Stuart. Why are you so late? They've been
> trying to reach you for hours.

>   STUART
>   (*Bewildered.*)
> Who has?

>   ELLEN
> There's a man here. (*She whispers.*) From the
> CIA. I think it's really important. (*Noticing all the
> books under Stuart's arms.*) What are all those?

>   STUART
>   (*Seeing a man waiting
>   in the living room.*)
> I'll tell you later.

DRIVER
(*Standing up.*)
Dr. Townley?

STUART
Yes.

DRIVER
(*Shaking hands.*)
Charles Driver, CIA. (*He shows Stuart his identification card.*) Is there somewhere we can be alone?

STUART
Certainly.

Stuart leads him to his study. As he passes Ellen he makes a strange face to show he is not very sympathetic to the James Bond atmosphere. Stuart closes the door to the study and motions Mr. Driver to sit down.

DRIVER
I'd like to make a phone call first.

STUART
(*Pointing to his phone.*)
Sure. Go right ahead.

DRIVER
(*Dialing with an almost comic slickness.*)
Bob... Charlie. He's here now. Right... No, there isn't time... No, I haven't yet. Just tell Burrows we've found him and I'll bring in the report as soon as I've got it... Right. (*He hangs up.*) Well, Dr. Townley, my office informs me that you have been doing a great deal of research on this new quasar.

STUART
Right.

DRIVER

I've been doing quite a bit myself. We're building up a good sized folder on it. Right now, though, we're interested in getting some additional information.

STUART

Such as?

DRIVER

We understand you haven't been able to accurately estimate this quasar's energy output, but we want to know if you think it's powerful enough to be affecting our atmosphere – perhaps like a solar flare.

STUART

Theoretically, yes.

DRIVER

In actuality?

STUART

(*Speaking cautiously, not certain what Driver is getting at.*)
There is no evidence of its having an effect.

DRIVER

(*Realizing that he will have to give more information than he had hoped.*)
Dr. Townley, we do have evidence of something affecting the atmosphere and we are trying to find out if the quasar might have anything to do with it.

STUART

What sort of evidence?

DRIVER
(*Reluctantly.*)
You understand that whatever information I give you is strictly confidential.

STUART
I understand.

DRIVER
For the last few weeks our radio communications and radar have been upset by a periodic interference. Until a few days ago this interference was almost imperceptible, but it has increased to a point now where our defense communications may be endangered.

STUART
Endangered in what way?

DRIVER
The interference has created lapses in our radio surveillance and probably in all our electronically controlled weapons systems.

STUART
(*Very interested.*)
Is it the same type of interference affecting commercial broadcasting?

DRIVER
(*Surprised that Stuart knows about this, he hesitates before speaking.*)
It seems to be. Network people here and broadcasters in Europe have been complaining for the last few weeks about a high frequency static or humming sound interfering with their transmissions. Until a few days ago they've been able to filter it

out of commercial telecasts, but now we are told it's beginning to go out on the air.

STUART
Couldn't it be jamming of some sort? Or a more local disturbance.

DRIVER
No. Our intelligence network has verified that this is worldwide. China and the Soviet Union are experiencing it too. We have ruled out all possibility of sabotage or atmospheric disturbance and we are now convinced that the origins of this interference must be outside our own solar system. Dr. Lovell and Jodrell Bank suspect it to be the quasar, and that you, more than anyone, will be able to help us.

STUART
Just because I noticed it first doesn't make me the quasar expert. Naturally we have a number of relatively complex theories about what this quasar is.

DRIVER
(*Interrupting him impatiently.*)
I've read most of these theories already and to be honest with you they're not what we're after. I know it may sound naive, but if it is the quasar, is it possible to stop, or neutralize its effects?

STUART
No.

DRIVER
Why not?

STUART
(*Reflecting for a moment.*)
Well, if the quasar is the cause, our trying to stop that amount of energy would be like flinging a grain of sand against a hurricane.

DRIVER
(*Frustrated by the answer and noticeably anxious.*)
We don't usually phrase things like that in our reports.

STUART
You asked for my opinion. I didn't say it was the quasar, but if it is, that's what we're up against. Has anyone said anything to the contrary?

DRIVER
(*Reserved.*)
We haven't finished checking it out yet.

STUART
Perhaps the only optimistic report I could offer would be that if it *is* the quasar, maybe the interference is just an isolated emission, like a solar flare. Maybe it will just fade away.

DRIVER
How likely is that?

STUART
I don't know. Mr. Driver, there is not really very much I can tell you at this point. I have a few theories of my own. They are not very complete, but we are continuing our observations and the information you have just given me may help put some things together.

> DRIVER
> (*Almost paranoid.*)
> This information is highly confidential.

> STUART
> Yes, I know. If I come up with something, you and your associates will be the first to know. I wish I could be more helpful. Of course, I'll make myself available for more questioning if you want.

> DRIVER
> (*Standing.*)
> Dr. Townley, we will be in touch with you. (*He pulls a card out of his wallet and gives it to Stuart.*) But if you need to contact us, call this number anytime, day or night. (*Stuart walks him to the front door.*) If, for any reason, we will not be able to reach you at your usual phone numbers, please let us know.

> STUART
> Right. (*They shake hands.*) Goodbye. (*He walks quickly down the steps.*)

Stuart returns to his study. He checks through the large assortment of books and positions them on his desk. He sits down, about to begin reading, when Ellen comes in.

> ELLEN
> What was that all about?

> STUART
> Secret.

> ELLEN
> Good or bad?

STUART
A secret.

ELLEN
I hate secrets. (*She is like a little girl whose friends are keeping something from her.*) Is it the quasar? Do they think it's affecting the televisions too?

STUART
You're on the right track but don't go any further. I have a lot of reading to do. (*Ellen glances at the pile of books.*)

ELLEN
My, my, look at these titles. *The Tibetan Book of the Dead*, *The Bible*. Is that why you were late?

STUART
I found an old lady who likes me.

ELLEN
Was it your charm or your money?

STUART
Both. Besides, her cat liked me.

ELLEN
So you bought her out?

STUART
She was aiding me in some research.

ELLEN
What about the psychiatrist?

STUART
He didn't have a simple answer, but he put me on to this. (*He points to the books.*)

ELLEN
But what did he say?

STUART
He said I had a death fixation.

ELLEN
And he told you to buy *The Book of the Dead*?

STUART
Not exactly. Ellen, listen, I've got a lot of reading here and I want to get started.

ELLEN
You're not being very communicative.

STUART
I'm sorry but it's really important.

ELLEN
(*Seemingly hurt.*)
Maybe if I stopped asking questions.

STUART
(*Defensively.*)
That's not it at all.

ELLEN
Are you going back to the psychiatrist? (*Stuart doesn't answer.*) Or did he say something to frighten you off?

STUART
Why don't you give me a chance?

ELLEN
Why don't you realize you're not alone in this house?

STUART
Now what are you talking about?

ELLEN
Stuart, you're not being fair.

STUART
What do you want?

ELLEN
I want to know what's happening to you.

STUART
Don't you think I want to know? I've told you everything I can put into words.

ELLEN
That's not true. You've hardly explained anything.

STUART
I've explained as much as I understand. Why don't you believe that?

ELLEN
What about the psychiatrist? He didn't just talk about death fixations. What did he say? What are all these books?

STUART
(*Getting hold of himself.*)
He said these... things... are not that... unusual. They've happened to other people. He related the experiences to... probably even religious experiences or... mystical experiences. (*Ellen looks at him almost sneeringly.*) I know it sounds crazy but... he mentioned some things and I think I have to follow them up. Maybe he's right. Maybe it's all in my head. But I have to know.

ELLEN
(*Concerned.*)
Are you going back to him? (*Stuart shrugs his shoulders. The response is ambiguous.*) Do you have an alternative?

STUART
I'm looking for one.

ELLEN
(*Picking up one of the books.*)
In these?

STUART
There might be something.

ELLEN
You can't play around with this. It's too serious.

STUART
Don't you think I know that? I'm not playing games. I'm trying to make sense out of something that doesn't make sense. Give me a few days. It's important.

ELLEN
(*With deep concern.*)
If it doesn't work... will you go back?

STUART
(*Understanding her concern but answering reluctantly.*)
If it doesn't work. (*He picks up a book.*)

ELLEN
(*Somehow relieved.*)
O.K. (*She starts to leave.*) I'll be outside. (*Stuart nods. She leaves, closing the door quietly.*)

Stuart is avidly reading the books from the large pile stacked on his desk. Many are open at specific pages for quick cross-referencing. The scene is composed of words, phrases, diagrams, paintings and drawings from the various books Stuart reads. In some we can see a striking resemblance to the experiences he has had, but in others there does not seem to be an obvious connection. Mystical paintings by Blake and Bosch are examined in detail depicting scenes of men confronting death, rising into Heaven, or being cast into Hell. Moving across the screen are passages from the books Stuart is reading. Stuart underlines various phrases. Many sentences, some obscure, some more relevant, cross the screen. It is impossible to determine Stuart's exact thoughts but it is obvious that he is excited and fascinated by many of the things he is reading. The many bits of information are like a puzzle that Stuart and the audience must assemble for themselves. Most importantly, the audience should realize the correlation between Stuart's own experiences and the vast storehouse of mystical and religious knowledge he is consuming.

We see Stuart sleeping with his head down on the desk and his reading light on above him. Ellen walks in silently. She puts her hand on his shoulder and gently wakes him.

                     ELLEN
                     (Softly.)
Stuart, Stuart.

                    STUART
            (Slowly opening his eyes
           and looking at her warmly.)
What time is it?

                     ELLEN
Two-thirty.

                    STUART
I must have been sleeping a while.

                     ELLEN
Come upstairs. You can't be very comfortable sleeping like this.

STUART
No. It's OK. I feel a little refreshed now. I want to get back to it.

ELLEN
Do you have a lot more to do?

STUART
I've only just scratched the surface.

ELLEN
(*Her tone is skeptical.*)
Find anything?

STUART
(*Excitedly.*)
It's unbelievable. A whole new world, Ellen. I know I've experienced some of the same things.

ELLEN
(*Worried and untrusting.*)
How can you be so sure?

STUART
(*Sensing her fear.*)
I know how it sounds. It's even hard for me to believe. But I understand it. It makes sense.

ELLEN
It doesn't make sense to me Stuart. It doesn't make any sense at all. How can you say you believe these things?

STUART
Because something like them happened to me, that's how. They're describing the same kind of experience.

ELLEN
That's crazy.

STUART
That's just it. It's not crazy. It's just different from what we know.

ELLEN
But Leo said they were hallucinations – and the psychiatrist confirmed it, didn't he?

STUART
Listen Ellen, let me try and explain. A hallucination is something you see that doesn't really exist. It's imaginary, right? (*Ellen nods weakly.*) Well, what I've seen isn't just in my mind. It does exist.

ELLEN
Anyone who has an hallucination says that.

STUART
But I mean it exists in the real world, scientifically.

ELLEN
I don't know what you mean.

STUART
(*Suddenly banging on his desk.*)
Look, look, this desk is solid, right?

ELLEN
Yes.

STUART
No, it's not! Theoretically, scientifically we know that it isn't. Seeing it as solid is the illusion. In reality it's made up of billions and billions of atoms, galaxies of them. Our

eyes just don't perceive it that way normally. What we usually see is just a small part of the physical reality – just one level. There must be infinite levels we've never seen. But I think I've begun to experience some of them.

                    ELLEN
           (Skeptical but interested.)
How is that possible?

                    STUART
I don't really know – but scientists have known for years that we use only a small part of our total brain capacity. It might be possible that something has opened up whole new areas of perception in me, whole new ways of experiencing things.

                    ELLEN
    (Intrigued by Stuart's argument,
 although not fully understanding all of it.)
Do you mean the quasar?

                    STUART
Well, these books talk about intense lights and high energy planes, very similar to what the quasar is, theoretically. There must be some connection.

Ellen looks directly and intensely at Stuart, as if trying to fathom what all this means. Stuart returns the look with a sense of warmth and confidence radiating from his eyes.

Stuart and Ellen are eating dinner in their kitchen. Stuart's mind is wandering again.

                    ELLEN
What are you thinking about?

STUART
Everything.

ELLEN
Me?

STUART
(*Playfully*)
Occasionally.

ELLEN
Do your books get into "love" at all, or is that too mundane? (*Stuart smiles and jokingly waves his hands in a "comme ci, comme ca" gesture.*) Well, I didn't really want to bother you with unimportant questions. I realize you have more pressing matters.

STUART
That's true. (*He smiles and continues eating.*)

ELLEN
Thanks

Stuart leans across the table and gives Ellen a purposely quick kiss.

STUART
Proof enough?

ELLEN
For a scientist? Hardly.

Stuart leans across the table again and gives her a very passionate kiss.

STUART
How's that?

ELLEN
Better.

Ellen smiles seductively when suddenly the phone rings. Her expression changes to one of real disappointment as she gets up to answer it.

>   STUART
> Probably one of your friends.

>   ELLEN
> Hello... yes. Yes, he is. Who's calling? Oh hi, Paul, I didn't recognize your voice. Just a moment. Stuart, it's for you. Paul Whitney.

>   STUART
>   (*Surprised.*)
> Hello Paul. Yes... (*Stuart's expression turns suddenly serious.*) When? Where did they take him? Yes. Thank you. I'll be there as soon as I can. (*He hangs up*)

>   ELLEN
> What's wrong?

>   STUART
> Paul found Elliot under the telescope in a state of shock. An ambulance took him to the hospital.

Stuart and Paul are walking down a long corridor in a downtown Los Angeles hospital. They walk quickly. Paul is very upset and has difficulty speaking.

>   PAUL
> Milton and the doctor are in there with him.

>   STUART
> How did it happen?

>   PAUL
> He came in excitedly early this evening and said something about wanting to check the quasar.

STUART
The quasar?

PAUL
I had to go down to the lab for some Van Allen filters. When I came back I found him on the sighting platform...

They enter a small room. Milton is waiting nervously. The doctor can be seen through the window examining the graph sheets. Something seems to be wrong. He enters the room where they are waiting.

DOCTOR
This is unbelievable. (*He turns to an assistant who has followed behind him.*) Is his wife still in the waiting room? (*The assistant goes to look.*)

STUART
(*To Milton.*)
Is Marcia here?

MILTON
She's very upset. They didn't want her to stay in here.

DOCTOR
We'll have to get her permission to give shock treatment.

MILTON
Is it that bad?

DOCTOR
I've never seen a brain wave pattern like it. Even in extreme epileptic seizure. It's a miracle he's still alive.

ASSISTANT
A nurse is with her. Should I bring her here?

DOCTOR
I'd better go talk to her there. (*Milton starts to go with him.*) No, please wait here. (*He exits.*)

MILTON
This is baffling.

STUART
Paul, when you found him, could he talk? Did he say anything?

PAUL
Not a word. He was just lying there, grabbing at the earphones like he was trying to get them off. But he didn't say a thing. His mouth and eyes were like (*Paul mimics a wide-eyed dazed expression.*). That's just the way I found him.

MILTON
Stuart, you don't know if maybe he had a past history of mental or emotional… you know, problems.

STUART
I don't think the problem is mental or emotional.

MILTON
But what else could cause something like this?

The doctor hurries back into the room and walks over to the attendants.

DOCTOR
Room 238. Dr. Michaels is waiting.

Elliot is rolled out of the room, down the hall and onto an elevator.

PAUL
Is shock treatment necessary?

DOCTOR
It's the only alternative.

STUART
(*Speaking after a moment of apparently deep concentration.*)
Doctor, what are my chances of having an electroencephalogram?

DOCTOR
(*Everyone is surprised.*)
What?

STUART
A brain wave test. The same as Elliot.

MILTON
Stuart? What is this?

STUART
I think it's important.

DOCTOR
Well... (*He hesitates for a moment.*) All right, let me get one of the interns. (*He leaves.*)

PAUL
Is there something wrong, Stuart?

STUART
That's what we're going to find out.

Stuart is shown going through the tests. The doctor is noticeably disturbed by the results and retests on another machine. The results are the same.

> DOCTOR
> If your colleague's test didn't confirm the results I would say it was impossible. But there it is. (*He points to the graphs.*)

> STUART
> How close are they?

> DOCTOR
> On paper, the same. The difference Dr. Townley, is that you are walking around, I have no idea how, and your associate is undergoing shock treatment.

> MILTON
> Stuart, can you explain what's happening?

> STUART
> (*Considering for a moment.*)
> Tomorrow, Milton. A conference at two o'clock. It's very important.

> DOCTOR
> Dr. Townley, I don't know what this is all about, but I must warn you that at any moment you may have need of medical treatment to prevent permanent neurological damage.

> STUART
> What effect would the shock treatment have?

> DOCTOR
> With luck, it would jar your brain back onto a normal level.

> MILTON
> Stuart, I don't think this can wait till tomorrow.

STUART
It will have to. I still have things to work out. (*To the doctor.*) When will we have the results of Elliot's treatment?

DOCTOR
We could have something soon.

STUART
Can I call you?

DOCTOR
Certainly. (*Stuart begins to leave. The doctor is surprised.*) Dr. Townley, I think it would be advisable to perform some additional tests.

STUART
So do I, but it will have to wait.

MILTON
Where are you going?

STUART
Home. Milton, stop worrying. Go home and get some sleep. I'll see you at two. And if you get in before I do, tell Iris to clean the conference room. We may have some big shots.

MILTON
Stuart, what's going on?

STUART
Two o'clock. (*And he leaves.*)

Stuart is sitting at the desk in his office, writing rapidly. Several books are open and lying in front of him. He looks up suddenly and then pushes the intercom button.

                    IRIS (V.O.)
          Yes, Dr. Townley?

                    STUART
          Iris, bring in that new report from Klein's
          office. O.K.?

                    IRIS
          O.K.

Iris enters with the report and puts it on Stuart's desk.

                    IRIS
          Anything else?

                    STUART
          No thanks... Milton in yet?

                    IRIS
          He called. Said he'd be late. There have been
          a lot of calls about Elliot.

                    STUART
          You haven't told them anything?

                    IRIS
          I just said he was doing fine.

                    STUART
          Good girl. (*She begins to leave.*) Don't get
          lost. It's going to get pretty hectic.

                    IRIS
          If you can't find me, I'll be under my desk.

Stuart smiles as she leaves. He opens the new report and scans it quickly. He looks at a passage for several moments and then his eyes wander off the page. He stares, absentmindedly, out the window. Suddenly Stuart notices that the walls of the room are beginning to move. He watches them curiously for a few moments before realizing that they are pulsating in rhythm with his breath. The pulsation increases rapidly until the walls are contracting to a suffocating closeness and expanding to a vast, almost limitless horizon. In a desperate effort to stabilize the environment, Stuart holds his breath. His hand reaches for the intercom button, heavily and slowly, as if weighted down by a thousand pounds. Still holding his breath Stuart's eyes begin to bulge and his face becomes red and full. As his hand nears the button the intercom breaks apart into a million moving molecular particles. Stuart looks very frightened. Suddenly his whole body explodes in slow motion into a thousand small spheres. It seems like a catastrophic disintegration yet strangely beautiful and awesome, each sphere containing a fragment of his image suspended and moving in space. At the same time the entire room dissolves into a mass of quickly spinning particles, as if we are seeing the molecular and atomic breakup of each solid form. As abruptly as they had disintegrated the molecules begin to reform. Only it is not Stuart's office that reappears but the hallway of his home. Stuart is amazed to find himself standing there. He rushes into the living room and sees Joan and Harry Robinson sitting on the sofa.

<blockquote>

HARRY

We were waiting for you, Stuart.

STUART

(*Yelling.*)

Where is Ellen?

JOAN

Come with us.

</blockquote>

They walk to a door leading to the pantry and open it. There is a flight of steps leading down behind it. Stuart starts down, but suddenly stops.

<blockquote>

STUART

There weren't any stairs here before!

</blockquote>

He turns around and looks at Joan and Harry. They have turned into monstrous Bosch-like demons. Stuart screams. They do not pay attention but continue walking him down the flight of stairs. He looks back hoping to escape and sees that the door behind him has disappeared.

STUART
Where am I? What is all this?

HARRY
You know where you are.

STUART
No! I don't know. How did I get here?

JOAN
You know how you got here.

STUART
No, I don't. I really don't! (*He seems hysterical and afraid, like a little boy.*) Where is Ellen? (*He calls her name like a child looking for his mother. They keep walking down the stairs.*) Why is this happening? I don't believe it! I'm just hallucinating. It's not real.

HARRY
If this isn't real, Stuart, what is real?

As they continue down the stairs they pass a door. Stuart violently breaks away from them and runs to it. He opens the door and runs inside. The room is large. In the center, rising out of the floor, is a small stand. On it is a button. Stuart stares at it, not knowing what to do. The door to the room is opening. He pushes the button and there is a sharp buzz. He has just pushed the intercom in his office.

IRIS
Yes, Dr. Townley? (*There is no answer.*) Dr. Townley? (*We hear a scuffle of chairs and then Iris and another secretary rush into the room.*) Dr. Townley, are you all right? (*Stuart just stares at them.*) Judy get some water, hurry. (*Judy runs out of the room and returns with a glass of water.*) Here, drink this Dr. Townley. (*Stuart doesn't drink the*

water.) Maybe we should take him to the
couch in the conference room.

They help him up and lead him to the door. They open it and we see the staircase again. Stuart looks down and then back at the secretaries. They are demons, caricatures of old hags with beaks like a bird. They mock him with their words.

IRIS
Right this way, "Doctor" Townley.

They walk down the long staircase. We reach the bottom and see a long narrow corridor. Stuart sees someone ahead of him, quite a distance away. He runs toward the human figure, but as he gets closer he sees that there are many people. Stuart's face turns white. It is the end of a long line. He recognizes the line, the people, the place. Instinctively he turns around to go back, but there is nowhere to go back to. We are in the same place as the opening of the film, the same sounds, the same faces, the same shot. Stuart is moved forward. He is shaking. A rope is placed around his neck. He sees the women in front of him as they slip and fall, their necks broken. Stuart is abruptly yanked forward and sees the other end of his rope being fastened to someone else. He cannot see the figure. Both men are suddenly pushed forward, tied irrevocably to each other. They are dragged toward the shining wires and shoved onto them. A look of abject terror is in their faces as they begin the perilous journey across. The noose dangles around their necks. They cross slowly, each step carefully measured and balanced. Their eyes do not leave the wire and they do not look at each other. Halfway across Stuart shoots a look forward, trying to see his destination. Instead of the safe landing area he had expected he sees only a dark, metallic wall. Even if he reached it there would be nowhere to go. For a moment he looks terrified and confused, like a trapped animal. His balance falters. His body twists and his head jerks up suddenly. The other man, startled, looks up too and their eyes meet for the first time in a moment of dumbfounded recognition. Stuart sees that he is bound to himself. The terror and distrust vanish from his face and his eyes reveal a look of sudden deep understanding and awakening. He stares at himself for a few silent moments and then in a decision of either madness or faith, the two Stuarts lean forward, embrace each other and dive deliberately, almost joyously, into the abyss. The two Stuarts come together into one body, as if finally uniting after a long and burdensome separation. At the point when the noose should choke him, at the moment of seemingly certain death, the rope continues unraveling and then flames into ashes, as he falls freely into a vast and limitless void. There seems to be nothingness at first, eternal blackness, until we begin to perceive a small white light in the distance. It comes closer, in a circular motion that slowly widens into a vast spiral, engulfing Stuart as it grows larger. As the spiraling white light reaches the audience, the blackness which defines it begins to turn red, then gold, then blue – a constant variety of colors, like those of the quasar. The colors become more pastel until they blend with the white space around them. The spiral gradually disappears and Stuart's falling becomes floating in ecstatic blissful light. The light rays form a river carrying Stuart into a new landscape, strange and surreal but not unfamiliar. We travel through avenues of gigantic vaulted archways suspended in space, porticos of undulating light, rows of marble pillars stretching into vast horizons. A magic kingdom opens before us, a glorious vision of heaven, of all the heavens that man has ever dreamed. Towering figures appear and surround Stuart as he floats between them. Saints in flowing robes, wise men, sublime images of gods and angels, primitive deities, ancestors of a thousand races. Suddenly the light bends and shoots upward, carrying Stuart with it. High above him, filling the whole of space, Stuart sees the archetypal image of the great God King, a vision of overpowering grandeur, almost terrifying in its magnificence. The great figure spreads out its arms as if to embrace and envelope the tiny being hurling toward him. Stuart's face is filled with joy and wonder. There is a great roar of thunder and bursts of lightning and the image of the God King begins to dissolve and disappear, but the outline of his form remains. Behind it, as if through an open door, a majestic sky and clouds appear. Stuart and the camera float through the body outline into the sky. The camera tilts down and an outdoor setting comes into view. Hills, trees and a parking lot. Suddenly Milton Klein passes through the frame. The camera pulls back and the outdoor setting is seen framed by a window and we realize that we are inside an office. Milton and Paul are pacing back and forth through the image, speaking nervously.

PAUL
When's Ellen supposed to get here?

MILTON
Iris called her. She said that she'd leave immediately.

PAUL
It's very strange. You'd think the ambulance would be here by now.

MILTON
It's a long drive. (*He pauses for a while and continues pacing.*) If I didn't see it with my own eyes I wouldn't have believed it.

PAUL
What can they do?

MILTON
I'm not sure. Shock treatment, I suppose.

The camera position moves slowly to Paul, who looks down and notices that Stuart is looking at him.

PAUL
Stuart. Don't worry. You're just hallucinating. Everything will be all right. Do you hear me?

We cut to Stuart from Paul's point of view. He seems astonished to find himself back in the room and is obviously trying to recapture the experience he has just had. He repeatedly opens and closes his eyes very slowly. He raises his hand into the air as if trying to explain something but it just floats there as his eyes close and a great smile forms on his face. Paul and Milton stare at him.

MILTON
Stuart, can you hear me? (*There is no answer.*)

PAUL
Stuart! (*Stuart slowly nods his head affirmatively. He is still smiling.*)

MILTON
Do you want some water?

> STUART
> (*Smiling as his eyes
> roll open, he speaks very softly.*)
> No. Nothing.

Paul and Milton look questioningly at each other. Stuart's head begins to move exploring his body, trying, it seems, to determine what position it is in. He begins to move his hands over his legs and then raises his palms in front of his eyes. He stares at them for a few moments and then flexes and unflexes his fists. He brings his hands onto his head, feeling his scalp.

> MILTON
> What's the matter? Are you feeling all right?

Stuart brings his hands down and looks directly at Milton and speaks to him, very softly in a controlled and beautiful voice.

> STUART
> I feel (*he pauses*) very well. (*There is another
> pause as he chooses his words.*) Very happy.

Paul and Milton seem worried as he speaks, not understanding his new tone of voice and suspecting him to be somewhat deranged. Stuart's expression is almost glowing, and they find it difficult to look at him.

Iris suddenly comes into the room and sees that Stuart is conscious.

> IRIS
> Dr. Townley! (*To Milton.*) Is he all right?

Stuart turns to Iris as she enters. He is startled for a moment, mistrustful, almost frightened. But then his smile returns.

> STUART
> Hello, Iris. (*She smiles at him, happy to be
> recognized.*)

> PAUL
> (*To Iris.*)
> Any word from the hospital?

IRIS
They said the ambulance should be here any minute. (*Iris hesitates, not quite certain what she should say.*) Listen, all of these people are beginning to arrive for the conference. What should I do?

MILTON
(*Realizing he has forgotten about it.*) Damn it, let me talk to them. I'll try and explain, somehow.

Stuart, too, suddenly remembers the conference and his face instantly grows more serious, more recollected.

STUART
Wait, Milton. Tell them to go to the conference room.

MILTON
(*Surprised and confused.*)
But you can't...!

PAUL
Stuart, you're not serious?

STUART
Yes, I am.

MILTON
This is absurd. You don't know what you're saying.

STUART
I know exactly what I'm saying. (*He turns to Iris.*) Tell them to go into the conference room. (*Iris turns to Milton for a signal, not sure who to listen to, but Milton is unsure of himself and unable to instruct her.*)

STUART
Go on Iris.

Iris leaves. Milton and Paul are obviously unable to reconcile Stuart's actions of several minutes ago with his present calm and strength.

MILTON
Stuart, you can't do this.

Stuart looks at Milton with a powerful and determined expression. Suddenly Ellen comes hurrying into the room. She is frightened. She looks rapidly at everyone in the room and then runs to Stuart, who stands up and embraces her.

ELLEN
Stuart, are you all right? What's happening? They made everything sound so terrible.

Stuart looks at Ellen. His face is filled with love for her as he embraces her with an unexpected exuberance.

STUART
I'm fine. (*Ellen looks searchingly into his face.*)

ELLEN
Did it happen again? (*Milton and Paul are surprised by the question.*)

STUART
Yes. (*He looks at Ellen with a sense of wonderment.*) It's even more than I dreamed it was.

MILTON
What are you talking about? Do you have any idea what happened to you? You weren't feeling fine twenty minutes ago. You were ranting and raving.

PAUL
Ellen, this is serious. Something has
happened to Stuart's brain. It's dangerous.
(*Ellen seems confused.*)

MILTON
(*Turning desperately to Ellen.*)
Ellen, listen to me. I spoke with Dr.
Curran.

ELLEN
Who?

STUART
Last night. (*Ellen nods her head, revealing
that she already knows.*)

MILTON
Do you know he said Stuart should be
confined? He needs tests. His mind is
operating abnormally. They need your
permission.

Ellen seems momentarily shaken but does not lose her composure.

STUART
Milton, why are you so afraid of anything
that might be abnormal? Listen, I know you
both mean well, but you don't understand.

MILTON
We don't just mean well, damn it. We don't
want you to lose your mind.

STUART
Neither do I. That's just the point.

PAUL
Stuart, really, be sensible.

STUART
I am being sensible. Really. Go to the
conference room. (*He speaks with unusual
confidence and power.*) I have some
extremely important things to say. I'll be
there shortly. I want to be alone with Ellen
for a moment.

They stay in the room for a few seconds, angrily, almost defiantly, until
Stuart gives them a harsh look and they leave.

ELLEN
Stuart, I'm frightened.

STUART
I suppose I would be too. But there's
nothing to be afraid of. I know what's going
on. Something is happening to my mind.
But it's not bad. Look at me! You can tell.
I'm fine. I really am.

ELLEN
Why did Milton say you were ranting and
raving?

STUART
I guess I was. But it's over now.

ELLEN
(*Looking at him, not sure
what to believe.*)
But maybe they're right – for your own
good. Isn't that possible?

STUART
No, Ellen. (*Looking deeply into her eyes.*)
Believe me.

Ellen looks at him. She doesn't understand what is happening but cannot
dismiss his confidence, his enthusiasm, his force.

ELLEN
Stuart, if you didn't seem so… (*She cannot find the words.*) What's going to happen now?

STUART
I'll know more after the conference.

ELLEN
Are you going to tell them what happened to you?

STUART
I have to.

ELLEN
They're not going to believe you.

STUART
I've got to try.

Stuart shrugs his shoulders to indicate it's a chance he has to take. Ellen realizes that she is going to have to take it with him.

STUART
I'll be home in a few hours. Everything will be all right. (*He holds her warmly.*)

Ellen walks down the corridor to the front door. Military personnel get out of their automobiles and approach the entrance. Two men in white uniforms stand at the desk with Iris. She signs a note of some sort and returns it to them. They leave. Stuart steps out of the door behind Iris' desk and walks to the conference room. The observatory conference room is not particularly impressive. It seems suited for meetings of less importance than the one Stuart is holding. The table in the center cannot seat all of the people who have been assembled, so many are sitting, delegate fashion, behind the first row of chairs. Stuart is standing at the head of the table, behind a small podium that is being positioned for him. Joining the observatory officials attending the meeting are men from the military and other government agencies. The talking subsides as Stuart begins to speak.

STUART

Yesterday evening at about eight o'clock, Elliot Borman, one of my assistants, was observing the quasar when suddenly he had a seizure or fit of some unknown nature, causing a radical change in his brain chemistry. He was given shock therapy in an attempt to restore his brain waves to a normal level. As of this morning, the treatment has been unable to alter this new brain frequency. The doctors advised continued treatment, but on my advice his wife has withdrawn her permission to give it.

PAUL

Stuart?

STUART

(*Motions for Paul to wait.*)
This is a graph of a normal brain wave (*He holds it up and pins it to the wall behind him. Then he holds up another.*) This is Elliot's. (*He pins it up.*) And this is mine. (*He places it alongside Elliot's. There is a low murmur in the room.*) Four nights ago, when you called me to observe the new fluctuations in the quasar pulsation, you may remember that Elliot claimed to see a luminous build-up that no one else saw. He said it was very faint. Then I looked. The build-up was no longer faint. It was growing into the most intense light I have ever seen. It was beautiful and terrifying. Suddenly the light broke into an overwhelming whoosh of colors that shot out through space, speeding toward me, rushing into my eyes, into my nervous system. It was like being electrocuted. I could feel every cell and atom in my body. I lost all sense of normal

consciousness. When I found myself back on the sighting platform, I was completely shaken.

MILTON
Why didn't you say anything then?

STUART
Because I felt what you are all probably thinking now, that the experience was all up here. (*He points to his head.*) Just my imagination. I couldn't believe that it had really happened.

MILTON
I looked. I didn't see anything.

STUART
I know.

MILTON
Why not?

STUART
Maybe you weren't ready.

MILTON
What is that supposed to mean?

STUART
It has something to do with receptivity. This the only way I can explain why some of us would have the experience and others wouldn't.

PAUL
Are you saying that Elliot had the same experience?

STUART
Yes. I spoke with him for a few minutes this morning.

MILTON
He was talking?

STUART
A little. He was still pretty frightened. You see, the vision can really shatter your hold on reality. Sort of like seeing a ghost. It's a whole new world.

One of the generals who has been fidgeting during the entire conference clears his throat.

GENERAL
Dr. Townley, are you certain these "stories" are relevant?

STUART
Very much so.

GENERAL
I'm afraid I don't see the connection. You aren't trying to tell us that this "star" out there is causing these... aberrations?

STUART
I am.

GENERAL
(*Shaking his head and chewing on the inside of his lip.*)
Do you know what you're saying?

STUART
I do. But let me say it. (*Stuart takes a drink of water.*) It is generally understood by most astronomers today that the universe was

created about fifteen billion years ago in a massive explosion we call the "big bang."

GENERAL
And what was there before the explosion?

STUART
Something we call a "cosmic egg." All potential energy and matter, unmanifested, very condensed.

GENERAL
And where did the egg come from?

STUART
(*Shrugging his shoulders.*)
We don't pretend to know. (*The general shakes his head as if enjoying a private victory.*) The first quasars we discovered were about nine billion years old, indicating that they were probably among the earliest things formed after the big bang. This factor, combined with their unbelievable distance and power, led us to hope that in studying them further we might unlock the door to those proverbial secrets of the universe. Then a month ago we discovered this new quasar – bigger, further away and older than the others. We have been unable to successfully measure its distance or age. But a week ago I would have estimated that it was probably formed not long after the big bang itself. However, my experiences in the last week, Elliot's experience, a lot of study and thinking have caused me to revise my estimate. I no longer feel we are observing something formed after the big bang but the explosion itself. I think we have discovered and are actually seeing the beginning of the universe.

There is a general disturbance in the room. People seem annoyed, skeptical and unconvinced.

                MILTON
Stuart!

                PAUL
That's insane!

                MILTON
Are you serious? How do you expect to substantiate that?

                PAUL
That's absurd. No one will believe it.

                STUART
I didn't expect it to go over very well. I'm still not finished, so save your comments until I am. I also believe that the energy radiating out of this quasar is creative and intelligent on every level of interpretation, that the universe is not a chance or haphazard formation but an evolving, organic whole. We are part of that evolution. Just as the seed or embryo from which we grew contained a blueprint for our growth and transmitted it by means of a genetic code from cell to cell, in the same way the cosmic egg, the seed of the universe, contained the plan of all potential development, a plan which is being transmitted throughout the universe which is still in the process of creation.

Stuart is slowly losing his hold on his audience. A number of generals are doodling on the pads in front of them. There is an undertone of whispering in the room. In contrast to the inattention, one man sitting close to one of the generals seems very absorbed in what Stuart is talking about.

STUART
A few days ago I got a massive jolt of that
transmission. Elliot too. And our visions
have revealed the universe to be more alive
and miraculous than we had ever suspected.
But these visions are not new. Mystics, seers,
wise men, have been experiencing them for
thousands of years. The same thing. All
religions seem to be based on them, on the
reality of the unseen, that which surpasses
all understanding. Christ, Buddha, Moses –
they all talked about it. An ineffable light.
Cosmic revelations. Until now, these visions
have only occurred to a few, those who were
receptive. But now the quasar is going to
change all that. Its energy is intensifying.
Our communication systems have already
begun to pick it up, and are broadcasting
it around the world. Even if we try to tune
it out, to turn off all the world's electrical
apparatus, the electricity in our brains will
begin to receive it.

MILTON
Stuart, stop this. You don't know what
you're saying.

STUART
I know what I'm saying and it's based on the
most profound experiences I have ever had.

MILTON
You're not being rational or professional.

STUART
Then you give me your explanation for
the alteration of my brain chemistry. You
explain why Elliot is in the hospital, why
our communication networks are being
disrupted. Milton, biologically this is as

far as we're going to go. The next step in evolution is the psychic step. The quasar isn't destroying us, it's triggering an advance. The door is opening and we win. Don't you see?

Obviously they don't.

Stuart and Ellen are sitting in their living room, not talking, staring at the wall, occasionally at each other. The long silence is broken by a jarring telephone ring.

STUART
I'll get it. (*He crosses to the phone and answers it.*) Hello… speaking… Yes… Thank you. I didn't think I'd gotten across to anyone… Oh really? (*Stuart seems extremely interested.*) Right. I understand… Yes, I think it's beginning to happen. People just have to realize that it's not just happening to them… Maybe if we could get together… Oh? (*Stuart's face turns almost white.*). Yes… I don't believe that. They wouldn't… (*Ellen comes over to Stuart.*) What do you suggest? (*Stuart looks at his watch.*) Yes… how urgent? (*Stuart's face grows very tense.*) Well, I appreciate your concern. Right, I understand. Well, thank you for letting me know. Goodbye. (*He hangs up.*)

ELLEN
Tell me. (*Impatiently.*) Stuart!

STUART
I think I've really hit some raw nerves. They want to… hospitalize me.

ELLEN
Who does?

STUART
The government, the military, I don't know. They think I know too much. I'm a security risk.

ELLEN
(*Confused.*)
Who was that?

STUART
Wouldn't say. Except he was at the conference. He believed what I was talking about. He's been having those dreams. (*Ellen seems a bit suspicious.*)

ELLEN
Stuart, let's go away.

STUART
That's what he suggested.

ELLEN
Please.

STUART
(*Making a rapid decision.*)
Pack your bag. (*Ellen is first surprised, then ecstatic as she hugs Stuart.*)

Stuart's car pulls out of the driveway and begins down the street.

ELLEN
Stuart, wait. Turn around. We forgot to call the camp. I want to let Mickey know.

STUART
We can call from the cottage.

                        ELLEN
            No, I want to call now. Please, Stu. It'll just
            take a minute. I'll feel better.

                        STUART
            O.K. But fast.

He turns the car around and begins driving to the house when he notices a
government car parked in front of it. There is a man on the porch ringing
the doorbell. He signals that there is no one home and three men, sitting
in the car, jump out and head for the house. Stuart and Ellen watch for a
moment, then drive quickly past the house in silence.

A close-up of a bubble fills the screen. We watch it as it moves upward
and then bursts. Another rises in the air, fragile and beautiful. The camera
begins to tilt downward and we see one perched on a plastic blower, the
kind that children use. Stuart is sitting on the floor of a country cabin,
looking intensely at the next bubble about to be launched. Ellen's voice
from the kitchen breaks the silence.

                        ELLEN
            Stuart, I'm worried about Mickey.

                        STUART
            Ellen, he's got the whole summer. He won't
            miss us at all.

                        ELLEN
            There's no way we can call?

                        STUART
            No way. Harry's right. It's better that they
            watch out for him. He'll be O.K. Things
            will probably cool down faster than we
            think. In a week or two this may all seem
            ridiculous. So let's enjoy ourselves. We've
            needed this. (*Stuart is still staring at the
            bubble balanced on the blower in front of
            him.*) I'll bet I can tell you exactly when this
            bubble will break. (*Stuart begins to imitate*

a rocket launching countdown as he stares at the bubble.) Five. Four. Three. Two. One. (*The bubble breaks a split second after "one" has been said.*)

ELLEN
(*Mildly surprised.*)
That was just luck.

STUART
Oh yeah? Watch me do it again. Five. Four. Three. Two. One. Zero. (*The bubble keeps floating.*) Minus one. Minus two. Minus three. Minus four. (*It breaks as he hits minus five.*) See, I told you I could do it!

ELLEN
But that's cheating.

The scene suddenly changes to both of them sitting outdoors on the grass, but the dialogue overlaps and continues.

STUART
Now's your chance to get even. You count this time.

ELLEN
You really are bubble crazy today.

Stuart begins to chew hard on the bubble gum in his mouth and starts to blow it up. The pink bubble expands slowly. Ellen begins the countdown.

ELLEN
Five. Four. Three. Two. One.

When she reaches "One" she pricks the bubble with a small twig hidden in her hand. It explodes in Stuart's face, covering his mouth and nose with a pink, sticky film. Ellen is laughing uncontrollably like a child. Momentarily stunned, Stuart is silent. Then he says in a soft, menacing tone, with his bubble-gum face, "Kiss me." Feigning disgust, Ellen moves away from him and starts walking toward the trees behind them. Stuart follows her in a mock robot-like movement, and then suddenly breaks into a fast run. Ellen is taken by surprise but instinctively darts away from him and disappears into the forest. Stuart chases her through the woods, catching sight of her, then losing her in the gigantic green maze of leaves and branches. But he keeps running furiously, even when she is completely out of sight, as if overwhelmed by a sense of movement and freedom in itself. When he seems to have definitely lost her he stops suddenly, trying to listen for her footsteps, but he hears only the ever-present crackle of the forest and an occasional bird. Stuart walks over to the lake and begins to wash the bubble gum from his face. We see Ellen slowly and silently sneaking up from behind, waiting to frighten or surprise him. But he has seen her reflection in the water and when she is right above him he reaches back and grabs her, lifting her on his back. She laughs and struggles to get free. Stuart is about to toss her into the water when she grabs hold of his belt. He loses his balance and they both fall laughing and splashing into the water.

We see the beginning of a fire catching from paper to kindling wood and finally to some larger logs. Stuart is lying next to it, absorbed in the rhythmic, mysterious dance of the growing flames. We can hear a shower in the background. We cut to a shot of Ellen getting out of the shower and drying herself. She walks into the living room and silently watches Stuart lying on the floor, chin on hands, gazing into the fire. It looks for a moment as if Stuart might have fallen asleep.

ELLEN
(*Looking at the fire.*)
It's so beautiful.

Stuart seems oblivious to her presence and lies motionless on the rug.

ELLEN
Stuart? (*Raising her voice slightly*).

He still doesn't respond and a wave of alarm suddenly engulfs Ellen. She rushes over to him. Stuart is startled and instinctively jumps up as she touches him.

STUART
What's the matter?

ELLEN
(*Relieved but still confused.*)
I don't know. Didn't you hear me?

STUART
No.

ELLEN
(*Apologetically.*)
I'm sorry. I guess I'm still edgy.

STUART
(*Nodding and looking
at her comfortingly.*)
Come here – you're shivering.

He puts his arm around her. Ellen sticks her toes up near the hot embers and wiggles them in a childlike way. She laughs, forgetting her fear as they watch the fire's light show being performed only for them. A few moments pass. They seem like little children as they snuggle up to one another.

There is hardly a movement, except for Stuart's hand gently stroking the nape of her neck. Ellen looks very beautiful, much younger than we have ever seen or felt her to be. She seems to radiate a strong warmth and glow. Turning her head slightly she looks at Stuart with her dark brown eyes. After a few moments they seem to get lighter, turning to blue, hazel, green and then grey. Stuart runs his fingers along her nose, eyes and lips with a gentle caressing motion, as if touching and really feeling them for the first time. He gently kisses her forehead, then her eyelids and nose, working his way sensuously down to her lips which he kisses softly at first but ever more passionately as they draw closer together. Their lips separate slowly as the embrace loosens, each looking deeply and lovingly at the other. Ellen's face seems slightly but noticeably different. It appears to be slowly, almost imperceptibly changing, as if revealing a new range of expressions hidden beneath its usual facade. Strangely and magically her features begin to modify as if someone were invisibly molding them again into a different face. The new face slowly emerges and solidifies into a distinct and unique personality, but lasting only a second, as the eyes, hair, nose, cheeks, lips and chin begin to dissolve again. Thinner lips this time, with a short stubby nose and blue eyes, then turning to oriental eves and a short flat nose with black hair. There is a constant flow of movement as the features dissolve into one another forming a continual galaxy of new faces. It is as if Ellen had contained all the possible faces of women since the beginning of time, almost as if she were all these women. Stuart kisses her again, holding her closely. The camera pulls back to different angles of the room revealing that it is not only Ellen's face that is changing, but her whole body as well. Within the continuous movement of their kiss and Stuart's hands caressing her hair, neck and face, Ellen's body is transformed into the bodies of a multitude of women, from long-haired blondes to curly-haired brunettes – thin and fat, young and old, peasant girls, sophisticated city types, whores, college girls, all colors and creeds, every conceivable woman, as the camera moves around the room viewing their embrace from all possible angles. Suddenly they are in a different room, half nude, with Stuart caressing her breasts, his hands moving up to her neck surrounded in the background by a green field and trees, then down her back, slowly, as they lie on a beach, continuing along her spine and around to her stomach as they move through many different rooms and environments, the women constantly changing within one continuous movement as their lovemaking becomes more intense. Both of them are nude now, gently touching each other, as the women merge into a oneness of arms, legs, backs, thighs, breasts and buttocks. We are lost in a world of flesh and shapes, movement and rhythm, as their lovemaking becomes more passionate, reaching its apex in a fantastic rush of a thousand faces and bodies that emerge from both of them, as if they had dissolved their own selves and become all men and all women at that moment. The flow continues, constant but slower now, as if their own bodies were searching for their unique shape and personality amongst the flood of a million others.

Stuart and Ellen become recognizable at moments. We begin to see Ellen's face again – briefly – only long enough to sense that it is not as open and soft as the others. There is a coldness, a fear, in it. The images stop changing, solidfying into Stuart and Ellen lying together, nude, in bed. Stuart turns over, dazed, exhausted, and seemingly asleep. A candle on the nightstand flickers wildly and suddenly goes out.

Ellen is on the telephone in the next room, frightened, hardly able to talk.

ELLEN
I don't know what to do. Milton, please hurry. He doesn't know me. I think he's going crazy... (*She tries to restrain her crying.*) Route 34, at Silver Lake.

Stuart's eyes are open. He is listening. He hears her hang up. She comes back into the bedroom.

STUART
You shouldn't have done that, Ellen.

ELLEN
Stuart... (*She pauses for a few moments. In a way, she seems afraid of him.*) I... I didn't know what to do... (*She starts crying again and runs over to the bed.*) I'm afraid... I'm afraid. (*She sobs uncontrollably.*)

STUART
(*Holding her close and caressing her head tenderly with his hand.*)
If there was only a way to show you.

ELLEN
I don't want to lose you. I'm afraid.

STUART
Is that why you called Milton?

ELLEN
It's not working. You've got to get help.

STUART
(*Tears forming in his eyes.*)
I need a different kind of help. (*Stuart is very upset but quiet. He seems hurt and lost and not sure what to do.*)

Ellen continues crying. Stuart rocks her in his lap, trying to comfort her. Slowly her crying subsides. There is a silence and Stuart sees that she is asleep. He waits until she is definitely breathing heavily and then slides out of bed. He goes to the kitchen, puts his clothes on, finds some notepaper and a pencil, and writes. Turning with the note in his hand to take it into the bedroom he discovers Ellen standing in the doorway, watching him.

>STUART
>(*Guiltily.*)
>I thought you were asleep.

>ELLEN
>(*Her face smudged with tears.*)
>Do you think I could really sleep?

>STUART
>(*Searching her face.*)
>I can't let them take me to the hospital.

>ELLEN
>(*Her eyes are watering.
>She holds out the car keys.*)
>You'll need these.

Stuart looks lovingly at his wife, profoundly moved by her gesture. She reaches up and gazes at his face as though it might be for the last time.

>ELLEN
>Don't be long.

>STUART
>I might not be back for breakfast.

>ELLEN
>(*Smiling slightly.*)
>I know.

Ellen sits at the cabin window holding back the curtain and watching as Stuart gets into the car. Her eyes are steady, gently observing his every move. The motor starts up and the car begins to advance slowly down the driveway. Ellen lets the curtain fall, dropping in front of the window. Stuart's departure is seen through it, two red tail lights shining through the lace design and disappearing.

Stuart heads down a deserted country road. He travels for a while over the bumpy surface until reaching the junction of a superhighway. Signs point west to Los Angeles and east to Nevada. Stuart pauses for a few moments, realizing for the first time that he doesn't know where he is going. A car honks from behind and Stuart quickly turns right, going east. For a short time there is a lot of traffic on the highway, headlights rushing toward him and cars behind him flashing their bright lights into his rearview mirror. An ambulance with a wailing siren and spinning red lights speeds past him heading in the other direction. As its shrill sound fades away, a strange and peaceful quiet begins to settle on the moving traffic, an almost musical silence. The car lights seem nearly to be floating over the landscape. There is no sense of speed. The highway narrows into two lanes and soon there are no other cars on the road but Stuart's. He passes a sign giving the mileage to Reno, Las Vegas and Death Valley. The night grows dark and ominous with thick clouds allowing only an occasional moon glow to penetrate through them. A bright light shines in Stuart's rearview mirror. The light blinds a few times and then a large, colorfully decorated hippie school bus passes him. Painted on the back of the bus is a big, funny looking face with a broad, quizzical smile. Stuart laughs to himself as he sees it. He watches as the bus speeds ahead and the smiling face gradually disappears. Stuart is left alone in the dark night. Stuart can see nothing but the thirty or so yards of the white dividing lines that his headlights illuminate. The lines rush at us hypnotically and we hardly notice at first that their rhythm is altering. Slowly, however, we realize that the lines are appearing less frequently. The intervals between them grow longer and longer and soon we are aware that there are no lines at all. There is only blackness. Stuart brings his car to a halt. He grabs a flashlight from the glove compartment and jumps out. He is mumbling about the "damn headlights" when suddenly he is blinded by them. They are still working. Stuart is mystified. He looks around for signs of the road but there is only hard, flat ground. Stuart stands staring in the glare of the headlights, a figure of confusion and frustration. He walks slowly back to the car, gets in and sits down. In a few moments he is lying on the seat, sound asleep.

A pink glow filters slowly through the front windshield. Reflecting faintly in the rearview mirror we can see what looks like sand, brownish-white particles catching the early morning light. Stuart wakes up slowly, shaking his head and lifting it up. He looks through the windshield. His eyes stare sleepily at a fixed point and then move around from side to side – uncomprehendingly. He quickly jerks his head to look around and the camera pans with him. Stuart is surrounded by desert. He gets out of the car and scrambles up to the roof. As far as he can see there is nothing but sand, rolling dunes and flatlands. There is no sign of a road. He climbs up a high dune, hoping to see further but the sight is the same: more dunes, valleys and a great flat plain stretching into the distance. He walks down the dune and into an area where the sand looks like an ocean of rippling waves. He circles the dune, expecting to get back to his car, but there is no sign of it. Frightened and completely bewildered, he realizes that he is lost. His face and back are perspiring heavily. He starts walking around the dune again, searching for the car. The morning sun has risen quickly in the sky and the rising heat waves shimmer in the air. Suddenly, a flash of light catches Stuart's eyes. He looks in its direction, squinting, trying to discover its source. Far in the distance something appears to be moving. Stuart walks toward it. The light hits his eyes again and he follows the movement of the object until it begins to take form and he realizes that it is a jeep speeding over the sand. Stuart begins to scream, running at it. The jeep keeps moving, drowning out his voice with its loud and raucous motor. Stuart yells louder. The jeep begins to move toward him. As the two get closer he sees that a man is driving it. A teenage boy is with him. They quickly drive up to Stuart.

                        JONATHAN
                        (*Calling out.*)
Hi!

                        STUART
Hi.

                        JONATHAN
What are you doing out here?

                        STUART
I got lost. I can't find my car.

JAMIE
(*Reaching for a canteen.*)
Would you like some water?

STUART
Sure. Thanks. (*He drinks quickly. Jonathan and Jamie smile as they watch him.*)

JONATHAN
Where did you lose it?

STUART
(*Pointing.*)
Out there, I think.

JONATHAN
(*Surprised*).
East?

STUART
I'm not sure.

Jamie hands his father a pair of binoculars.

JONATHAN
Let's see. (*He scans the eastern horizon and sees nothing.*) Do you remember where the sun was? Were you walking toward it or away from it?

STUART
(*Thinking for a moment.*)
It was behind me.

JONATHAN
(*Nodding his head.*)
Good enough. Hop in. Let's see if we can find it. (*Stuart jumps in.*) By the way my name's Jonathan. This is my son Jamie.

                    STUART
        I'm Stuart.

They shake hands and then start off. They drive for a while and stop.

                    JONATHAN
        Are you sure it was in this direction?

                    STUART
            (*Frustrated and annoyed.*)
        No, I'm not sure. (*To himself.*) What is all
        this? You don't just go around losing cars.
        Damn it! (*He takes the binoculars and jumps
        out of the jeep. He climbs a small dune and
        views the area. He sees nothing and returns
        to the jeep, dejectedly.*) This is absurd! I have
        to find it!

                    JONATHAN
        What's your hurry? Where you going?
        (*Stuart stops a moment and realizes that
        he doesn't know where he's going.*) It's not
        gonna go anywhere. (*Comfortingly.*) Why
        don't you come back with us? You can wash
        up and relax. It'll still be there.

Stuart consents, realizing he has no other choice. He gets back in the jeep and they turn in the direction they had originally been heading. The desert views, from the highlands to the valley floor, are exhilarating. Jonathan drives wildly and exuberantly over the desert sands, tackling steep dunes and the roughest of terrain for the sheer challenge of it. At first Stuart holds on for dear life as Jamie and Jonathan nearly fly out of their seats with every bump. Their laughter and enjoyment is contagious, however, and soon Stuart is also rising and falling freely as they speed onward. Stuart can see a small house in the distance appearing and disappearing as they roll over the dunes. They approach it, rapidly. Finally they arrive and the jeep stops. The house is made of stone, hand hewn, strong and sturdy. Near it are some service sheds and a large family garden.

                    JONATHAN
            Jamie, go inside and tell your mother we've
            got a guest for breakfast. (*Betsy, 9, and
            Michael, 4, come running from the house
            and throw their arms around their father.*)
            Michael, Betsy, this is Stuart.

They turn spontaneously to Stuart and hug him unabashedly, playfully. Stuart is surprised and warmed by this unexpected reception. They hold his hands as they walk to the front door. They walk into the kitchen. Margaret, Jonathan's wife, is washing some dishes.

                    JONATHAN
            Margaret, this is Stuart.

                    MARGARET
            Hi, Stuart. (*She wipes her hands on a towel
            and shakes hands with him.*) We don't get
            many guests here. It's a pleasure.

They walk to the table.

                    JONATHAN
            Is Willy eating this morning?

                    MARGARET
            I've set a place for him.

The children finish setting the table and filling the glasses. Everybody sits down. Margaret puts a stack of pancakes on everyone's plate, a specific number for each person. She gives Stuart three and then, realizing that he will want more, adds another. There is an empty place at the table. They eat without speaking, very conscious of their food. The table movements are dance-like, almost choreographed. Food is passed and received spontaneously, without asking. Stuart is slightly uncomfortable by the silence and suspicious of the almost poetic gracefulness of the family. There is a sound of footsteps and Stuart looks up and sees an old man approaching the table. He notices Stuart and smiles warmly.

                    JONATHAN
          Willy, this is Stuart.

Willy smiles again and Stuart smiles back, easily. Margaret gets up and
puts some pancakes on Willy's plate and he too begins eating silently,
without distraction.

                    JONATHAN
                   (*To Stuart.*)
          When you're finished you can take a bath if
          you like. Then I've got some clothes you can
          put on.

                     STUART
          Well, I don't know…

                    MARGARET
          As long as you're here, be comfortable.

                     STUART
          Yes, but…

                      JAMIE
          (*As if picking up on Stuart's hesitation.*)
          I can go look for your car some more.

                    JONATHAN
          Get some water for the tub first, Jamie.

                      JAMIE
          O.K.

Jonathan and Stuart head up a hill past the sheds. They're standing
overlooking some cultivated fields.

                    JONATHAN
          The irrigation trenches run from there to
          there. We could have run them further, but
          then we'd take a chance on overproducing
          and maybe lowering the water table. We

had to drill over eight hundred feet for it. Doesn't rain much of course, so we're tapping water that took thousands of years to accumulate.

STUART
I didn't know it ever rained here.

JONATHAN
Two or three times during the winter. We're going to build a cistern to catch it when it comes. Boy, when it comes, you've never seen anything like it.

STUART
How's that?

JONATHAN
Flash floods. Sweep right over the desert floor. Wash everything away. That's how we lost our first place. It was just carried off. And then we built another one, but after a while it stopped giving us what we needed. I had my eye on this place for about a year and so we decided to try again.

STUART
But why do you stay out here?

JONATHAN
It's peaceful and quiet. (*He pauses and we can actually hear the intense silence.*) Come on, I want to show you where I've been working.

Jonathan and Stuart are seen in a beautiful cave full of mysterious and colorful mineral formations. The feeling is one of an exquisite Renaissance cathedral.

STUART
It's magnificent.

JONATHAN
That's one of the problems, At first we didn't want to touch it, to take anything. But we made our peace with it, like taking the thousand-year-old water.

STUART
So you're a prospector?

JONATHAN
Of sorts. Every month or so we sell off a load of these crystals and that provides us with the essentials. (*He looks around at the great display.*) We should be able to go on forever.

The family is sitting at the dinner table. They have finished their meal.

JAMIE
Tomorrow I'll try out by the ridge. That's the only other place I can think of.

JONATHAN
Of course, Stuart, if you want, we can drive you into Allensville. They've got a phone there and you can probably get a ride back with no trouble.

WILLY
He's not looking to go back.

MARGARET
Well, you're welcome here as if it's your own place, as long as you're happy with us. (*Stuart smiles.*)

It is early morning when Stuart rises. The sunlight is already filling the room. He looks over to where Jamie and Michael sleep. They are not there. He gets up and dresses quickly and hurries into the kitchen. There is no one there either. He walks around to the sheds, to Willy's room looking for everyone, but they are not around. He goes into the living room and sits down in a large stuffed chair. The room is very comfortable and Stuart relaxes for a few moments, but then his mind begins to wander. He fidgets in the chair, obviously not enjoying the silence or being alone with himself. Suddenly, as if they had been there all along, the family appears.

MARGARET
Good morning, Stuart. I'm sorry you didn't sleep well. (*She kisses his forehead.*) Breakfast is almost ready.

STUART
Where were you all?

MARGARET
We get up early. We wanted you to sleep.

Betsy and Michael come running into the room and sit on Stuart's lap. They hug him warmly.

BETSY
We're going to have a wonderful day, Stuart.

STUART
How do you know?

BETSY
(*Speaking very sweetly.*)
I can tell.

MICHAEL
She says that every day.

                    JONATHAN
          Morning, Stu.

                    STUART
          Morning, Jonathan.

Betsy jumps off Stuart's lap and takes Michael piggy back into the kitchen. Stuart and Jonathan follow. They sit down at the table. Jamie walks in very quietly. His eyes are wide and very clear. He moves slowly as he approaches the table and sits down. He seems very distant. When he notices Stuart he smiles fully, with great affection.

                    JAMIE
          Good morning.

                    STUART
          Morning, Jamie.

Jamie continues smiling but makes no attempt at further conversation. As at dinner the night before, no one is talking. Margaret brings the food to the table and begins serving. Stuart notices that no place has been set for Willy and that his chair is standing against the wall. He is about to ask why when he begins to hear the quasar hum filling his head. He tenses immediately and looks nervously around the room to see if anyone else notices it. They do not appear to be affected.

                    STUART
               (*Standing up awkwardly and
                excusing himself.*)
          I... excuse me... I'll be right back.

He hurries out of the kitchen to the front of the house. The sound has grown louder. He begins walking toward the sheds and notices the sound increasing. He looks around suspiciously. He puts his hands over his ears and takes them away again. The sound's intensity remains the same. He begins walking out toward the desert as the hum intensifies. As he walks up a nearby hill it begins to grow almost unbearable. He rounds the top and looking below notices Willy, sitting very still and erect, looking out into the endless horizon. The sound rises higher and higher until it passes beyond the range of hearing and there is only a reverberating silence.

Stuart stares down at Willy for a long time, then turns abruptly and walks back to the house. He stops for a moment outside the kitchen door and tries to regain his composure but it is obvious that his head is filled with many questions. He moves through the kitchen door and stops, almost in a trance, as he looks at the family eating. Margaret looks up at him.

                MARGARET
                (Gently.)
Willy's dying.

Everyone looks at him as he stands there.

                STUART
         (With great difficulty.)
    I don't understand any of this...

                JONATHAN
(Leaving the table and coming over to Stuart,
  he speaks with a true sense of compassion.)
Yes, we know. Although you understand
far more than you realize. It will only be a
matter of time before you can accept it. It's
always new and strange at first.

                STUART
  (Placing his hands tightly on Jonathan's
shoulders and looking piercingly into his eyes.)
Who are you? What is happening to me?
(He begins squeezing Jonathan's arms.) Am
I still hallucinating? Where am I? What is all
this?

An expression of panic flashes across Stuart's face. He lets go of Jonathan, and hurries outside. Jonathan follows and takes hold of him firmly. Stuart relaxes for a moment and Jonathan takes his head in his hands and brings it before his face. He stares calmly and with great strength into his eyes.

                JONATHAN
    Relax, Stuart... Trust us...

STUART
(*Looking hard at Jonathan.*)
Do you understand what's happening to me?

JONATHAN
Yes.

STUART
The sound? The visions?

JONATHAN
Yes.

STUART
But how?

JONATHAN
These experiences aren't new. You're not the only one. You know that.

Stuart pauses, his eyes darting from side to side. He takes a deep breath and sighs.

JONATHAN
You can't be what you were, anymore. You have to accept that. You have seen too deeply into reality to deny what you know.

STUART
I'm not trying to deny it. (*He pauses, reflecting on the last few weeks. He grows very quiet inside.*) Now what? What am I supposed to do? Just wait? (*He pauses again.*) This is all so… well… I never expected anything like this in my life.

JONATHAN
No one ever does… Stay with us, Stuart. You can help us with our work, if you like. Your work will take care of itself.

Willy and Stuart are seen working in the garden. The work is hard and strenuous, but Stuart is thriving on it. He looks younger and healthier now than he has before. Margaret, singing to herself, is hanging clothes on a line to dry. Michael is helping her by carrying the clothespins. Betsy is sitting nearby, sewing. Suddenly Michael runs away from his mother and jumps down on the ground, grabbing for something in the sand. He comes back triumphantly carrying a small lizard by the tail. He offers it to his mother as a gift. She accepts it gratefully.

MARGARET
What should I do with him? (*Michael shrugs his shoulders.*) Should we eat him? (*Michael makes a face.*) Want to put him in your bed so you can sleep with him?

MICHAEL
No.

MARGARET
Well, what should we do with him?

MICHAEL
Can we give him a bath?

MARGARET
I don't think they take baths.

MICHAEL
Never? (*He is very intrigued.*)

MARGARET
Well, not that I know of. (*She smiles.*) Listen, why don't you give him some lunch? O.K.?

MICHAEL
O.K.

MARGARET
Take him to the field and let him have any bug he wants.

> MICHAEL
> (*Already heading for the garden.*)
> O.K.

Jonathan, passing by Willy's bedroom, notices Margaret putting up window curtains.

> JONATHAN
> (*Angrily.*)
> What do you think you're doing?

> MARGARET
> (*Innocently.*)
> Willy took them down.

> JONATHAN
> (*Pulling them down again.*)
> Then leave them down!

He throws the curtains on the bed. There is an uncomfortable silence. Jonathan's anger seems very out of place. Margaret looks at him searchingly. He lowers his eyes. We sense that he is under a great deal of stress. Margaret walks over to him.

> MARGARET
> Jonathan, I was wrong. But the problem is your anger, not the curtains.

> JONATHAN
> (*He begins to reacts angrily, but stops himself.*)
> You're right. I guess I haven't accepted it yet. Not really. I must be more upset about it than I realized.

> MARGARET
> (*Looking at him lovingly.*)
> Don't hold onto it. Let it go.

She walks over to the curtains and begins to refold them. Jonathan watches her for a moment and then gets up and goes over to her.

JONATHAN
Here, let me help.

Jonathan and Stuart are in the kitchen pouring kerosene into several lamps. Willy is in the living room adjusting the gas heater. Margaret is sitting in a hard back chair, helping Michael on with his sweater. Jamie and Betsy are sitting on the floor near Willy. Michael runs over to them and they playfully toss him back and forth. He enjoys it and laughs as he pivots and rocks trustingly from one to the other. The room gets much brighter as Stuart and Jonathan enter with the lamps. They place them on the various tables around the room and sit down. Everyone seems very relaxed and comfortable after a good dinner. Stuart watches the children playing. Willy seems very quiet and restful sitting in front of the heater. Margaret gets up and takes a shawl from a shelf and drapes it around her shoulders. She also drapes one over Stuart's legs. Jonathan folds his feet underneath him on the chair. Stuart smiles happily at the simple comfort of the evening. He looks out the window at a sky filled with stars. The sound of the quasar is faintly heard, as if coming from very far away. The room seems to grow subtly darker. The orange light from the heater radiates a warm glow that envelopes Willy. Everyone sits quietly, looking at him. Stuart's eyes move rapidly around the room. He becomes aware that Willy is breathing very deeply, with great control and that everyone else in the room is breathing in rhythm with his breath. As Stuart attempts to regulate his own breathing he notices that the humming sound is now starting to rise out of each of the people in the room, only at a different pitch. An aura of light surrounds everyone, although each has a different color and intensity. As Willy directs his attention to each individual their sound pitch begins to change, raising or lowering until it merges with his own. With the change of sound is a visual change in the aura, the dimmer colors growing brighter and brighter until radiating a brilliant golden light similar to Willy's. Stuart is having difficulty. The color around his heart is very dim and seems to be retarding the color change around the remainder of his body. Suddenly the color around Willy's heart grows very dark as Stuart's grows brighter, as if Willy is absorbing it. When the dark spot is completely within Willy's aura it explodes and the aura grows brighter still. The humming sound which emanates from Stuart rises to Willy's pitch and now everyone is operating on the same level. The auras begin to expand around each person like a magnetic or electrical force field until they all interconnect and everyone in the room is seen as part of unified system. For a moment, certain vibrations seem to be silently transmitted between the energy centers and then the fields slowly recede back into the auras as the auras fade almost imperceptibly into the normal light of the room. Everyone is sitting as they were before, quiet and relaxed. Willy is having difficulty unfolding his legs. Jonathan goes over to him and Stuart follows. They help him stand up. It is obvious that his strength is leaving him rapidly. Margaret comes over and kisses him and he bends over so that the children can kiss him too. Everyone looks at each other with great love. There is a beautiful understanding between them. Stuart and Jonathan help Willy to his room.

            WILLY
    That was very good for you Stuart. You
    learn quickly. (*Stuart seems very pleased.*)
    Try and meditate like this every day. With
    practice you will be able to sustain it longer.
    Then you can go deeper.

They help Willy into bed and both kiss him good night. Jonathan blows out the light and he and Stuart step out into the brisk night air. They walk for a short while, in silence.

            STUART
    How long does Willy…?

            JONATHAN
        (*Shrugging his shoulders.*)
    We don't know. Willy wants to keep that to
    himself, I suppose.

They walk for a bit. They pause while Stuart regards the star-filled sky.

            STUART
    Do you think the quasar is really triggering
    an effect?

            JONATHAN
        (*Putting his hands in his pockets.*)
    Yes, I think so. (*He waits for a moment, for
    the right words.*) The inner world… and
    the outer world… are reflections of one

another. Man stands in the balance. People
think the mind is up here (*he points to his
head*) but it's really all around them. There
is a stage when you realize that. For us, my
family, Willy, the source of the sound came
from within. For you, it came from without.
It makes no difference. The sound is the
same. We are fortunate to be alive at such a
moment, when the inner and outer worlds
come together.

STUART
But what is the sound? Is it the residue of
the explosion?

JONATHAN
The Hindus call it the "OM" sound,
the sound of creation. The Bible calls it
the "WORD." "In the beginning was
the WORD." I guess astronomers and
physicists have their own terminology.

STUART
(*Reflecting for a moment.*)
What will happen to the others when the
quasar begins to affect them?

JONATHAN
Stuart, that can't be your concern now.
When you've learned to understand it and
can handle it, then you'll know what to
do. Without the discipline, you'll exhaust
yourself in insanity. A quiet mind will be open
to receive. Those who haven't learned this
will spend all their energy fighting their own
instincts. I think you were right to warn your
associates of a change. What you forgot to tell
them was the need to prepare themselves.

                    STUART
          So Noah has to build an ark to survive the
          storm.

                    JONATHAN
          Yes, within him.

They walk for a few moments in silence.

                    STUART
          You know, I have a family.

                    JONATHAN
          I assumed you did. Your thoughts seem to
          be there as much as they are here.

                    STUART
          (*Smiling for a second, then growing serious.*)
          Does one have to give up everything?

                    JONATHAN
          You only give up the attachment. As long
          as it does not possess you, you can have
          anything – your family, money. But when
          you can't let go of it, then you are trapped.

                    STUART
          When do you think I'll be ready to go back?

                    JONATHAN
          When you no longer need to. You'll know
          when.

It is morning. The family is finishing breakfast. A place has been set for Willy and his chair is at the table, but it is empty. Everyone seems conscious of Willy's absence. Stuart is seen about to pass something. He picks it up, eyes Margaret for a second, then passes it to Jamie. Jamie smiles but shakes his head "no."

MARGARET
(*Laughing and reaching out for it.*)
No, no, you were right the first time.

STUART
(*Grinning.*)
Well, I had the feeling. I just didn't have the direction.

JONATHAN
You're picking it up.

They end their meal and move to the various chores waiting for them. Stuart, Jonathan and Jamie go to the jeep and drive toward the mine. Inside, they work diligently and without speaking. They are chopping at one of the walls and removing large crystal structures. Suddenly, spontaneously, they all stop. Jonathan closes his eyes for a moment and lays down his tools. Stuart and Jamie do the same. They follow him out of the cave and see Betsy in silhouette, waiting for them. They all get into the jeep and head quickly back toward the house. Margaret is waiting for them, with Michael in her arms. Jonathan approaches her.

MARGARET
He's asking for fresh milk.

She follows Jonathan into Willy's room. He expects to find Willy under the covers but sees him instead trying to move his bed so that it faces the window. Jonathan goes to help him but Willy motions not to. He turns the bed with great effort and then gets in it.

MARGARET
Your bath will be ready in a few minutes.
(*Willy smiles.*)

WILLY
(*He looks at Jonathan.*)
Do you think you can get that milk?

JONATHAN
It'll be a while.

                    WILLY
        Not too long.

                  JONATHAN
        I better go right away. (*Willy nods his head.*)

                    WILLY
        Have you ever seen such a beautiful day?
        (*Jonathan smiles and leaves the room.*)

                  JONATHAN
                  (*To Jamie.*)
        Stay with your mother. Stuart you can come
        with me if you like.

                   STUART
        Sure.

They both get into the jeep and speed off into the desert. When they return Margaret and Jamie are sitting outside Willy's door looking very distant but very happy, almost blissful. Little Michael is playing in front of the house. He seems to be turning somersaults until suddenly he is standing perfectly on his head. He stays up for a moment and then falls down. Betsy is coming out of Willy's room as Jonathan approaches. She too seems very distant and is smiling ecstatically. Jonathan hands the container of milk to Stuart and motions for him to take it in.

                   STUART
        I think maybe you should?

                  JONATHAN
        I'll go in next.

Stuart takes the milk in to Willy who is sitting crossed-legged at the end of his bed. Stuart takes the glass from the table and fills it with the warm milk. He hands it to Willy, who smiles. He closes his eyes and goes deep inside himself and after several moments, begins to drink the milk. Willy looks radiant, bathed and fresh. Stuart stares at him and suddenly feels tears rolling out of his eyes. He is about to start crying when Willy smiles at him.

WILLY
You're sad because I'm dying. (*He places his hand softly on Stuart's head.*). If you knew what dying was you wouldn't feel sad. (*Stuart looks at him tenderly.*) Sit over there. (*He motions to the other end of the bed.*) Relax. (*Willy smiles at Stuart again and Stuart is nearly transfixed by the warmth of it.*)

As he gazes deeply into Willy's eyes, the walls of the bedroom slowly begin to vanish, opening into a limitless desert vista. A blinding sun shines above them in a white sky. The sand seems bleached by its intensity. Stuart and Willy sit motionless on the sand. Willy directs Stuart's gaze up into the sky, where there is a strange sense of objects rushing at Stuart, diffused and unformed. The white dividing lines on the highway speed toward him and disappear. He recognizes an image of his wife moving rapidly. The sky becomes a projection of endless images. Stuart zooms forward into his past as it unfolds before him. Scenes of the actual film appear. He sees the picnic cove, the conference, the abyss, etc. They are all seen from Stuart's point of view. The images are amorphic, vaguely hollow and incomplete. Stuart attempts to arrest the flow of certain images and they begin to grow more solid, almost real. He sees his wife walking toward him, bringing the letter from Mickey. The sense of her presence is powerful, almost too poignant for Stuart to bear. In the background we can hear Willy's voice instructing Stuart. His words are in counterpoint to some of the visuals but refer more generally to the entire progression of Stuart's experiences throughout the film. The instruction is heard intermittently for the duration of the scene.

WILLY (V.O.)
The less you try and understand, the more you will know. Flow with the universe within you. The less you try and hold on to, the more you will have. Merge with the intelligence that created you. Trust the shape of your hands and the rhythm of your breath. You know their ancient wisdom. Accept your destiny. The life force is a billion years older than you. It created you.

You are the sacred vessel that contains it. Learn from it. Feel a part of it. Allow it to flow through you and you will flow with it. Breathe deeply and consciously. Quiet your mind. Do not listen to your thoughts and they will go away. Surrender to the life force. Everything is energy. Your human consciousness is only one plane of many. Time and space exist in infinite dimensions. Allow your mind to expand and experience them all. Beware of attachment. Become attached and you stop flowing. Death is a natural process of life. Do not be afraid to give up what you have. Something greater will take its place. There is no end to the flow. Each stage is a necessary one. Try and avoid an essential step and you lose your way. Confusion and fear are the result. Avoid the fear and you become more afraid. Then you are trapped. Energy becomes negative. Madness is infinite also. Recognize the challenge and confront the fear. Re-channel the energy. Make it positive. At the moment of true confrontation the fear becomes illusion. You created it and you can destroy it. Go through the fear and you will be free. There are many pitfalls along the way. Heaven is just as much an attachment as Hell. Both are inner projections of your fears and desires. Rise above them. Recognize that they are just one stage. Go through them and then surrender them. There is much more beyond. This is an ancient journey. You are one of many. Each person has the seed. Only few realize it.

We watch scenes of Stuart's life as they unreel before us, important events and obscure recollections constantly moving back in time. As Stuart grows smaller, the camera's view gets closer to the ground. Furniture seems huge. We see the side of a crib with toys dangling and large distorted heads peering down at Stuart as an infant. The image begins to blur. There is a great shriek of a baby crying and then blackness. We are pulled into a strong rhythmic movement, a constant contraction and expansion in a strange visceral world of pulsating fluids and forms. The movement stops abruptly and we see the small and tender face of a fetus looking fearful and bewildered moments before its birth. The image slowly dissolves and we see him at an earlier stage of development, the eyelids sealed and joined together. Through a series of slow dissolves we see the entire fetal growth in reverse. The fully developed fetus gets smaller and smaller as the magic and beauty of its development unfolds before us. Soon it loses much of its recognizable human features. We are plunged into what looks like space with a milky way of star clusters swirling around the fetus. Hardly more than an inch long now, his head seems monstrous, completely dwarfing the rest of the body. He seems human and not human. Back further in time, only a few days old, his form is now jelly-like, reminiscent of other creatures, other times. Suddenly his shape becomes round, like a capsule, with a great amount of change occurring within its center or nucleus. The multicelled organism reduces cell by cell, like bubbles popping into small configurations, returning finally to the first cell, the magic seed, throbbing orgiastically with the secrets of human growth. The cell rests quietly for a moment as if listening to the strange, pre-verbal sounds that seem to be speaking to it, as if it were being prepared for re-entry into a higher order. Suddenly, without warning, there is a wild rush inward, as if everything were being pulled together, to one super-condensed point, by some unbelievable force. A fantastic array of forms, cellular, molecular, even atomic, seem to be jamming together into one intense mass. It is like seeing the effects of a bomb explosion in reverse and slow motion, imploding to the moment of ignition. In a furious rush the cell is sucked into itself, bursting into an ocean of life without form, a chaos of pure and intelligent energy. Stuart as an individual entity no longer exists. His being merges in the infinite sea of cosmic consciousness. A billion moving energy particles overwhelm us with their beauty, enveloping us in a symphony of free-flowing color. The vibrant life energy consolidates, defining itself in constantly changing patterns and designs growing out of one another inexhaustibly and at an incalculable speed. The amount of intricate forms seems unlimited. We feel that we are witnessing the building blocks of the universe magically revealed before us. The designs become even more complex, like mandalas of a thousand moving particles coalescing into one shape and then another. Great religious symbols and motifs appear and disappear in the ever-changing patterns. The source

energy of the universe dances and spins in total, joyous harmony. We
begin to hear the sound of the quasar, growing louder and louder, as the
particles become more frenzied and ecstatic, forming a prismatic flow
of energy. The hum of the quasar begins to modify into other sounds,
as if we are hearing nuances in the uniform frequency that we could not
hear before. The sound blends into many sounds – waterfalls, trumpets,
thunder, choirs. As our awareness of the sound increases, the prismatic
particles rushing towards us become bleached, intense white and we
are engulfed in an ethereal display of light, highly potent, almost alive,
vibrating before our eyes. It is the quasar, the same light we have glimpsed
in the observatory and in the television scene. Stuart discovers the center
of the universe in the center of himself. The effect of this pulsating energy
mass is almost supernatural, as if we were not simply perceiving the light,
but becoming part of it. The effect is visceral and kinetic. It actually
seems to affect our brains, physically activating a whole new sense of
visual and emotional experience. We find ourselves either flowing with its
beauty and intensity or defending ourselves from its seemingly terrifying
strength. The intensity of the experience begins to diminish as the quasar
light condenses into a brilliant star-like formation hovering before us.
Gradually we become conscious of a nebulous, transparent shape forming
around and enclosing the quasar. The form continues molding itself until
we are able to recognize it as a human shape. It is still totally transparent.
It is floating on its back, its head projecting towards the audience and its
body and legs extending into the screen. We can see through the head of
the body, into the quasar suspended in the center near the solar plexus.
The body begins to rotate slowly pivoting around the quasar. The arms
and legs start to move and the image turns upright in a cross-legged
sitting position. The quasar light radiates through the entire form as it
sits suspended in a black void. Slowly the body surface grows opaque
and colors appear, moving to different areas, pink and fleshy tones filling
in the face, darker colors forming hair and clothing. The various facial
features slowly come into being, forming many different faces as they
settle into place. Certain faces seem momentarily recognizable: Milton,
Ellen, Jonathan, Margaret, Willy and then Stuart's image resting as the
final shape. The void in which he is still floating begins to manifest color
and form, sand and sky, a familiar earthscape and then the room becomes
visible and solid. Stuart looks like his old self except for one detail – his
eyes. They are constantly changing color prismatically, like the quasar.
He looks in front of him. Out of invisible space, Willy begins to appear,
just as Stuart did, but his face is not recognizable as it turns and molds

itself into a hundred rapid faces, finally stopping at Willy's features. They look directly at each other, both pairs of eyes radiating the quasar colors. Only tears obscure the light in Stuart's eyes. They say nothing. There is nothing to be said.

It is dusk. The desert is very quiet. Stuart bends down and picks a flower from the sand. He walks over to a large pile of logs and sage brush. Willy's body is lying on top. All the members of the family gather around the pyre. Michael suddenly starts crying and runs to take Willy's hand. Jonathan lifts him up and lets him kiss Willy and then passes him to Margaret, who holds him lovingly. Jonathan takes a torch and lights the pyre and it bursts into flames. The camera follows the great cloud of smoke into the evening sky.

Stuart is sitting next to the house carving a piece of wood. The setting sun casts a warm glow on his face. He seems peaceful and very content. We hear the sound of the jeep approaching but Stuart does not react until it stops in front of him. Jamie and Betsy jump out and run to him.

BETSY
We found it!

Stuart looks at her, not understanding for an instant what she is referring to. Then he realizes. He looks up at the family standing around him. They all know he is going to leave.

The whole family is sitting in the jeep bounding over the desert. We can see a metal object gleaming in the last rays of sunlight. As they draw nearer we recognize Stuart's car. They pull up alongside it and get out. Stuart goes over to the car and gets in. He tries the ignition. It sputters for a few moments and then turns over. Michael claps his hands excitedly. Stuart laughs and climbs out of the car. They just stand looking quietly at one another and then Michael runs to Stuart and hugs him. Betsy and Jamie follow. Stuart comes over to Margaret and Jonathan. They regard each other with deep emotion and they, too, embrace.

JONATHAN
We'll be with you.

Betsy holds onto her mother's dress acting for the first time like a little girl. She is trying not to cry.

>**JONATHAN**
>I'll lead you to the road. I don't know how you lost it in the first place. It wasn't that far away.

Stuart gets back in the car and they get into the jeep. They drive to a narrow road spottily covered with the shifting desert sands. Jonathan points Stuart in the right direction and they wave goodbye. Stuart glances back occasionally as the jeep rides out of sight. His car moves swiftly down the road. He comes to a big curve and notices that he is branching into a larger highway. The white dividing lines begin to rush at the car. The night is falling rapidly and soon they are all that he sees, line after line speeding hypnotically toward him. In the distance a pair of red tail lights seem to be moving slowly down the highway. As he approaches he is stunned to see the smiling face on the back of the hippie school bus. Stuart stares at it with a sense of wonder. Suddenly he begins to realize that he may never have been lost in the desert, that he may never have left the highway. As he passes the bus and the dividing lines continue to rush at him he starts to feel that the entire experience with the family may have been simply in his mind.

He drives for quite a while in deep contemplation. For a long time there is no sign of life along the side of the road and then an occasional sign passes by, or a gas station. A few old houses also begin to appear in between the long, barren stretches of sand. In the distance he sees a neon sign. All that can be made out is the word "DINER." Stuart turns off the highway and parks alongside a large trailer truck. He walks into the diner. There are five people at the long counter and the booths are about half full, occupied mainly by couples. The atmosphere is quiet, except for a middle-aged woman talking rapidly and excitedly to herself. Stuart walks over to one of the booths and sits down. He picks up the menu, placed in between the sugar and the ketchup, and begins looking at it. A large man, probably a truck driver, approaches Stuart's table. He has a cold, hard look on his face.

TRUCK DRIVER
                   (*Slowly and angrily.*)
            This is my seat.

Stuart looks up at him. Although not afraid of the man, he sees that it is pointless to argue with him. He looks directly at him.

                       STUART
            Sorry.

He gets up slowly and moves to the next empty booth. Nobody seems to have noticed their exchange of words. The woman at the counter continues talking. A couple sitting in front of Stuart is very quiet, deeply absorbed in something. The young man is looking down intently as he begins to pour the sugar into his spoon. We see the spoon from the young man's point of view and watch as the first sugar granules tumble slowly in midair like a beautiful, snow-white waterfall of crystals. In the background we hear a voice.

                        VOICE
                  (*Softly and gently.*)
            Julie, Julie, wake up. There's somebody
            waiting.

Stuart turns in the direction of the voice and sees a young girl in a waitress uniform sitting behind the counter. An older woman is above her, shaking her easily, as if trying to wake her. But the girl's eyes are open all the time. She gets up slowly, dazed, and walks over to the fountain to fill a glass of water. She walks toward Stuart's table. When she gets closer we can see that she is in a state of complete bewilderment and terror. Her head seems about to burst, similar to the way Stuart's looked before it exploded in his office. She puts the glass of water on the table. Her hands are trembling and her eyes seem to be moving in many different directions. She gives a shy, almost apologetic look at Stuart and backs slowly away, going over to a chair in the corner and sitting down. The older woman comes over to Stuart and begins wiping his table and making excuses for the other waitress' behavior.

                    WAITRESS
          It's really getting to her. She's been like that
          for a week. Tense. You know? What'd you
          like?

                    STUART
          You have a salad?

                    WAITRESS
          Sure. That all?

                    STUART
          Yeah.

                    WAITRESS
          French or Russian?

                    STUART
          Oil and vinegar.

                    WAITRESS
          Right.

She goes back behind the counter. Stuart gets up and walks over to Julie and sits down in a chair next to her. He looks at her intently as if about to speak but he doesn't say anything. His eyes begin to change colors as the quasar manifests itself within him. Julie's eyes suddenly meet his and at the moment of contact her head jerks back violently, uncontrollably. As it settles back we notice that she is beginning to change. We can see the blood vessels and nerves appearing through her now transparent image, just as we saw Stuart's when he first sighted the quasar. The light flows through her body briefly and then her form begins to recompose itself. Her face looks subtly different, relaxed and soft. There is a faint sparkle in her eyes as she stares wondrously at Stuart. A beautiful smile forms on her face. Stuart smiles back. He warmly strokes her head, gets up and goes back to his table. The other waitress brings Stuart his salad. She notices Julie smiling.

                    WAITRESS
Will you look at that. (*She puts the salad down.*) Anything else?

Stuart shakes his head and she goes back to the counter. Somebody puts on a radio. We hear the stations being switched. Everyone turns around, looking in the direction of the sound. It is a small transistor that a young boy at the counter is listening to. The truck driver gets up and quickly goes over to him, furious, hardly able to contain his deep anger.

                    TRUCK DRIVER
Shut that goddamn thing off. You know it's dangerous.

The kid turns around, his eyes wide open and glowing, radiating a sense of complete well-being, looking directly at the truck driver. He nods his head a little and turns it off. As he walks back to his seat we see the truck driver clearly. He is frightened, trying desperately to contain the panic raging within him. Stuart is looking at his salad. He has not yet begun to eat. He is very quiet and still. Suddenly the quasar sound begins to manifest in the diner. The old woman at the counter tenses and stops talking for the first time. The truck driver jumps up furiously and charges at the young boy.

                    TRUCK DRIVER
I said turn it off!

He grabs the radio out of his hands and smashes it on the ground. The sound is still there. His heart seems to stop beating. He freezes. The sound of the quasar continues to increase. He tries to walk back to his seat, but the room chaotically fragments around him. A thousand separate pieces seem to fly at him as he clings to the closest table. Finally managing to sit down, his face grimaces as he tries with all his might to prevent the tension within him from exploding. We see the spoonful of sugar that the young man had started to pour earlier – full now, rising out of the metal spoon like a white mountain. It drops into the light brown coffee with a splash, reverberating like a stone dropped into a silent and still forest pond. A couple sitting at the counter stare lovingly at each other, caressing tenderly, uninhibited by the people around them. The old woman is sitting motionless but calm, looking like an ancient statue. The young boy is bending down to pick up his broken radio. Within the slowed-up motion of his movements we are around him, on top of him, below him, within the action from multiple vantage points, all continuous, flowing, a simple motion expended sensuously into an ecstasy of movement. The camera pulls back so that we see the full interior of the diner. Nothing seems different. The boy has picked up the radio and is returning to his seat. The counterman is pouring a Coke. The young man is stirring his coffee. The hum of the quasar disappears. We see the truck driver, his head buried in his hands. He lifts it up slowly and cautiously. He is wide-eyed. Tears are rolling down his cheeks. He looks confused, but somehow a little softer, gentler than before. In his eyes we can see a vague glow and know that he has experienced something greater than he has ever known before. He stares into the empty space before him. Captured most fully in his expression is the underlying sense of awe. He stares out at us for a long time. And then blackness.

Teratoma

1. FLOATING VIRUS. (SUBJECTIVE P.O.V.)

White sunlight is gradually obscured by clouds. The camera moves gently through the billowing forms. Patches of blue appear and disappear. There is a sense of floating on currents of wind. Green hills and treetops materialize below. The camera swoops down over them. A large institutional building sprawls over a section of flat land. The camera moves toward it. Surrounding the building is a high wire fence. The camera passes through it. The building grows larger and menacing as it approaches. The camera glides over rough brick walls and barred windows. One of the windows is open just a crack. The camera slides in. The hospital room that it enters appears vast in size. The camera hugs the wall, moving effortlessly from floor to ceiling. From the camera's point of view everything is enormous. A glass of water on a nightstand appears the size of a lake as the camera skims the surface. The Kleenex tissues seem monumental in dimension as the camera rides through their sensuous folds. Loud footsteps and a door opens, casting a bright light into the shadows of the room. Emerging from the light in the doorway is a mythic figure, a towering woman in white robes and wings seeming to grow from her head. She moves into the room as the camera floats away from her. The more distant perspective reveals that she is a NUN in traditional habit for hospital attendants. She walks over to a female PATIENT lying in a massive bed. As she walks the camera moves on the currents of air displaced by her motion. As she stops by the patient, the camera comes to rest. The SISTER raises the patient's head. She is a middle-aged woman with crossed eyes and a moronic appearance. The camera moves slowly toward her. Her face begins to grow in size until it is of gigantic proportions. The camera skims her face like a fly on Mount Rushmore. The SISTER holds a cup with two pills inside it. She taps lightly on the patient's lips and her mouth opens. The camera moves toward her mouth. Great yellow teeth part and reveal the inside like a dark, forbidding cave. Two monstrous capsules enter the mouth, resting on the vast plane of the tongue. From inside the mouth the camera peers out and observes as a massive paper cup draws closer. Like a tidal wave the liquid in the cap rushes forward propelling the camera image down the long tunnel of the esophagus into darkness.

2. TITLE AND OPENING CREDITS.

3. ASYLUM. MAIN GATE.

MRS. JOHNSON is standing outside the main gate of Saint Sebastian's Home for the Mentally Incompetent. She is carrying a black leather doctor's bag. SISTER THERESA approaches from the main building.

>   SISTER THERESA
> Mrs. Johnson?

>   MRS. JOHNSON
> Yes.

>   SISTER THERESA
> So good of you to come. (*She unlocks the gate, invites Mrs. Johnson to step in, and then locks it again.*) Won't you follow me, please?

They walk toward the main building.

4. ASYLUM CORRIDOR.

The two women walk down the long hallway as free-roaming PATIENTS gather around them and stare quizzically at MRS. JOHNSON. Various ATTENDANTS try to pry them away.

5. OFFICE OF MOTHER SUPERIOR.

MOTHER SUPERIOR MARY ROSE is looking through a book of medical illustrations. There is a knock at her door.

>   MOTHER SUPERIOR
> Come in.

SISTER THERESA and MRS. JOHNSON enter nervously. MOTHER SUPERIOR rises to greet them.

>   SISTER THERESA
> Mother, I would like you to meet Mrs. Johnson. Mrs. Johnson, this is Mother Superior Mary Rose.

MOTHER SUPERIOR
It's a pleasure to meet you.

MRS. JOHNSON
(*Dryly.*)
Likewise.

MOTHER SUPERIOR
It's a blessing for us that you could come. We have been very troubled.

MRS. JOHNSON
Frankly, I was surprised to be called.

MOTHER SUPERIOR
The situation is both confusing and embarrassing for us.

MRS. JOHNSON
Can you describe it?

MOTHER SUPERIOR
This is difficult for me. You see... one of our patients is pregnant. A forty-year-old woman... Mary Foster. She has been with us for fifteen years. Brain damaged. (*She finds it hard to look directly at Mrs. Johnson.*) There are no men allowed on these grounds. We do all of our own work, even maintenance. I have no explanation. It is baffling.

MRS. JOHNSON
Men are determined creatures. I am never surprised. Without them, I would not be so gainfully employed, so who am I to complain? (*She smiles. Mother Superior does not.*) Tell me, how many months is she?

> MOTHER SUPERIOR
> (*Awkward and emotional.*)
> We weren't sure when it happened at first.
> We didn't believe it really. But as the months
> wore on we could not deny it... We were
> afraid to have a doctor. It would have been
> damaging... You must forgive me. I feel
> I have sinned. I could not report... I had
> hoped to call a midwife when the time came
> and dispose of it all quickly and quietly.

> MRS. JOHNSON
> And so I have come. I assume then that it is
> that time.

> MOTHER SUPERIOR
> (*Head bowed.*)
> She is... eleven months pregnant. (*Mrs.
> Johnson regards her curiously.*) We waited
> and waited. There was no labor. I expected
> it any day.

> MRS. JOHNSON
> I think you should take me to her.

> MOTHER SUPERIOR
> I have sinned. I know I have sinned. Forgive
> me.

> MRS. JOHNSON
> That is not my profession.

6. PATIENT'S ROOM.

The light is turned on. The patient, MARY FOSTER, closes her eyes tightly to cut off the brightness. She is the same woman seen in the opening sequence of the film.

> MRS. JOHNSON
> Is she violent?

SISTER THERESA
Never.

MRS. JOHNSON
Does she speak?

SISTER THERESA
Hardly.

MRS. JOHNSON
(*Patting her stomach.*)
She certainly looks big enough for eleven months, I'll say that. Wouldn't be surprised if it was twins. (*She looks around the room.*) I'll need some hot water and fresh towels. As many as you can get.

SISTER THERESA
Right away.

As she opens the door to leave, several PATIENTS poke their heads inside to see what is going on. They are pulled away by some of the SISTERS, who appear no less curious.

MOTHER SUPERIOR
(*Innocently.*)
Is she going to have it... now?

MRS. JOHNSON
I doubt it. I just need to check inside... feel what the situation is. (*She pulls a stethoscope out of her black bag and presses it to Mary Foster's stomach. She moves it from place to place.*) Not good. (*She rolls Mary Foster over and listens through her back. She moves the stethoscope many times but keeps coming back to one spot.*) Strange. Very strange. I've never heard anything like it. I don't know what it is.

> MOTHER SUPERIOR
> What do you mean?

> MRS. JOHNSON
> A grinding…. Odd. (*She appears concerned.*)
> But I can't find a heartbeat.

SISTER THERESA returns with water, followed by SISTER MARIA carrying towels. Again, MRS. JOHNSON washes her hands carefully. They push PATIENTS from the doorway.

> SISTER THERESA
> Do you need anything else?

> MRS. JOHNSON
> Yes, if you don't mind. Each of you hold
> up her legs. (*The Sisters are not sure what
> to do. Mrs. Johnson positions them but they
> are awkward and uncomfortable.*) Let's see
> what's going on in here.

MRS. JOHNSON begins to probe inside MARY FOSTER. Her arm moves slowly, professionally, as she explores the unseen space within. MOTHER SUPERIOR does not watch. Neither do the SISTERS. MARY FOSTER looks afraid but does not move. The SISTERS struggle for a moment with her legs.

> MRS. JOHNSON
> Hold still.

MOTHER SUPERIOR turns to watch, uneasily. MRS. JOHNSON'S face registers concern, curiosity, caution. There is a deep quiet in the room. Finally MRS. JOHNSON withdraws her arm and turns to those standing beside her.

> MRS. JOHNSON
> There is no child in there.

> MOTHER SUPERIOR
> But what…?

MRS. JOHNSON
I suggest that you get her to a hospital right away.

7. AMBULANCE.

An ambulance drives quietly out of the Asylum gates. MARY FOSTER is lying on a stretcher inside it. Her eyes indicate the dimensions of her confusion and fear. MOTHER SUPERIOR is with her, praying.

8. HOSPITAL EXAMINING ROOM.

DR. KLAVIN is examining MARY FOSTER. He taps and presses on her protruding belly. The expression on his face is very grave.

9. OPERATING ROOM.

MARY FOSTER is anesthetized and prepared for emergency surgery. A NURSE, holding a clipboard, enters the words "Emergency Tumor Extractions – Dr. Klavin," in appropriate boxes on the form before her. Other NURSES and ATTENDANTS work busily, almost mechanically, at their well-rehearsed chores. The preoperative detail is studiously observed. DR. KLAVIN approaches the sleeping PATIENT and makes a long, steady incision below her navel. The camera shies away from the actual cutting, observing, instead, the people's faces. Occasionally there is a clinical glimpse of internal body mechanisms. Traditional dialogue – "Scalpel," "Sutures" – interrupts the sounds of the operation, scissors cutting, sponges patting, fluids gurgling. It is through watching the faces of DR. KLAVIN and his associates that the horror of what is inside MARY FOSTER is first apparent. All eyes fixate on her open abdomen in disbelief. No one moves. Slowly DR. KLAVIN begins to reach inside, as though to take hold of it. Suddenly there is a gnawing, grinding sound and his hand recoils. Only now do we see fear on their faces. A kind of paralysis affects them all. Finally DR. KLAVIN reaches for a pair of uterine forceps and guides them slowly forward. He opens them widely to encompass a large object. When the forceps make contact there is a powerful movement and the sound of cartilage and bone gnashing. DR. KLAVIN seems hard pressed to hold on and one of his ASSISTANTS grabs another pair of forceps to help him. Slowly, it is extracted. As it rises into camera, the NURSES back away. Suspended before them is a monstrosity, an unearthly creature with shiny black skin. Tufts of long hair extend from different parts of it and an oily substance lubricates its dark coat. It has no face, no eyes, no limbs. Only one feature distinguishes it: teeth. The creature is embedded with sharp pointed teeth protruding from folds of flesh that act like gums and a powerful musculature that serves as jaws.

                    ASSISTANT
           What is it?

                    NURSE
           It's horrible.

                    ANESTHESIOLOGIST
           It's not human.

                    DR. KLAVIN
           It's the most awful thing I've ever seen.

                    ASSISTANT
           What is it, then? A tumor?

                    DR. KLAVIN
           God only knows.

10. FLOATING VIRUS. (SUBJECTIVE P.O.V.)

The Chicago skyline appears off of Lake Michigan. The camera is floating toward it. It glides effortlessly through the canyons of the city between the hovering walls of glass. It sails past metal girders and windows that do not open. It observes the giant people inside, moving silently. It peers down at the street below. An updraft carries the camera soaring high over the towering buildings. It floats and darts around the machinery and building apparatus on the rooftops, the water systems and air conditioning plants. The camera moves toward an air intake system at the very pinnacle of one of the great sky scrapers. Suddenly, it is sucked into darkness. Brief flashes of light indicate that it is moving rapidly through the innermost mechanisms of the building. Just as suddenly, it is expelled into a bright space, a great chamber occupied by massive figures causing violent air currents as they move through it. It is an office. The camera bobs wildly as the towering figures pass by. With effort, the camera glides down toward a desktop and begins to explore the surreal landscape of typewriters and pencil boxes. The typewriter mechanism is particularly fascinating as the camera passes through the keyboard and down into its inner workings. Unexpectedly, there is a great turbulence and the camera turns to see a gigantic face with vast, puffed cheeks blowing at it. The camera hides beneath the ribbon as a colossal brush begins sweeping huge meteors of erasure particles in all directions. The storm subsides. The camera rises toward the face above it and narrowly avoids being attacked by a barrage of typewriter keys rushing furiously at the whiteness behind it. Spiralling upward, the camera encircles the great face before it, flying past the eyes, over the hair, around the nose. It explores delicately the rim of the nostrils and then shoots inside, traveling through the hairs and filtration system of the nose and into blackness.

11. OFFICE INTERIOR.

HORACE RHIMER stops typing for a moment and looks out the window. He seems deeply pensive. After a short while he turns back to the typewriter and begins typing rapidly. Again, he stops. His eyes are tearing and he reaches for a tissue in the bottom drawer of his desk. A buzzing sound pierces through the atmosphere and, abruptly, silence falls on the office. All eyes turn toward the front as JAMES SUGARMAN, a tall black man in a neatly tailored suit, commands everyone's attention.

> SUGARMAN
> Attention, please. Attention. I have an important announcement to make. *(An older woman is still finishing a last piece of paperwork.)* Jody, can I have your attention too, please. *(She flinches and puts down her pen.)* This is important. Word has just come in that the Washington office has just passed the $5 million mark. *(A great flash of disappointment surges through the office. Faces droop. Expressions sag.)* Now listen, it's not over yet. We still have another month. We're not doing that badly. *(He steps a little to the side, revealing a chart with a graph ribbon stalled at $3,500,000.)*

We're third place now, but I know we can do it. We can overtake Los Angeles in a week's time, easy. And Washington's not unbeatable. It's just a question of attitude, folks. That's all it is. We've got to pump up that old winning spirit. I know we've got it in us. We showed them last year. We can show them again. It'll mean a big push. But that's not new to us. We're pushers. We're fighters. Aren't we, team? (*He looks around the office. Heads nod without conviction.*) Come on, what kind of answer is that? That's not a winning response. How can we expect to hit $6 million with that kind of attitude? Now let's try it again. Are we fighters? Are we? (*A few voices yell back affirmatively.*) That's better, but come on. Are we the greatest? (*More voices join in.*) That's getting there! Are we going to show those Washington sons of bitches that we're number one? (*Even the old ladies are starting to warm up. It's a struggle for them but the juices are flowing.*) Who'll get that week in Las Vegas? Who'll lie in that Las Vegas sun? Who'll it be? Let me hear it. (*The office chorus begins to chant, "We will! We will!"*) That's what I like to hear. Hey, how about it? Let's sing the company song. Let's sing it so they can hear it right through the ceiling. Let the big boys hear it upstairs. Come on everybody. Up on your chairs.

There is something unreal in the sight of sixty-year-old ladies climbing up on top of chairs to sing a corporate anthem, but up they climb, some grabbing hold of drapes, others balancing on desktops. The younger and more athletic members of the office staff tiptoe on top of telephone books balanced on their desks. It is a heartening sight. Even HORACE RHIMER is poised to sing.

ALL
(*The singing incorporates
choreographed hand movements.*)
We reach for the moon.
We reach for the sun.
We'll never stop
Till we're number one.
We'll fight till we drop
Till our very last breath
To protect from injury
And insure against death.
We'll fight every day
Till the end of our life
To take away worry
To take away strife.
We don't fear life's currents.
We sell the greatest insurance.
Proverbial Life, Proverbial Life, Proverbial Life.

SUGARMAN
Wow! What's gotten into you all? With this kind of spirit, how can we lose? When you're hot, you're hot! Come on team, let's do it again. Let the whole city hear you!

The office staff begins a new round, all except HORACE RHIMER. His face is broken out in a cold sweat and he is looking faint. Carefully he climbs down from his desktop perch, as those nearby eye him with suspicion. He walks dizzily through the singing throngs toward the water cooler. JAMES SUGARMAN, judging by his glance, does not approve. From the water cooler HORACE watches as the office settles back into its pre-pep rally routine. Slowly, he makes his way to SUGARMAN, who catches him just before he enters his office.

SUGARMAN
What's up Horace?

HORACE
I don't feel well. Hit me all of a sudden.

                    SUGARMAN
Yeah, you don't look so hot. Got anything
you can take?

                    HORACE
I think I wanna go home.

                    SUGARMAN
Oh yeah? Well, what about the Pinsky deal?
Can you get that covered?

                    HORACE
It'll wait till tomorrow.

                    SUGARMAN
Okay, if you feel it's okay. I hope you feel
better.

12. RHIMER HOME.

HORACE RHIMER is sitting in the living room of his suburban home. A thermometer protrudes from his mouth. His wife, FLORENCE, is standing over him and glancing at the second hand on a clock hanging over the mantlepiece. When it reaches 12, she extracts the thermometer. She has difficulty reading it and carries it over to the window.

                    FLORENCE
103. Horace, I'm going to call.

                    HORACE
What for? What's he going to tell you?

                    FLORENCE
I don't know what he's going to tell me.

                    HORACE
I know just what he's going to say. Same
thing he always says. Horace...

13. DOCTOR'S OFFICE.

>   DR. WORDEN
> You've got a bug.

>   HORACE
>   (*To his wife.*)
> What did I tell you?

>   FLORENCE
> What kind of a bug?

>   DR. WORDEN
> A bug… a virus.

>   HORACE
> A cold.

>   DR. WORDEN
> An infection. Something's in your system and your body's trying to fight it off. I'll give you a little penicillin, you go home and take a rest, and you'll be as good as new in a couple of days.

>   HORACE
> I feel rotten.

>   DR. WORDEN
> So nu? You're sick. What do you expect?

14. RHIMER HOME.

HORACE is lying in bed. His eyes are red. His nose is red. He is surrounded by used tissues and lozenge wrappers. His nightstand looks like a pharmacy.

>   HORACE
> I think it's spreading.

                    FLORENCE
Do you want some more soup? A cup of
tea?

                    HORACE
My chest. I feel it in my chest.

                    FLORENCE
I'll put honey in it.

                    HORACE
Not my throat, my chest. (*He pats his chest.*)
It hurts all over.

                    FLORENCE
Do you want some Vicks? I'll rub it in.

                    HORACE
No, I hate the smell.

                    FLORENCE
That's because it's good for you. Let me put
some on.

FLORENCE unbuttons her husband's pajama-top chest. She begins to rub it in.

                    HORACE
Ugh. What a mess.

                    FLORENCE
You'll feel better.

                    HORACE
Ow! Ow!

                    FLORENCE
You know, I think maybe you have boils
under the skin. Like right here. (*She moves
her hand on his chest.*)

                    HORACE
    Ouch.

                    FLORENCE
    I think it's boils. The skin even looks a little
    red. Maybe your body is just trying to get
    rid of some poisons.

15. RHIMER BATHROOM. NIGHT.

HORACE turns the light on in the bathroom. He walks over to the mirror and unbuttons his pajama top. Several boils have appeared on his chest.

He scratches around them. There is an expression of disgust on his face. FLORENCE calls to him from the bedroom.

                    FLORENCE
    Horace, what are you doing?

                    HORACE
    Nothing. (*He turns on the tap water.*) Just
    getting some water.

                    FLORENCE
    Are you okay?

                    HORACE
    Yeah, I'm okay?

                    FLORENCE
    What's wrong?

                    HORACE
    Nothing's wrong.

                    FLORENCE
    You weren't sleeping well. You were talking
    in your sleep.

                    HORACE
I was? (*He stops to think for a moment.*)
What was I saying?

                    FLORENCE
I don't know. Just gibberish. Do you think
your fever's back?

                    HORACE
No.

                    FLORENCE
Take some aspirin.

                    HORACE
I'm not hot.

                    FLORENCE
Let me feel your head.

HORACE walks back into the bedroom.

16. RHIMER BEDROOM.

FLORENCE is lying in bed. HORACE approaches her slowly as though thinking about something. He stops.

                    HORACE
You just reminded me of this dream I was
having.

                    FLORENCE
Come, sit down. Get back in bed.

                    HORACE
I was walking through our back yard. It was
a spring day. Early spring. The ground had
just started to thaw.

FLORENCE
Lean over. (*She places her hand on his forehead and then nods her head.*) I don't even have to touch it. It's on fire. You must take some aspirin.

HORACE
Wait. Let me just finish. It was horrible. I kept looking at the ground. I kept thinking I was going to see flowers popping up. Then, all of a sudden, I saw the ground kind of caving in in one spot. I wasn't sure what was happening. I kept watching it. A little hole formed and I knew something was going to come out of it. I was afraid because I thought it was going to be a rat or something like that. But I couldn't take my eyes off of it. Suddenly a little head started to come out, like it was being born. I stared at it to figure out what it was. It was like a groundhog or woodchuck. After the head these two little front paws came out. For a moment I thought it was cute, but then it opened its mouth and it had these long fangs and these claws unfolded from the paws. I got scared and wanted to run but then I noticed that the ground behind it was heaving. (*He breathes heavily and uses his hands to demonstrate the swelling action that took place.*) I couldn't believe it. And then this great hairy form began to rise out of the earth and I realized that this little groundhog head was attached to a gigantic body and it was growing out of the ground.

FLORENCE
You're making me sick.

HORACE
It was awful.

FLORENCE
Take some aspirin.

HORACE
But you know what was most frightening?

FLORENCE
What?

HORACE
I realized that the creature was inside me.

FLORENCE
I thought you said he was in the earth.

HORACE
Right. That's true. (*He points to his head.*) But he was in my dream.

FLORENCE
(*Nodding her head as though
to appease him.*)
Take some aspirin and try to sleep.

She rolls over and goes back to sleep. Horace scratches inside his pajamas and then heads for the bathroom.

17. RHIMER KITCHEN.

HORACE is sitting at the breakfast table, fully dressed. FLORENCE is sitting across from him in a housecoat.

FLORENCE
Well, I don't approve, I don't care what you say.

HORACE
I can't not go in. That Pinsky deal…

FLORENCE
Pinsky schminsky. Nothing is worth your health.

HORACE
No one else can do it.

FLORENCE
You look awful. You feel awful. I'm sure they'd understand. What's another day?

HORACE
It could mean the deal.

FLORENCE
You're making a mistake.

18. HORACE SITTING AT HIS DESK.

He looks weak. His skin is mottled. He is not doing his work. Suddenly, he stands up and feels dizzy. He balances himself for a moment, holding on to the back of the chair. He starts walking down the aisles of desks and then backtracks. He looks confused. One of the secretaries notices his confusion.

SECRETARY
What are you looking for, Horace?

HORACE
(*Sheepishly.*)
The men's room.

SECRETARY
(*Giving him a strange look.*)
It's right over there. Are you feeling okay?

HORACE nods his head "no."

19. RHIMER HOME.

The doorbell rings and FLORENCE goes to answer it. She opens the door and sees HORACE and two POLICEMEN.

> POLICEMAN
> Mrs. Rhimer? (*She nods her head.*) I don't think your husband is feeling too well. I suggest you get him to see a doctor as soon as you can.

> FLORENCE
> What's wrong? What happened?

> HORACE
> (*Deeply disturbed.*)
> I couldn't find my way home.

> POLICEMAN
> We found him over in Beechwood Estates. He kept circling around the same block. Kind of upset the neighbors.

> HORACE
> I kept looking for our house.

> POLICEMAN
> I really do suggest you get him to a doctor.

They walk him into the house and sit him in the living room. FLORENCE accompanies them back to the front door.

> FLORENCE
> I don't know what to say.

> POLICEMAN
> That's okay, ma'am. Good day.

They leave. FLORENCE goes back into the living room. HORACE has taken off his jacket and is pulling off his tie.

                        FLORENCE
            Honey, are you all right?

                        HORACE
            (Tears forming in his eyes.)
    I'm sick.

                        FLORENCE
            (Frightened.)
            I'm going to call the doctor.

She runs to the kitchen and pages through a little red address and telephone book. She turns to "W" and scans down the page for Dr. Worden's number. She finds it and begins dialing. The phone is about to ring when she hears HORACE calling her.

                        HORACE
            (Panicked.)
       Florence! Florence!

She drops the phone and comes running into the living room. HORACE has removed his shirt and is staring down at his chest.

                        FLORENCE
        What's wrong?

                        HORACE
    Look!

                        FLORENCE
       The boils?

                        HORACE
    Look!

He points closely at one of the boils.

Two hairs seem to be growing out of it. She stares at them for a moment before she realizes that they are moving. She gasps and pulls back. All over his chest and belly, thick black hairs seem to be moving independently.

>   HORACE
>   (*Fearful.*)
> They're moving. They're alive. (*He looks
> as though he wishes to step out of his own
> body.*)

>   FLORENCE
>   (*Alarmed.*)
> What is it?

HORACE shakes his head. FLORENCE looks closer.

>   HORACE
> Oh God.

>   FLORENCE
> They're growing out of the boils.

FLORENCE reaches down and touches one of the hairs. It responds. She jumps back. She stares at the hairs in disbelief. She reaches back down and touches one again. It begins to sway back and forth as though sensing her finger. She tries to pull on one.

>   FLORENCE
> Does that hurt?

>   HORACE
> It's numb. I can't feel anything.

FLORENCE moves closer to one of the boils and the hairs protruding from it. She moves her fingers between them. Without warning, the two hairs coil around her finger. She tries to pull back but is caught in their unexpected grip. She shrieks. HORACE stiffens. She begins tugging at the hairs trying to free her finger. The hairs hold tighter.

                    FLORENCE
Oh, Jesus.

With a powerful muscle action, FLORENCE pulls her hand back, tugging at the hairs, and suddenly yanking them out of her husband's body. Their grip on her finger loosens. She holds the hairs up to her face. Attached to them is a gruesome, insect-like form. She screams and shakes her arm, tossing the tiny creature to the floor. HORACE appears to be in a state of shock. FLORENCE looks down at the floor and notices that the creature is crawling on her living room carpet. She raises her foot and with an unexpected yell comes smashing down on it.

20. MEDICAL CONFERENCE.

A medical slide of a microscopic image is projected on a screen.

                    DR. WORDEN
          This is an image of one of the boil-like sacs
          extracted from Mr. Rhimer's upper chest.
          As you will notice, it has an egg-shaped,
          larval appearance. In all, 38 of these sacs
          were surgically removed from Mr. Rhimer's
          chest and abdomen. The largest of these was
          no more than one inch in diameter. (*Slides
          continue to change, illustrating the lecture.*)
          The sacs each contained living creatures
          of insect-like description, although not
          insects in any sense of the word. There were
          a number of features which distinguished
          them from insect forms. First, and most
          startling, they were made entirely of human
          tissue. They were not parasites or foreign
          organisms, but grown from the body
          itself. Second, they were very incomplete
          organisms containing only rudimentary
          organs incapable of sustaining life outside
          of the body for more than several minutes,
          which, in fact, was the case. It is possible,
          had they been allowed to grow, that they
          may have evolved into more complex

structures, but we had no intention of using Mr. Rhimer as a testing ground. Third, while it is convenient to call them insects, the fact is that they are unlike any insect form that I know of. I have consulted with several specialists in insect studies and shown them these slides. Two of their responses were interesting to me. One is that this creature is unclassifiable by any standards we now have. It defies all categories. And second, according to one eminent paleontologist Dr. William O'Connell of MIT, we may be dealing with the rebirth of a prehistoric organism. How it has come to be reborn, how it is transmitted, is a mystery. But the history of medicine is filled with mysteries.

The lights come up on a large room. It looks like a hotel ballroom. A hundred or so chairs have been placed near a podium at one end of the room. Only about fifteen people are sitting on them. On the podium, along with DR. WORDEN, are HORACE and FLORENCE RHIMER and two MEN in business suits. One of the officials approaches the microphone.

>   OFFICIAL
> Well, thank you, Dr. Worden. We'll now open this seminar up for questions. (*He pauses.*) Are there any questions? (*There is a long, embarrassing silence.*)

After a short while, a hand goes up in the back of the seating area.

>   OFFICIAL
> Yes. In the back row.

>   DR. VACARRO
> (*Standing up.*) I'm Dr. Vacarro from Battle Creek, Michigan. I don't have a question. I just wanted to say that it is unfortunate that Dr.... (*He glances down at his program.*)

Worden was unable to preserve any of the specimens about which he is reporting. Although his slides are interesting, it is difficult to accept much of the information when there has been so little clinical research. His findings are interesting, however. Very curious. (*He sits down.*)

DR. WORDEN stands and approaches the microphone. The OFFICIAL stands aside.

DR. WORDEN

I'd like to respond to that, to Dr. Vacarro. As was stated before this lecture and in the conference notes, I am a general practitioner, not a researcher. I decided to address this gathering simply to report this strange case which came to my attention. I thought perhaps that someone here might find what I had to report useful. I hope that is true, although judging by the attendance this morning it seems that medical discoveries of this nature are not a major interest in the field.

21. CONVENTION DINNER.

DR. WORDEN, HORACE and FLORENCE RHIMER are sitting at one of many tables in a large dining room filled with medical conventioneers. There are several other people at their table engaged in their own conversation.

HORACE

Well, at least we got a free trip to New York.

DR. WORDEN

And the food's not bad.

                    FLORENCE
I've had worse.

                    DR. WORDEN
You wonder sometimes how the medical
profession survives, with so many closed
minds.

                    HORACE
Even the ones who showed up were half
asleep.

                    FLORENCE
Hung over. You could smell it on the way
out.

                    DR. WORDEN
I must confess, I expected it to be front-page
news. This has been a good lesson for me.

DR. RONALD PARISH, a well-dressed man in his mid-thirties, approaches their table.

                    PARISH
Dr. Worden?

                    DR. WORDEN
Yes?

                    PARISH
My name is Ronald Parish. I'm head of
Virology at the Center for Disease Control
in Atlanta.

                    DR. WORDEN
          (*Looking at his name tag.*)
How do you do? Yes, I'm familiar with
your work. I suppose we all are. (*He turns
to Horace and Florence.*) He was one of the
people... Well, let me put it another way: his

department was responsible for the swine
flu and Legionnaires' disease programs.

                    PARISH
I'm not sure responsible is the right
word.

                    DR. WORDEN
Let me introduce a patient, or should I say, a
friend of mine. Friends, that is. Horace and
Florence Rhimer. Doctor Parish.

They all shake hands and exchange greetings.

                    PARISH
Yes, I saw you all this morning.

                    HORACE
You were there?

                    PARISH
Oh, yes. I wouldn't have missed it. I pick
up more things at these conventions. It's all
like a big puzzle to me. I just keep collecting
pieces. Sometimes pieces come together.
Usually they don't. But when they do... (*He
makes a gesture to indicate total pleasure.*)

                    HORACE
Did you pick up any pieces today?

                    PARISH
Sure. I don't know if they'll ever fit
anywhere, but I was very interested.

                    HORACE
Like what?

PARISH
Oh, your symptoms interested me. The fact that it was so much like a viral infection.

DR. WORDEN
That's how I diagnosed it.

PARISH
I think any good physician would have done the same. But your memory loss intrigued me, and the numbness. It took, what... 48 hours for it to set in?

HORACE
I don't know. That's what's so strange. I didn't know I wasn't feeling them. I could feel around the boils, the skin itched, and when Flo pushed on them I could feel them, but otherwise I wouldn't have known they were there. I would never have known something like that was growing inside me. To tell you the truth I think that's the scariest part, that something like that could be going on and you wouldn't even know it.

FLORENCE
Except for the virus symptoms.

HORACE
Yeah, but you could just think that was a cold.

PARISH
Well, you don't look any the worse for wear.

FLORENCE
Oh, he was amazing! He came out of the operating room cheerier than I was.

HORACE
(*Smiling.*)
I was just happy to be rid of them.

PARISH
(*Patting Horace on the back.*)
I'll bet you were.

22. FLOATING VIRUS. (SUBJECTIVE P.O.V.)

The lights flashing on the movie marquees over 42nd Street look like so many suns in distant galaxies as the camera floats past them. It is night, and giant human forms make their way down the street as the camera weaves between them. The camera rides the summer air into a seedy hotel lobby. It circles fake marble pillars and glides over the desert terrain into a squatty ash tray. The flickering light of a television screen compels it and the camera rides toward the vibrant image. The closer it gets the more the picture disintegrates into its electronic impulses devoid of form or content. The sound of the violent police drama coming from the set fades as the camera floats deeper into the lobby. Two statuesque black ladies with bright red lipstick enter an elevator. The camera swirls behind them. It moves though the vast space of the elevator as though charting its way though a sudden new universe that has just come into being. Just as it gets the lay of the land the door opens and a new world appears, a dark corridor with dim lights like distant beacons calling it forward. The camera floats out into this new space, riding along the baseboard and traveling up to explore the dazzling radiance of a 60 watt light bulb. Gradually it withdraws, moving along the walls, observing the fading floral wallpaper and the lunar landscape of the chipped plaster walls. The darkness between the light bulbs is interrupted by a pattern of light emanating from an air vent atop an old door. The camera rises up to it and passes inside. The new space is filled with shadows that dance on the walls as the giant figure of an old man commands their movements. His gestures are small but the whole room responds as he makes them. He is eating. As he raises his fork, a shadow moves and an old couch appears. As he drinks a glass of water, a shadow falls and a picture of Jesus emerges in the light. The camera moves tentatively in this strange place, slowly drawing toward the dish of food from which the old man eats. Macaroni transfigured. The camera rests in the center of this soft, tubular world and watches as a fork moves toward it like a glistening spaceship. Poised for docking, the camera rises with the fork and makes the short trip to the mammoth portal opening above. Crusty lips and tobacco teeth open for the arrival and the camera enters the darkness of yet another world.

23. HOTEL LOBBY.

The old man, MR. ROBINSON, is sitting in front of the television, sleeping. Suddenly he begins coughing, and wakes up. He gathers the phlegm into his mouth and spits it into an ashtray. An OLD WOMAN sitting near him makes a look of disgust. He gives her a dirty look. He changes his position in his chair and tries to fall back asleep. Moments later he is coughing again. He looks annoyed.

24. HORN & HARDART AUTOMAT.

MR. ROBINSON carries a pot of hot water and a cup past the cashier, who nods as he passes. He walks over to an empty table and sits down. Moments later someone else sits at the same table, so he gets up and moves away. He sees an old newspaper resting on an empty chair. He scurries over to it and brings it back to his table. He puts the paper aside for a moment and reaches for the catsup. He takes the bottle and empties a fair portion of it into his cup. With ritualized movements he places a spoon in the cup along with the catsup and then pours in the hot water, stirring as it enters. He seasons the brew with salt and pepper and then settles back to drink and read his paper. Then his coughing starts. He rubs his throat with his hands, trying to appease the discomfort. He tries to force his tongue back into the soreness. Nothing seems to work. He tries to drink his catsup concoction, but it burns his throat. He throws his newspaper on the floor and leaves.

25. MR. ROBINSON'S ROOM.

The old man is lying tossing in his bed. Sweat pours from his brow, his eyes, his glands. He coughs incessantly. Someone knocks angrily on his wall.

> ANGRY VOICE
> Shut up and die already.

The old man raises his fist at the wall.

26. HOTEL CORRIDOR.

MR. ROBINSON is wandering the halls in his underwear. Two hookers pass him, making as wide of an arc as possible. One of them yells at him.

>   HOOKER
>   Get out of the halls! You're killing my
>   business!

27. HOTEL LOBBY.

MR. ROBINSON wanders through the lobby. He has removed his undershirt.

The HOTEL CLERK comes up to him.

>   CLERK
>   Mr. Robinson, are you okay?

>   MR. ROBINSON
>   Listen, I don't bodder you, you don't
>   bodder me, unnerstand?

>   CLERK
>   Well, listen, you can't walk around like
>   that.

>   MR. ROBINSON
>   Wadda ya mean? In Miami I stay at the
>   Fountain Blue and I walk around the
>   halls like this all the time. You think I go
>   swimmin' with a shirt and tie?

>   CLERK
>   This is not the Fountain Blue.

>   MR. ROBINSON
>   You're telling me! Hotel Scumbag. That's
>   what this is.

                    CLERK
    Come on Mr. Robinson. Let's go back
    upstairs.

                    MR. ROBINSON
    Take your hands off me. You queer or
    somethin'?

                    CLERK
    You can't stay in the lobby like this.

                    MR. ROBINSON
    You afraid I'll ruin your reputation?

He starts coughing again. The CLERK looks concerned and reaches out to help him. The OLD MAN pulls away from him and struggles to the elevator. The doors open and he goes in. The doors close.

28. MR. ROBINSON'S ROOM.

MR. ROBINSON is lying in bed, holding his stomach and moaning. Intermittently, he coughs and tries to clear his throat. Suddenly he is seized with the urge to vomit. He retches violently over the side of the bed, but has dry heaves. The attack over, he rolls back into bed. He is making strange sounds with his throat as though trying to expel something. His eyes are rolling around in his head. Again the vomiting attack occurs. Again he leans over the bed. The camera moves close to his face and then in toward his mouth. His whole body heaves and suddenly a strange sinewy form begins to emerge from his mouth. He heaves again and it grows longer. The OLD MAN'S eyes peer down in horror. A snake-like creature with a forked tongue and no skin is being born. He retches again, uncontrollably, while trying to pick himself up. The creature extends another inch into the world. In total panic the OLD MAN begins to scream but the creature blocks his vocal chords and only a dull cry emerges. Picking himself up as best he can the OLD MAN struggles to the door. He is naked. He tries running down the hall but falls to give birth to still more of this creature. Its head has no eyes. Its tongue searches the darkness. Another inch comes forth. The OLD MAN frantically grabs it and tries to yank it out but it will not come. It slithers around in his hands. In terror the OLD MAN begins to run.

Teratoma 167

29. STAIRWELL.

The OLD MAN surges down the stairs, madly, dizzily as the creature flails in the air before him.

30. LOBBY.

The OLD MAN crashes through the lobby. HOTEL RESIDENTS back against the wall at the sight of him. The CLERK rushes from behind the desk, offended by the OLD MAN'S nudity. He grabs him by the shoulders and spins him around. The creature shoots out at him. The CLERK falls back, his face frozen in fear. The OLD MAN stumbles to the doorway.

31. 42ND STREET. NIGHT.

The OLD MAN breaks onto the sidewalk and dashes madly through the crowds. The CLERK chases after him. Peoples faces are confused and frightened. Police sirens add to the confusion. Red flashing lights and yellow neon blur as the OLD MAN runs. The CLERK tackles the OLD MAN at the corner of Times Square. People make a wide circle around them, eyes popping at the sight they see. The OLD MAN heaves again and the creature is expelled. The crowd gasps. Several flash lights pop as someone takes pictures of the scene. The creature starts to move. It is over three feet long and three quarters of an inch thick. People back away. Some begin to run. The OLD MAN is crying. The CLERK stands to stomp the life out of the strange creature but it moves quickly. The crowd parts. The creature moves blindly toward the curb. Before anyone knows what is happening it disappears into the blackness of a sewer drain.

32. CENTER FOR DISEASE CONTROL, ATLANTA.

The heads of various departments from the Center are seated in a conference room around an oval table. They are passing around photographs of the strange creature on the New York street. There is an expression of perplexity on nearly everyone's face. RONALD PARISH, head of Virology, studies the photographs closely and then looks to ARTHUR JENKINS, Director of the CDC.

PARISH
You know, Arthur, from what I can tell this thing is not unlike the one they reported in that asylum down in South Carolina.

JENKINS
I thought you sent one of your men down there.

PARISH
Yeah, but it was destroyed already. God knows what they did with it. All we got was hearsay. Even so, this picture does look a little like what they described, except for the teeth maybe. This one looks pretty clean.

DR. CARL RAYMOND raises his hand and ARTHUR JENKINS nods to him.

RAYMOND
You know what I think we're dealing with here? Teratogenesis. I think this may just be a teratoma.

DR. LORETTA SILLER looks annoyed.

SILLER
"Just"? What do you mean "just"?

RAYMOND
Well, obviously it's not exactly a perfect teratoma.

SILLER
That's an understatement. A teratoma is a cancer, a tumor.

RAYMOND
But there are similarities. Teratomas have a bizarre appearance and exhibit differentiated

cell growth. It's not all that unusual for them to have grown hair or teeth.

JONATHAN EBBINGHAUS, Director of the Venereal Disease Program, interrupts.

> EBBINGHAUS
> Forgive my ignorance, but I don't know what you're talking about. I've never heard of these things... teratomas.

> RAYMOND
> It's just a particular form of cancer. Most cancer is caused by a proliferation of cells, right? It's as if they go crazy and start duplicating themselves at a breakneck pace. They grow so fast they create these things... tumors.

> EBBINGHAUS
> Cancer I know. Teratomas, that's what I don't know.

> RAYMOND
> In teratomas, instead of the same cells reproducing themselves we have a whole rash of cells gone wild, producing strange, sometimes monstrous combinations. Tumors with eyelashes, for example, or fingernails, are not uncommon.

> SILLER
> You are leaving out two important factors. One is that they occur in the uterus. That means that they are found in females. Another is that they do not emerge from people's mouths and crawl along the streets of New York.

RAYMOND
I admit that pokes some holes in my theory.

SILLER
Pokes? I'd say it tears it to shreds.

RAYMOND
Still, there are some fascinating similarities and I don't think they should be dismissed because of a few discrepancies.

SILLER
Discrepancies. I've never known anyone to be so understated.

RAYMOND
Do you have a better theory?

SILLER
I don't have any theories. It's too early to have theories. Jesus, we only know of three incidents separated by thousands of miles and three months.

JENKINS
I agree with you, Loretta. It's too early to develop theories now. I certainly don't want to make any assumptions, but at the same time I don't want to be caught short. I want to keep a monitor on these things if they happen again, and be ready to move if we have to.

PARISH
Who? What department?

JENKINS
An interesting question.

PARISH
That's why I asked it.

JENKINS
The problem of course is that since we don't know what it is, I don't know who should cover it. *(He points to Tom Alderman.)* Tom, should I give it to you? Maybe it's a parasite. Maybe it should be your baby. Or are we dealing with an epidemic? *(He looks at Wendel Frampton.)* Wendel, maybe it should be *your* baby. Who knows, but God forbid, it could become an epidemic. Then there's the viral symptoms…

PARISH
I've thought about those.

JENKINS
I'm sure you have.

PARISH
They could easily be coincidence.

JENKINS
But what if they're not? They've been there in a hundred percent of the cases.

PARISH
But in real figures that only means that three people had colds.

JENKINS
Followed shortly by the presence of these strange… God knows what to call them.

PARISH
That does not establish cause and effect.

JENKINS
Well, it doesn't disestablish it either, does it Ron!

PARISH
I'm getting that old sinking feeling in the pit of my stomach. Why are you looking at me like that?

JENKINS
How come you're always a step ahead of me?

PARISH
It takes one to know one, Arthur, and my answer is no. We're stretched to the limit. Give it to John-Boy. Let *them* play with it.

EBBINGHAUS
(*Up tight.*)
Venereal Disease? What does this have to do with Venereal Disease?

PARISH
What the hell does it have to do with viruses? I can tell by your eyes that I haven't got a choice.

JENKINS
Well…

PARISH
Don't give me one of your "wells." Be straight.

JENKINS
Ron, there really isn't anyone else right now that can handle it.

PARISH
You know Arthur, I'm going to request a permanent transfer into Venereal Disease.

JENKINS
Why so?

PARISH
It just seems the best place for me to be, since I'm always getting screwed.

33. EXTERIOR ELEVATOR. PEACHTREE CENTER.

RONALD PARISH and his girlfriend, SYLVIA STRIKER, are riding in an outside elevator to a restaurant on top of Atlanta's elegant Peachtree Center. An elderly COUPLE, apparently tourists, are riding with them.

PARISH
Right to the wall. I tell you, he screwed me right to it. In front of everybody. Right up the ass.

The old COUPLE pretend not to hear and work their way, unobtrusively, to the far wall of the elevator.

SILVIA
So you've been two timin' me, huh? Gettin' a little on the side? Right?

PARISH
You got it baby.

SYLVIA
Gettin' it on with your boss?

PARISH
Right on.

SYLVIA
Right in.

                    PARISH
          Deep. (*He makes a full-blown Italian
          gesture with his arm.*)

                    SYLVIA
          Well, my mama always told me you could
          trust a man who didn't lie about his affairs…
          especially when he gave you all the facts and
          figures.

                    PARISH
          Your mama had a dirty mind.

                    SYLVIA
          Amen. Her dirty mind made this
          conversation possible.

34. PEACHTREE ROOFTOP BAR.

PARRISH and SYLVIA are seated at a cozy table overlooking Atlanta. PARRISH lifts his martini in a toast.

                    PARISH
          To your mama's mind.

                    SYLVIA
          I'll drink to that.

There is a sudden, high-pitched ringing sound.

                    PARISH
          Damn!

All heads in the bar turn in their direction as PARISH reaches down to his belt and turns off his electronic paging device.

                    SYLVIA
          Can't pretend it didn't happen, huh?

He shakes his head no. She nods in acceptance. He stands up and walks over to the HOSTESS.

> PARISH
> Where's the nearest phone?

> HOSTESS
> Right over there.

> PARISH
> Thanks.

He walks over to the phone and dials. He waits impatiently while it rings. He has many nervous habits. He taps out a rhythm on the telephone receiver with his fingernails, while grinding his teeth.

> PARISH
> Hello, Virology please, extension 2401.

35. PARISH'S VIROLOGY LAB.

DORIS BLUMENTHAL, an assistant to PARISH, answers the phone.

> PARISH (V.O.)
> Hello, Doris? What's up?

> DORIS
> Ron, hi. Where are you?

> PARISH
> Peachtree. Why did you beep me?

> DORIS
> Sorry to disturb you. I just got a call from Jenkins.

> PARISH (V.O.)
> Sonofabitch! *Now* what does he want?

                    DORIS
Oh, some story just came over the wire
services about some woman in a little village
in Mexico. She died yesterday.

                    PARISH (V.O.)
Yeah? So?

                    DORIS
They claim she had horns growing out of
her head.

                    PARISH (V.O.)
Jesus Christ, it was probably some fungus.
What did he have to call me for? Tell him to
call Henry if he's so excited.

                    DORIS
He wants you to send someone down there
right away.

                    PARISH (V.O.)
Damn! Who? We can't spare anybody for a
trip like that.

                    DORIS
Well, I was thinking...

                    PARISH (V.O.)
What? You want to go?

                    DORIS
No. Actually, I thought *you* might like to.
You love these mystery things.

                    PARISH (V.O.)
Maybe, but I don't have time to go
pussyfooting around Mexico. Hey, what
about what's his name? That new guy you
just hired... Pierce?

                    DORIS
Sidney.

                    PARISH (V.O.)
Yeah. What about him?

                    DORIS
He's still pretty green.

                    PARISH (V.O.)
So let him get his feet wet. It'll be good for
him. Tell him I picked him specially. You
take care of it, Doris. I know you can handle
it.

36. VIROLOGY LAB.

DORIS is six feet tall and weighs over two hundred pounds. SIDNEY PIERCE is five foot seven and weighs about 120 pounds. They are sitting in a corner of the Virology lab. SIDNEY has the personality of a stand-up comic.

                    SIDNEY
No. No. Absolutely no. I wasn't hired to
do fieldwork. I have hay fever. And asthma.
And I can't eat spicy food. Besides, I never
travel. I don't believe in it. It's not good for
the digestion.

                    DORIS
Dr. Parish asked for you specifically.

                    SIDNEY
For *me*? He doesn't even know me. He
interviewed me for three minutes and all
that time he was on the telephone ordering
lunch. He wouldn't know me from a tuna
fish sandwich.

                    DORIS
He's a busy man.

                    SIDNEY
I am too. Tonight I'm supposed to take my
mother to the A&P for a cottage cheese
sale. How could I explain that I have to go
to Mexico to look at some dead woman's
horns? What would *your* mother think if
you said something like that to her?

                    DORIS
My mother's dead.

                    SIDNEY
Oh, I'm sorry.

                    DORIS
Sidney, I don't know what to say. We need
you to go. Desperately.

                    SIDNEY
I don't know what to say either. My mother
would never forgive me if I left her like this.
She loves cottage cheese.

DORIS stares at SIDNEY curiously.

                    DORIS
Are you putting me on?

                    SIDNEY
Would I kid you?

                    DORIS
I don't know. I'm thinking I don't know
you at all.

                    SIDNEY
I'm a hard person to know.

DORIS
Why is that?

SIDNEY
Don't push me too fast. It's hard for me to say these things.

DORIS
What things?

SIDNEY
I've never told this to anyone before. I'm afraid of people. That's why I work with viruses. They don't make any demands. You don't have to take them out to dinner or figure out what kind of gifts to buy them. Viruses make great companions. But the best thing, and don't ever tell anyone I told you this, you can sleep with twenty million of them at the same time. How's that for a little erotica?

DORIS is laughing.

DORIS
Who writes your material?

SIDNEY
I'm sworn to secrecy.

DORIS
You're very funny.

SIDNEY
You really think so?

DORIS
Yeah, I do.

SIDNEY
(*Nodding his head.*)
Huh. But I'm not joking. I really don't want to go.

DORIS
Sidney, there's no one else.

SIDNEY
How about the janitor? (*She smiles.*) I've never been on an airplane. I have a terrible fear of heights. I get dizzy stepping off a curb. What if her horns are contagious? I wouldn't look good in horns. I don't even look good in a hat. I'd frighten people. I'd lose every friend I ever had... my mother. Think of the tragedy. (*He pauses a moment.*) Maybe I should reconsider. I'll do it. On one condition.

DORIS
What's that?

SIDNEY
You tell her. And you may have to buy her cottage cheese.

37. MEXICAN VILLAGE.

The church bells are ringing. It is high noon and townspeople are retiring for their siestas. SIDNEY PIERCE is walking down the center of the dusty road that runs through the town. He is singing "The Streets of Laredo" to himself. People eye him suspiciously. He is very conscious of them and seems paranoid and nervous. Near the end of the strip he sees an OLD WOMAN in a black shawl beckoning to him. He looks around to see if it is really he who is being summoned. She insists with her finger that he come over to her. As he approaches, she motions him to go behind the house. He is hesitant, but she does not let up. With very tentative footsteps, he inches his way around the house. A cloth, draped over the door, is pulled back, and a hand motions him to enter. He takes a deep breath and follows it. It is dark inside and it takes a few seconds before he notices the old woman standing in the corner holding a large rock in her hand. He freezes. She motions for him to sit down. He sits. She begins trying to talk to him.

> OLD WOMAN
> Diablo. Diablo. Comprende? Diablo.

> SIDNEY
> (*Confused.*)
> Diablo to you to.

> OLD WOMAN
> Diablo. Diablo.

She looks frustrated. She puts the rock down and holds her hands up to her head with her fingers pointing up like horns. SIDNEY looks interested, as though he understands, and she seems pleased.

> OLD WOMAN
> Diablo. (*She nods her head in a "yes" motion.*)

> SIDNEY
> (*Nodding back, although not sure why.*)
> Diablo.

Suddenly she picks up the rock as though she is going to throw it.

SIDNEY ducks rapidly to the floor.

> OLD WOMAN
> (*Yelling at Sidney.*)
> No! No! Diablo.

SIDNEY looks at her curiously but not yet convinced enough to stand up. She begins prancing around the room acting out a strange drama. First she pretends to have horns. Then she bends down to pray. She stands up and makes horn gestures again. Then she makes the motion of throwing the rock. The entire charade is lost on SIDNEY, judging by his expression.

> OLD WOMAN
> Diablo. Morte. Diablo. Morte. Comprende?

> SIDNEY
> You'll have to forgive me but I don't understand anything you're trying to tell me, which is too bad since you're the first person who has been willing to talk about the horns. (*He makes a horn gesture.*)

> OLD WOMAN
> Diablo. Morte.

> SIDNEY
> Where is diablo? (*He tries to make a "where is" gesture.*)

The OLD WOMAN pretends to hit herself with the rock and then falls to her bed.

> OLD WOMAN
> Diablo, goodbye. Adios.

> SIDNEY
> Where, adios?

She stares at him blankly.

> OLD WOMAN
> No comprende.

Suddenly a young BOY's voice can be heard from outside the house.

> BOY'S VOICE
> Meester Seedney! Meester Seedney!

The OLD WOMAN is startled and quickly shoos SIDNEY out the door. He walks to the front of the house and sees the BOY.

>   BOY
> Meester Seedney! Phone. Phone. (*He waves for
> Sidney to follow and he does.*)

38. HOTEL LOBBY.

SIDNEY enters the lobby of a small hotel. In the far corner is an old phone booth. He is directed to it.

>   OPERATOR (V.O.)
> Meester Seedney Pierce?

>   SIDNEY
> Yes.

>   OPERATOR (V.O.)
> Go ahead please, Atlanta.

>   DORIS (V.O.)
> Sidney? Sidney? Is that you?

>   SIDNEY
> Yes. It's me.

>   DORIS (V.O.)
> We've been trying to reach you for two days.

>   SIDNEY
> Well, I haven't been on the golf course, I can tell you that.

>   DORIS (V.O.)
> What's going on down there?

SIDNEY
That's a good question. If you find out,
let me know. We got here three days ago,
me and Carlos, the guy from the Health
Department in Mexico City. We had to fly
in on a little plane. They don't have any
roads. But that won't stop me on the way
back. I'll hitchhike through the jungle if I
have to but you won't get me back in one of
those two-seaters. No sir. This is the most
godforsaken place I've ever been. You can't
even buy a Hershey bar. And you didn't
tell me they didn't speak English. The only
Mexican words I know are "Adios amigo"
and "Dorito corn chips."

DORIS (V.O.)
What about the woman? Did you find her?

SIDNEY
Nobody will talk about it. Even the police.
Carlos flew back to Mexico City to get some
papers from higher government officials to
get the police to cooperate. I've been waiting
here for two days. He said he'd be right
back. Right back. How long is "right back"
in Mexican? I figured he meant a couple of
hours. It's not that I'm bored, mind you.
Just going to the toilet keeps me pretty well-
occupied. I've even begun to enjoy it. Gives
me something to look forward to. Hey
Doris, do you speak Mexican?

DORIS (V.O.)
What do you want to know?

SIDNEY
What is "diablo"?

                    DORIS (V.O.)
    Diablo?

                    SIDNEY
    Yeah.

                    DORIS (V.O.)
    I think it means "devil." Why?

                    SIDNEY
    Some old lady kept yelling it at me. I
    couldn't figure out what she was saying. I
    thought it meant "kiss me," but she looked
    too old for that.

CARLOS and a POLICE OFFICER walk past the lobby door. The
hotel CLERK points them to SIDNEY in the phone booth. SIDNEY
notices them approaching.

                    SIDNEY
    Hey Doris, you've brought me luck. Carlos
    is back. Tell Dr. Parish that I'm coming back
    on the first land vehicle out of here. Tell him
    to expect me in about two years. And I want
    double time on weekends.

                    DORIS (V.O.)
    Sidney, call us when you find something
    out. And take care of yourself.

                    SIDNEY
    Thanks. See you soon.

He hangs up. CARLOS comes over to him.

                    CARLOS
    It's all arranged. I'm sorry it took so long.
    These are not easy matters.

SIDNEY
I got that impression.

CARLOS
Come. We go now.

SIDNEY
I'll meet you outside. I need to get my bag and freshen up a bit.

CARLOS
Freshen up? What is that?

SIDNEY
Oh, how do you say in Mexican (*he rubs his fingers together as he tries to conjure up the appropriate phrase*) "take a sheet"?

CARLOS
For sleeping, you mean?

SIDNEY
Carlos, my friend, some things you cannot translate.

39. MEXICAN VILLAGE STREET.

SIDNEY, CARLOS and the POLICE OFFICIAL are walking down the main street. It is very quiet and there are no people to be seen. The POLICE OFFICIAL keeps looking behind him.

CARLOS
It turns out that we have stumbled upon something that people did not want us to know about.

SIDNEY
What is that?

                    CARLOS
A murder.

                    SIDNEY
Whose?

                    CARLOS
The woman with horns.

                    SIDNEY
Murdered? By who?

                    CARLOS
The people in the town.

                    SIDNEY
The people? All of them?

                    CARLOS
She went to church to pray for forgiveness.
She thought a demon was inside her... She
was asking Christ to cast it out. They believe
in miracles here. And in demons. While
she was inside the horns grew longer. They
stoned her to death when she came out.

                    SIDNEY
How barbaric! I thought this was a civilized
country.

                    CARLOS
There is no such thing. In all the world you
will not find one.

A loud pistol shot rings out. The POLICE OFFICIAL spins around, his gun already in his hand. SIDNEY notices that there are MEN with rifles stationed on roofs along the street. One of them holds up his hand and points to a window across from him. Another MAN appears behind them and runs toward the window, his gun pointing at it. He kicks the door open and goes inside. Moments later he emerges dragging a dead body by the hair. He waves to the man on the roof across the way. They smile. SIDNEY'S face goes ash white. He stops moving. CARLOS motions for him to continue, but he doesn't move. CARLOS goes over to him.

>CARLOS
>It's all right. We have protection.

>SIDNEY
>Why didn't you tell me? I didn't know it would be dangerous.

>CARLOS
>There is no danger. Come.

>SIDNEY
>I can't.

>CARLOS
>Come.

>SIDNEY
>I can't walk.

>CARLOS
>What's wrong?

>SIDNEY
>I need to go to the men's room.

>CARLOS
>You what?

>SIDNEY
>I need to go to the men's room. (*Carlos looks confused.*) Bathroom. (*Carlos stares at him questioningly.*) Toilet.

>CARLOS
>(*Understanding the word.*) Oh.
>(*Understanding the predicament.*) Ooohh.

(*He gives an embarrassed look that offers no advice.*)

Another shot rings out. Everyone turns. A cry is heard coming from one of the homes. A MAN runs toward it. Everyone waits. Moments later he appears and gives an all-clear sign. CARLOS turns to SIDNEY.

>CARLOS
>You must come.

SIDNEY nods in agreement and walks uncomfortably between CARLOS and the POLICE OFFICIAL. They stop at a house in mid-block. They do not knock.

40. PEASANT HOUSE. INTERIOR.

The three men enter the house. An OLD PEASANT WOMAN is inside. She is dressed in mourning. CARLOS speaks to her for a few moments in Spanish. SIDNEY looks around the room. It is filled with candles, The OLD WOMAN begins crying. CARLOS comforts her. SIDNEY reaches into his bag and pulls out a camera. He begins assembling the flash attachment. The OLD WOMAN sees it and screams, rushing at him as if to smash the camera. CARLOS grabs her and speaks with her again. He keeps mentioning the words "America" and "Doctor." She quiets down. CARLOS comes over to SIDNEY.

>SIDNEY
>Does she have a bathroom?

>CARLOS
>Oh no. They don't have bathrooms here.

>SIDNEY
>Well, what the hell do they use?

>CARLOS
>The field. You must wait.

>SIDNEY
>I don't know if I can.

CARLOS
We only have a short time. We are in the middle of a very difficult situation. The old woman is distraught. She wants her daughter buried. The townspeople want her burned. They have not reached a compromise.

SIDNEY
I thought we were going to ship the body...

CARLOS
Not possible. The government will not allow it for one, and the townspeople would kill us before we got away. They are very proud. This does not reflect well on them. Even now we have only moments before we must flee. So please let us look at the body quickly. I will distract the mother while you take pictures.

SIDNEY
Can I take a piece of the horn?

CARLOS
Quickly.

41. PEASANT HOUSE. BEDROOM.

SIDNEY enters the bedroom by pulling aside a cloth hanging over the narrow doorway. This room too is filled with candles. On the bed in the corner is a draped figure, although the form beneath the covering is difficult to relate to a human shape. CARLOS can be heard restraining the OLD WOMAN in the other room. SIDNEY moves cautiously, and still uncomfortably, forward. The POLICE OFFICIAL stands at the door, watching. SIDNEY approaches the bed. He reaches for the covering and gently pulls it back. He gasps at the sight. He had not expected so massive a growth. The woman's head is crowned with a twisted mass of antlers. Her face is battered almost beyond human recognition. SIDNEY turns away as though about to be sick. CARLOS interrupts him.

                    CARLOS
        You must hurry.

SIDNEY turns back and lifts the camera. His hands are shaking so badly that he has difficulty focusing. He snaps a series of pictures. As each flash fills the room, the OLD WOMAN groans in the other room. SIDNEY puts the camera away and pulls a container from his black bag. It is wrapped in plastic. He puts on a pair of sterile gloves and removes a pair of scissors from a protected sealer. Slowly, he approaches the antlers. His hand reaches out to touch them. When the first contact is made, SIDNEY'S whole body shudders. He must force himself to touch them again. He holds on with great difficulty. With his free hand he manipulates the scissors to remove a portion of the antlers. The scissors have no effect. He unwraps a knife from a similar sealer and attempts to use it to cut the antlers, but it is too ineffective.

                    CARLOS
        Come, please.

SIDNEY is sweating. He appears disturbed and anxious. Suddenly, he reaches out with both hands, closes his eyes, grabs one of the antlers in two places, and, in a mighty effort, breaks it in half.

42. FLOATING VIRUS. (SUBJECTIVE P.O.V.)

The camera swirls around the antlers. It passes through and around the antlers as they take on monumental proportions. In the distance the massive form of SIDNEY PIERCE seems more a canvas of abstract patterns than a whole being. It seems hard to assemble his movements into a coherent image. He appears to be placing his instruments back in their containers and the section of antler in a special bag. The camera moves in close to him. It wastes little time. It floats past his eye, over his glasses, then rushes into his mouth.

43. RONALD PARISH'S OFFICE.

SIDNEY and DORIS are sitting in two comfortable chairs facing PARISH at his desk. SIDNEY is recounting his adventure.

SIDNEY
There were four guards on either side of us when we got out of the house. They formed like a phalanx. The townspeople were starting to come out of their homes. You wouldn't believe the hostility on their faces. I really didn't think we would make it out of there. We began at a fast walk and ended at a full run. Suddenly I realized we were heading straight for the airfield. I was really crazy by then. I kept yelling that I had to go back to the hotel. Carlos was thinking I had to go to the bathroom, but I had forgotten all about that. Actually it was just some bourgeois instinct. Something in me felt that I needed my bathrobe. I'm running for my life and all I can think of is my bathrobe and my Robert Hall shirts that I paid $4 for. Can you imagine? I was ready to give up my life for a three-year-old bargain. And I didn't even like them especially. The sleeves were too long. I still can't believe it. I mean, if I had bought them at Bloomingdales, then maybe I could consider it, but Robert Hall – you knew I had to be crazy.

PARISH
(*His eyes wet with laughter.*)
Where did you find this guy? What are you doing here? You belong on the stage somewhere.

SIDNEY
Oh, I just work here for a joke.

PARISH
Oh yeah?

             SIDNEY
Yeah. I mean, imagine me on Johnny
Carson. Can't you just picture the
introduction? (*He imitates Ed McMahon.*)
And now, direct from the Virology labs at
the Center for Disease Control, it's Sidney
Pierce! (*Doris and Parish crack up.*) I'll do
anything for a laugh. So it takes a few years
out of my life. What's life for?

             PARISH
Sidney, I've been in Virology for ten years
and never heard a single person crack a joke.

             SIDNEY
Who needs it? Ten years in Virology *is* a
joke.

PARISH smiles. That's not something he can laugh at.

44. VIROLOGY LABORATORY.

SIDNEY, DORIS and a battery of TECHNICIANS are performing tests. SIDNEY seems very serious when he is working. DORIS keeps looking over at him and then returning to her microscope. She seems distracted. Finally she gets up and goes over to him.

             DORIS
Anything interesting?

             SIDNEY
Oh, so-so.

             DORIS
Same.

             SIDNEY
You know what bothers me?

DORIS
What?

SIDNEY
Oh, I don't know. Just all that effort to get that thing and I only get this tiny little sliver. (*He looks down through his microscope.*)

DORIS
See anything?

SIDNEY
Nothing much. A McDonald's Hamburger sign. An ad for a topless bar. The usual.

DORIS
Let me look.

SIDNEY
It takes a special eye.

DORIS
Oh yeah, let me see.

SIDNEY
What? McDonald's or the bar?

DORIS
Neither. Your eye.

SIDNEY
Any particular one?

DORIS
No I like 'em both. Either one. (*He looks her in the eye.*) You know they're awfully red. Are you aware of that?

SIDNEY
Sort of. I'm used to it. It's just my allergies.

DORIS
(*Concerned.*)
You're sure?

SIDNEY
I've had 'em for thirty years or so. I ought to know 'em by now. (*Changing the subject.*) Hear of any results yet? You'd think someone would find something.

DORIS
Just that report from downstairs.

SIDNEY
Which one is that?

DORIS
Where they confirmed that the horn was made of human tissue. You heard that, didn't you?

SIDNEY
Nope. I don't get special reports. Just what filters down.

DORIS
Well, that's what they found. Just regular human tissue growing into something that it had never been before. It's awfully strange. It scares me really. Turns my stomach, in a way. (*She pauses.*) Speaking of stomachs, what do you say we have dinner tonight? If you're not busy or anything? (*He is surprised and suddenly looks very shy.*) Please don't turn me down. It took me a whole week just to get up enough courage to ask.

SIDNEY smiles, wrinkles his shoulders and nods yes. DORIS beams.

45. CHINESE RESTAURANT

SIDNEY and DORIS are sitting in a half-empty Chinese restaurant. DORIS is eating with chopsticks, SIDNEY with a fork. Suddenly SIDNEY sneezes.

                    DORIS
          Bless you. You sure you're okay?

                    SIDNEY
          Terrific. Terrific.

                    DORIS
          I expected you to tell me you were allergic
          to chop suey.

                    SIDNEY
          Just to monosodium glutamate. But that's
          all right. I love the way it tastes. Sometimes
          when cook dinner I sprinkle a little on my
          finger just to lick it off. And I'm always
          astounded at what it does for broccoli. (*She
          stares at him.*) I'm sorry. I'm not so good
          at small talk. I haven't had much practice.
          I'm much more at home with philosophical
          discussions.

                    DORIS
          Proust? Kant? Kierkegaard?

                    SIDNEY
          Rod McKuen, Studs Terkel. (*She nods her
          head knowingly.*) I carry on these long
          philosophical discussions with my turtle.

                    DORIS
          He must be very wise.

SIDNEY
Very. He's mastered the greatest of all teachings. "If someone thinks you're smart, keep your mouth shut." He never says a word. Pure genius. You can see it in his eyes. (*He sneezes again.*)

DORIS
I think you're getting a cold. You look very flushed. Let me feel your forehead. (*She leans over the table and touches his brow.*) I think you're sick.

SIDNEY
Really? I feel... (*He sneezes.*)

DORIS
I think we should get you home.

SIDNEY
Now? But I haven't gotten my fortune cookie.

46. DORIS BLUMENTHAL'S CAR. INTERIOR.

DORIS is driving. SIDNEY is sitting opposite her slumped over in his seat. He is breaking open a fortune cookie.

DORIS
What does it say?

SIDNEY
I can't read it.

DORIS
Want me to turn on the light?

SIDNEY
Wouldn't help. It's in Chinese.

DORIS
Turn it over.

SIDNEY
Ah ha. Very tricky.

DORIS
So?

SIDNEY
I'll take you up on your offer now. (*She smiles and turns on the light. He glances at it quickly.*) Okay, turn it off.

DORIS
What does it say?

SIDNEY
It's personal.

DORIS
Oh come on.

SIDNEY
I'm embarrassed.

DORIS
You don't have to be embarrassed with me. As a sign of friendship.

SIDNEY
Oh, okay. It says I have a heart as big as all outdoors.

DORIS
Is that true?

SIDNEY
I never looked. (*He sneezes.*)

47. HOSPITAL ROOM.

An X-ray image of SIDNEY'S chest appears on the screen. A DOCTOR is examining it. SIDNEY is lying in a hospital bed. PARISH and DORIS are standing next to the DOCTOR.

>   DOCTOR
> Nothing. It looks clean.

>   SIDNEY
> I told you it was just a cold.

>   PARISH
> We couldn't afford to take chances.

>   DOCTOR
> I would like to take another picture in a couple of weeks, though, when you all get back.

>   PARISH
> Why's that? Precaution?

>   SIDNEY
> Get back?

>   DOCTOR
> No. It's nothing really. His stomach seems to have an extra pocket to it. Nothing serious. Probably congenital. But I'd like to look at it again.

>   SIDNEY
> Get back from where?

>   DORIS
> How about his heart? Does it look enlarged to you?

DOCTOR
No. Quite normal, really.

DORIS
Not as big as all outdoors, huh?

DOCTOR
Well, not physically anyway.

SIDNEY
Get back from where?

DORIS
He's blushing.

SIDNEY
I am not. I have a fever.

DORIS
You haven't had a fever in two days. Face it, you're all better.

SIDNEY
Get back from *where*?

PARISH
Africa.

SIDNEY
Africa?

PARISH
A viral epidemic. We're all going down.

SIDNEY
What do you mean, *all*? I'm a lab assistant. I'm just supposed to work…

> PARISH
> We need every man we can get. We're short-staffed.

> SIDNEY
> But I don't have anything to wear! All my summer shirts are in storage.

> DORIS
> We have some beautiful new blue smocks.

> SIDNEY
> They have strange diseases down there, tsetse flies, elephantitis, where your feet swell up like tree trunks. I have enough trouble buying shoes as it is. I can't go there. I haven't had my shots yet!

> PARISH
> Yes, you have. (*He smiles at Sidney*). They were given to you yesterday. Sidney, there's no way out.

> SIDNEY
> Who's going to tell my mother? She'll never understand. We were supposed to watch *Kojak* together! She'll never forgive me. Not in a million years.

48. AFRICA.

A needle is inserted into a small jar of serum. The jar empties. The hypodermic injection is administered as the camera pulls back to reveal a large team of CDC PERSONNEL in blue robes giving shots to what appears to be a mile-long line of black AFRICANS. SIDNEY, DORIS, and PARISH are prominent among the faces. There are no large buildings around. They are out in the bush. One BLACK MAN is standing next to a nearby hut. He has an angry expression on his face. The camera occasionally cuts back to him. He does not move. PARISH notices him and asks a BLACK OFFICIAL about him.

                        PARISH
            Who is that?

                        OFFICIAL
            The tribal doctor.

                        PARISH
            He doesn't like us, does he?

The OFFICIAL shakes his head.

49. CAMPSITE.

SIDNEY, PARISH, DORIS, and OTHERS are sitting near some tents. The sun is setting. They look tired. No one is talking. SIDNEY'S stomach begins to growl. No one pays much attention at first, but it becomes so obvious after a while that someone has to say something.

                        PARISH
            Can't you just tell it to shut up?

                        SIDNEY
            We're having a very important conversation.
            (*His stomach growls again and Sidney
            nods his head as if in response. His stomach
            answers in turn.*) It's always done that, since
            I was a kid. It was terrible in school. The
            teacher would ask if anyone had a question
            and my stomach would always answer.
            (*Sidney makes the sound of a stomach saying
            "yes."*) He used to call on my stomach more
            than me. All A grades for my stomach. (*His
            stomach growls again.*) Now *that* was an
            important message. (*He stands up.*) If you'll
            excuse me.

                        PARISH
            Again?

SIDNEY shrugs his shoulders and rushes off behind the tents.

50. CAMPFIRE.

The CDC PERSONNEL are sitting around a campfire eating dinner – everyone, that is, except SIDNEY.

> DORIS
> You should eat something.

> SIDNEY
> If I felt it would stay inside long enough to do me some good, I would, but it won't, so why bother? I can just sit here and enjoy the smell. What day is today?

> DORIS
> Sunday.

> SIDNEY
> That's what I thought. (*He looks at his watch.*) *Kojak*'s on in half an hour. (*He looks mournful.*)

> DORIS
> (*Trying to comfort him.*)
> It's already Monday in the States.

> SIDNEY
> You mean I missed it?

> DORIS
> Afraid so.

He looks even more depressed. Suddenly a group of AFRICANS approaches the campfire. They are yelling loudly. The leader of the group is the TRIBAL DOCTOR. The BLACK OFFICIAL stands as they approach. The group begins looking down the rows of white faces as though looking for someone. The BLACK OFFICIAL walks over to them. He is pushed aside, They keep staring until they see SIDNEY. They stop. SIDNEY is surprised. The TRIBAL DOCTOR comes over to him and begins yelling in his own tongue. He is pointing at SIDNEY'S stomach. The group with him begins chanting. The BLACK OFFICIAL approaches and tries to speak with him but the TRIBAL DOCTOR enters into the chanting.

>SIDNEY
>What are they doing? What are they saying?

>OFFICIAL
>They say you have... the curse.

>SIDNEY
>He must have seen me in the bushes. Tell him, damn right I've got the curse. Tell him, I don't know what they call it here, but in Mexico it's known as Montezuma's Revenge.

>OFFICIAL
>They are trying to exorcise it from you.

>SIDNEY
>Tell him that if he can do a better job than Kaopectate to go right ahead.

A number of BLACK SOLDIERS come running toward the scene, their rifles drawn. They fire up into the air and the chanters run off screaming. PARISH and OTHERS quickly gather around SIDNEY.

>PARISH
>What precipitated that?

>DORIS
>I'm still shaking. That was terrifying,

>OFFICIAL
>I must apologize. Superstition has not yet vanished from many of our people.

>SIDNEY
>But what did they see in me?

OFFICIAL
They see many things we will never understand.

For a short while there is absolute silence and then the group disperses to continue with their meal. Everyone is talking about the incident. Only SIDNEY remains silent.

51. TENT. INTERIOR.

SIDNEY, PARISH and a number of other MEN are sleeping in a tent on narrow cots. The sounds of insects fill the night air. Suddenly there is another sound, a cry or wail. It is low and muffled. It sounds far away. In a moment it is gone. The sounds of insects return. None of the men seem to be sleeping well. When the wail returns PARISH'S eyes open, He looks around the tent. The cry stops. The sound of snoring and the sounds of insects merge. Once again the cry is heard. SIDNEY'S eyes, too, open. He listens for a moment until it fades away. He seems afraid. Gradually his eyes close, and he sleeps.

52. CDC TRANSPORT PLANE.

The Center for Disease Control's private transport plane is heading back for the United States. All CDC PERSONNEL are on board. SIDNEY is sitting with DORIS toward the back of the plane, next to the emergency exit. SIDNEY has one hand on the panel for the emergency door handle.

DORIS
I wish you wouldn't keep your hand there.

SIDNEY
It gives me security. Some people suck their thumbs, some stroke their blankets. I hold onto the emergency exit.

DORIS
But for eighteen hours?

SIDNEY
Do you have a better idea?

DORIS
Well... you could hold my hand.

SIDNEY
Hmm... Well, you can have my free hand if that'll make you feel better. But I really can't spare this one.

DORIS
One's better than none. (*He gives her his hand and she holds it with both of hers. She seems very content.*)

The CAPTAIN of the plane comes out of the crew cabin and approaches PARISH. He bends over and begins speaking with him. PARISH seems very concerned by what he hears. They have a brief exchange and then the CAPTAIN returns. PARISH stands up and takes a microphone. He is very upset.

PARISH
May I have your attention please? Something important has just come up which is going to alter our plans a bit. Instead of landing in Atlanta as scheduled we are rerouting the plane to South Carolina. We are being faced with what may be a very great emergency. Some of you are familiar with the strange creatures... births, I guess is the only thing I can call them. I am afraid to report that there has been an outbreak. A group of nuns in the asylum where the first of these creatures was reported has now contracted them. I'm afraid this may give rise to the worst of my fears, that whatever these strange things are, they are contagious.

53. HOSPITAL. QUARANTINE SECTION.

PARISH is standing outside of a window looking into the quarantine ward of a hospital. In the ward are a number of women and, in a screened-off area, two men. DR. RICHARD HOWE and DR. STANLEY PEARL are standing next to him. Two sisters, SISTER ANNA MARIA and SISTER CARMELA, are with them also.

> DR. PEARL
> The man over there is Dr. William Klavin. He was the doctor who performed the operation on Mary Foster. And the other man was his anesthesiologist. The woman on the far left is Mother Superior…

> SISTER CARMELA
> Mary Rose.

> DR. PEARL
> (*Nodding.*)
> Right. And then Sister Theresa. The other two women are patients in the Asylum.

> SISTER CARMELA
> Carole Edmonds and Dorothea Small.

> DR. HOWE
> They all exhibited symptoms of viral infection. Dr. Klavin and Sister Theresa both suffered memory loss. What brought them to our attention, however, were the tumors. They are all large in size and all protrude from the body. None of them are in the same location. They range from the thigh to the neck.

> DR. PEARL
> What first alerted us was the rash of cases all from the same location, but it was Dr. Klavin who put it all together. It was he who suggested that we call you.

> DR. HOWE
> The X-rays tipped us off too. Most tumors are static, easy to photograph. These kept moving. We could never get a clear picture. I've never seen such rapid activity going on inside the body. Even fetal growth. I've never seen anything like it.

> DR. PEARL
> We were also frightened by the idea of an infectious growth. It seemed unsafe to operate.

> PARISH
> Gentlemen, I appreciate your precautions. We are dealing with something that is potentially very dangerous and we cannot be too careful.

54. HOSPITAL OFFICE.

PARISH is in the office of the head of the hospital. He is sitting behind a big desk talking on the telephone. The small room is crowded with people including SIDNEY and DORIS. They are sitting on folding chairs, table tops and the floor. PARISH is nodding his head affirmatively.

> PARISH
> Okay. Okay. Right. Okay, Arthur. Top priority. Gotcha. Right, we'll take care of it. See you tomorrow then. Good enough. Thanks. Bye. (*He turns to the group.*) Well, we're going to take 'em to Atlanta. NASA, is flying down the Astronauts' Space Recovery Station. We'll perform the operations over in Maximum Security. That way we'll be able to keep our eye on this thing from beginning to end. Doris, I want you and your group to get back to Atlanta right away and take care of the necessary preparations. (*He looks at a man sitting on*

the floor.) Elliot, I want you to head up a team of investigators here. I want detailed reports on every person, every animal that had contact with these people or even with that first woman... what's her name, Foster. Mothers, fathers, taxi drivers, whatever. I want careful observations. And at the first sign of a sniffle, even a sore throat, I want these people brought up here to the quarantine section. We're taking no chances. Can you take a group to New York and do the same with the Robinson case? Doris, contact the Mexican health people. We'll let them take care of the one down there. Who's up for Chicago? Tom, can you do it? (*He nods "yes."*) The guy there is... Horace Rhimer. And get right to the doctor who performed his surgery. Worden, I think the name is. Check it out at the Center. We've got all the records. And listen, I apologize to everybody. I know we were all anxious to get home, but some things can't be helped. We can't afford to take chances. (*He looks over to a man by the door.*) Dr. Randel, forgive me for overrunning your hospital like this. I realize it's an imposition. But we're going to need access to a lot of telephones and working space. Do you think that's possible?

DR. RANDEL
No problem. I'll take care of it right away.

PARISH
Terrific. There's no time to lose.

55. AIRPLANE LANDING.

A gigantic NASA transport plane lands at the airport outside of Columbia, South Carolina. It taxis to a cargo area. The bottom of the plane opens and the Astronaut's Recovery Station is wheeled off. It is like a giant bus. Several CDC MEN are there to meet it.

56. HIGHWAY AND ROAD TO HOSPITAL.

The Recovery Station drives down the expressways and highways leading to the Columbia General Hospital.

57. HOSPITAL EXTERIOR.

A work crew is awaiting the Station's arrival. It is driven into place along one of the outside walls of the hospital. A special hydraulic lift on the station goes into action and raises the entire unit up to a second story window. A team of MEN instantly begins sealing the entrance to the Station so that it is airtight around the window.

58. HOSPITAL, SURGEONS' QUARTERS.

PARISH, DR. PEARL and DR. HOWE are being fitted into astronaut-like space outfits. PARISH has a serious expression on his face. The DOCTORS seem amused by it all.

59. HOSPITAL, QUARANTINE WARD.

PARISH and the DOCTORS are led into the quarantine ward. The ASYLUM patients are terrified when they see them. SISTER THERESA comforts them. They are greeted by DR. KLAVIN, the ANESTHESIOLOGISTS, and MOTHER SUPERIOR. A knock on the window indicates that the Station is ready for them to enter. PARISH and DR. PEARL help everyone to fit through the window without too much difficulty. DR. PEARL is the last one to enter. PARISH remains outside. The DOCTORS take air hoses from the roof of the Recovery Station and connect them to their suits. When they are functioning they signal to PARISH. He waves good luck and then closes the airtight outer door. The Station slowly lowers back to the ground.

60. HOSPITAL EXTERIOR.

Four police cars surround the Recovery Station. Sirens wailing, they speed off the hospital grounds and onto the highway.

61. CDC OPERATING ROOM.

The image inside the operating room is surreal in its impact. The team of DOCTORS, ASSISTANTS and LABORATORY TECHNICIANS are all dressed in space suits and connected by red umbilical cords to oxygen systems on the ceiling. The operation is in progress. Everyone communicates through small headset devices. The only words that pass back and forth are technical. The camera does not observe the operation but glimpses what is taking place in the helmets worn by the DOCTORS and ASSISTANTS. The camera also observes their expressions through their plastic visors. It is obvious that even to these professionals the tumors they are operating on are fearsome.

62. MAXIMUM SECURITY LAB. ANTECHAMBER.

PARISH and ARTHUR JENKINS are suiting up to enter the Maximum Security Laboratory.

> PARISH
> You won't believe it when you see them. They are astounding.

> JENKINS
> Are they still... alive?

> PARISH
> The tissue died within hours.

> JENKINS
> It's the diversity that amazes me. The combinations. And the complexity of development. Incredible. The reports are incredible.

> PARISH
> Come on.

63. MAXIMUM SECURITY LAB. INTERIOR.

PARISH and JENKINS are looking at a large sealed bottle. Inside is a tumor. PARISH turns the jar until suddenly it is possible to make out the appearance of...

                    JENKINS
Fingers.

                    PARISH
Eighteen of them. No thumbs, by the way. They were all moving when it was cut out. Gruesome, huh?

                    JENKINS
What have the tests shown?

                    PARISH
Most of them are perfect fingers, cartilage, cell tissue, everything. A percentage of them, though, don't make it. They're missing one thing or another – muscle, ligaments, nails.

He puts it down and goes over to another jar.

                    JENKINS
I feel like a kid at a circus sideshow. Remember those?

                    PARISH
I hated them. Here, look at this.

                    JENKINS
What is it?

                    PARISH
Muscles. All different kinds. For half an hour after they were removed they kept contracting and relaxing, over and over again.

JENKINS
Bizarre.

PARISH
You're telling me.

64. MAXIMUM SECURITY LAB. EXAMINATION ROOM.

PARISH, DORIS and SIDNEY are working in a special room in the Maximum Security area. Objects to be studied are placed in a glass enclosure and handled with special gloves that are fitted onto the outside of the enclosure. The enclosure frees them from wearing space suits.

SIDNEY
If it's a virus, I haven't found a thing. Not a trace. No antibodies in the blood. No chromosome change. Everything looks normal.

PARISH
Then how is it spreading?

SIDNEY
Don't get excited. Just because we haven't found them doesn't mean they're not there. They're tiny, you know. We're just going to have to keep looking. But you would think there would be antibodies. It doesn't seem the body would let them in without a fight.

DORIS
None of the blood samples give any indication of new antibody formation. If we could just find them, if we could just determine what mechanisms the body was putting into effect to protect itself against these things, then we would have a chance of figuring out what they are.

                    SIDNEY
It's rare for something to invade the body
and not be attacked.

                    DORIS
Well, we know there is a fever. That's one
sign of a battle. Maybe we just have to
search more during the fever stage.

                    PARISH
Could it possibly not be a virus?

                    DORIS
Sure, that's possible. But something is
tricking those cells to start growing these…
things. What starts a cancer growing? If we
knew the answer…

                    PARISH
But cancer's not contagious.

                    DORIS
We assume.

                    PARISH
And this is.

                    DORIS
Ron, face it. It's still early in the ballgame.
We don't know what we're dealing with. We
don't have any answers.

He nods his head in agreement. He looks depressed.

65. JENKINS OFFICE.

JENKINS is sitting at his desk. PARISH is pacing the floor.

                    PARISH
So what should we do?

JENKINS
Do you think we should alert the press?

PARISH
Are you kidding?

JENKINS
Wouldn't they be the best means...?

PARISH
For what?

JENKINS
Well, how do you think we should inform...?

PARISH
Who? About what?

JENKINS
The public? Shouldn't we...?

PARISH
Are you crazy? What good would that do? Do you want to create a panic?

JENKINS
Doctors? The medical profession?

PARISH
How?

JENKINS
Mail?

PARISH
Do you think it would work? Could we keep it quiet?

JENKINS
Do we have any alternatives?

PARISH
What do you think?

JENKINS
Telegrams, maybe?

PARISH
Can you imagine what that would cost?

JENKINS
Wouldn't it be faster? I mean, is this an emergency or isn't it?

PARISH
Who knows?

JENKINS
So when will we know?

PARISH
Who knows if we'll ever know?

JENKINS
Do you see any reason why we shouldn't act as if it is?

PARISH
I don't. Do you?

JENKINS
(*Shaking his head "no."*)
So then, what do you think of telegrams?

PARISH
Why not?

66. PARISH'S OFFICE.

PARISH is on the telephone, engaged in a heated conversation.

                    PARISH
Alexi, relax. Please, just listen to me. We're not keeping anything from you. I swear. No, I don't think of us as autonomous. I know we're members of the World Health Organization. Alexi, I'm not trying to keep this from anyone, except the public. It's too early to get anyone else involved. Listen, we sent you the telegram didn't we? We're not trying to hide it from you. It's just not a world problem yet. Okay... Okay. You're right on that. But how in God's name do you think we can organize a global assault at this point in the game? Answer me that? Good God, Alexi, there have only been eight cases. Eight. There are four billion people on this planet. How the hell...
(*Parish's secretary interrupts.*)

                    SECRETARY
                    (*Whispering.*)
Excuse me. Tony Majors of CBS wants to talk to you. He says it's urgent.

                    PARISH
Hold on a second, Alexi. (*To his secretary.*) Tell him I'm very busy.

                    SECRETARY
He wants to have lunch with you in half an hour.

                    PARISH
Tell him I already have a luncheon engagement. I'll talk to him tomorrow. I'm sorry, Alexi. Where was I?

SECRETARY
(*Whispering.*)
He's seen the telegram.

PARISH
Oh shit! Excuse me, Alexi. Just tell him it was a simple notification, nothing unusual, and certainly not worth a story.

SECRETARY
He wants to know why you sent out eleven million of them.

PARISH
Goddamn it. Why can't anyone keep a secret? Alexi, I'll have to call you back. I know this is important but something just came up that's just as important. I'll talk to you soon. Take care. Okay. I promise. (*He hangs up.*) Tell Tony to meet me here in half an hour.

67 CDC CAFETERIA.

PARISH and TONY MAJORS are walking through the cafeteria lunch line.

MAJORS
I'm always afraid to eat the food here. I can't help thinking I'll come down with some deadly infection.

PARISH
We should be so lucky.

MAJORS
Ron, lookit, you've got to understand, if I fall, there are hundreds behind me to pick up the banner. It's our job. We carry the public's trust. (*To the countergirl.*) How's

the pot roast, sweetheart? (*She shrugs.*) Any
unknown toxins or contaminants in the
mashed potatoes? (*She blushes.*) What are
you doing for dinner tonight? (*She doesn't
answer.*) Do you mind if I invite her for
lunch?

                    PARISH
Tony, I've only got half an hour.

                    MAJORS
Oh, I keep forgetting you poor executives
and your peptic ulcers. Got to keep
lunch bland. Nothing too spicy or over-
stimulating, right? (*To the girl.*) Sorry,
sweetheart. Maybe some other time.

68. CAFETERIA DINING AREA.

PARISH and MAJORS are sitting at a small table, eating.

                    PARISH
Tony, there's no story. It's as simple as that.

                    MAJORS
Infectious tumors – no story? I've been
around too long, Ron. I won't buy it.

                    PARISH
We've had eight, nine cases. There's no real
correlation yet.

                    MAJORS
Just enough to send out a few telegrams to
several hospitals and medical clinics, right?

                    PARISH
Listen, the only way we're going to
know if there is anything happening is to
examine the broadest field possible. This is

preventive medicine, Tony, that's all it is. If anything comes out of it, you'll be the first to know.

                    MAJORS
You can bet on that, whether the story comes from you or not.

                    PARISH
Tony, cool it, okay? For all we know, it's already over.

69. SIDNEY PIERCE'S APARTMENT.

The night calm is disturbed by a ringing telephone. The sound of several objects falling to the floor precedes the sound of the telephone being answered.

                    SIDNEY
Hello? Hello?

Another crashing sound is followed by a night light going on. It illuminates SIDNEY. He is sprawled on the floor holding a lamp in one hand and the phone in the other.

                    SIDNEY
Hello? Who is it please?

                    DORIS (V.O.)
Sidney, it's me, Doris.

                    SIDNEY
Oh Doris, hi. So nice of you to call. I'm sorry for all the commotion. I've never had a phone call in the middle of the night before. It's very exciting. What can I do for you?

                    DORIS (V.O.)
Oh, Sidney. (*She begins crying loudly.*) Sidney.

SIDNEY
I'm still here.

DORIS
(*Trying to catch her breath.*)
I need to see you.

SIDNEY
Me?

DORIS
I need someone to talk to. Can I come by? I really need to. I'm desperate. I'm in pain.

SIDNEY
You don't think maybe a doctor would be better? I don't have any fresh aspirin or anything.

DORIS
It's emotional.

SIDNEY
Emotional? It's emotional and you want to see *me*? Are you sure you have the right Sidney Pierce? Maybe you have the wrong number.

DORIS
Sidney, please. I need you. May I?

SIDNEY
May I? May I! Yes, you may. Take two giant steps. (*Clasping his hand over the phone.*) My God. What am I saying? "Take two giant steps." (*Removing his hand.*) Sure. I'll be right here. I have nowhere else to go. I'll just be waiting for you.

> DORIS
> Oh, thank you. Thank you. I'll be right over. (*She hangs up.*)

> SIDNEY
> (*Hanging up.*)
> A moron. She must think I'm a moron. "Take two giant steps." I haven't said that since I was seven, "May I, yes you may." (*He looks around his apartment. A look of horror registers on his face.*) This place is disgusting. How can I let her see it looking like this? I know, I'll talk to her in the hall. On the stairs. That sounds romantic. Romantic. Oh God. Do you think? I haven't shaved. I'm out of deodorant. What should I wear?

SIDNEY runs to his closet and begins pulling out clothes. He pulls out a suit, considers it a moment, then discards it. He pulls shirt after shirt out of his drawer, debates them for a second, then stuffs them back. He pulls a bathrobe off of a hook and tries it on over his underwear. He looks in the mirror but does not seem satisfied. He takes off his undershirt and tries again. He brushes the few hairs on his chest so they can be seen above the neckline. He walks back and forth debating his image. While he is walking, he picks up whatever he finds lying in his way: two TV Dinner containers, a stepladder, and assorted magazines and newspapers. Finally, all assembled, he positions himself on his bed to wait. The camera rests on shots of his turtle, swimming. When the doorbell rings SIDNEY is fast asleep. His body seems to sit up before he is awake. He suddenly realizes what is happening and rushes to the door. There is no one there. The buzzer sounds again before he remembers to buzz the downstairs door. He runs to the kitchen to push the button. He can hear the door open and DORIS climbing the stairs. She arrives. Before he has a chance to say anything, she is crying. He leads her to the sofa and takes her coat.

> DORIS
> I'll be all right. Just give me a minute. Thank you for letting me come.

SIDNEY
(*Feeling awkward.*)
Sure. Can I get you something?

DORIS
Coffee would be great.

SIDNEY
(*Embarrassed.*)
I don't have any. I never drink it.

DORIS
Tea?

SIDNEY
(*Shaking his head "no."*)
My stomach. How 'bout some Instant Tang?
(*She nods "okay."*) I hope you don't mind
if it's a little warm. The water her doesn't
get very cold. I've got Ovaltine too if you'd
prefer.

DORIS
That sounds good.

SIDNEY
Hot or cold? Or I should say hot or
lukewarm?

DORIS
Doesn't matter.

SIDNEY
Whatever you want. I aim to please.

DORIS
Oh Sidney... (*She breaks down crying again.
Sidney looks confused, as though not sure
whether to go after the Ovaltine or back to
the couch.*)

SIDNEY
(*Going to Doris.*)
What's wrong? What is it?

DORIS
I'm lonely. I'm just very lonely. (*She cries and reaches out for Sidney's hand. He lets her take it. He is obviously uncomfortable.*) I'm sorry. There was just no one in the whole world I could tell that to. You're the only person I feel I can talk to. (*She cries again.*) And cry to. I don't know why I feel that. Just something about you, something I know I can trust.

SIDNEY
I don't know what to say. I can't even think of a joke. Nobody's ever said anything like that to me before. Not even my mother.

DORIS
Can I ask you a difficult question? (*He nods.*) I don't know if I can do it.

SIDNEY
Try me.

DORIS
Do I turn you off? I mean, that I'm so big? You can be honest. I just have never been able to ask anyone that before. You don't have to answer if you don't want to. I just needed to ask it.

SIDNEY
You want me to be honest? (*She nods her head "yes."*) This is hard for me too. Doris, I love big women. I lust after them. I always have. I was just afraid they would laugh at me. I could never say anything. My whole

life. I've always been so small, so puny. And I've always been shy. It's my biggest hangup. Can I tell you something? (*She nods her head again. Tears are pouring down her face.*) You turned me on the minute I saw you. I mean it. You're the biggest reason I wanted to work for CDC. I'm serious. When you asked me to go out to that Chinese restaurant... I couldn't believe it. I could never have asked, not in a million years. I was so happy. I still get angry when I think how I got sick. And on the airplane when I held your hand. That was a big moment for me. I don't know if you noticed but I let go of the emergency exit after half an hour. Now that's saying something. Doris, I am really happy you came up here tonight. I can't tell you how happy I am.

DORIS is sobbing as SIDNEY talks. When he is finished she reaches out and kisses him. They stare at each other wide-eyed for several moments and the scene blacks out. In the darkness we hear the last sounds of their lovemaking, then silence. After a moment we hear DORIS whispering.

                  DORIS
I thought you said you were shy.

                  SIDNEY
I thought I was. What can I tell you... I surprised myself.

                  DORIS
You're wonderful, Sidney. You're very wonderful.

                  SIDNEY
You're pretty great yourself. Doris, can I ask you a question?

> DORIS
> What?

> SIDNEY
> Do you still want your Ovaltine? (*She laughs.*)

> DORIS
> Save it till morning.

> SIDNEY
> That's what I hoped you'd say.

The room is silent again. The outline of the sleeping couple is made visible by the light of a neon sign outside the window. After a short while we hear the sound of crying. It is familiar. It is the wailing sound that awoke Parish in Africa. It goes away for a moment and then begins again.

> DORIS
> Sidney... are you crying? (*He does not answer.*) Sidney... I hear someone crying, or moaning.

Doris reaches for the nightstand and turns on the light. She looks at SIDNEY. His eyes are wide open. He seems upset. She stares at him quietly. Suddenly the sound comes again, the crying. DORIS looks frightened. She looks at SIDNEY. He looks away. She leans over and places her ear to his stomach.

> DORIS
> Oh my God.

70. CDC ISOLATION CHAMBER.

SIDNEY is lying on a hospital bed. He is sweating. DORIS, in a space suit, is sitting by him. A monitor is positioned over his stomach, recording the sounds that are coming from inside him. The sounds are frightening in their nearly human content. PARISH and the DOCTOR who had treated SIDNEY before enter the chamber in their space suits. The DOCTOR is carrying several X-ray plates. They approach SIDNEY.

DOCTOR
How's the patient?

SIDNEY
Very impatient. It's going to drive me crazy. I can't tell you what it feels like having something like that coming from inside me... I just want to crawl out of my body. I just want to get out.

DOCTOR
Well, I don't think we can help you to get out, but we're going to get that thing out of you as quickly as we can.

PARISH
We've got some pictures of it.

DOCTOR
Remember that extra pocket I thought I saw on your stomach? In that last set of pictures we took? Well, it seems to be more a part of your lungs than your stomach and it's grown to about six times the size. In two months that's pretty remarkable, I'd say. People don't grow that fast.

SIDNEY
What is it? Why is it making those sounds?

PARISH
We'll have a better idea tomorrow.

DOCTOR
We'll operate at 7 a.m. I've got some medication that will help you sleep till then. I imagine all that whining down there must be keeping you awake.

He hands two pills to SIDNEY. DORIS gets him a glass of water.

                SIDNEY
Will you stay with me? (*She smiles and nods her head.*) I'm scared.

                DOCTOR
Well, you get a good night sleep. We'll see you bright and early.

                PARISH
Take it easy, Sid. It'll be all right.

They leave.

                DORIS
Sidney, do you want me to call your mother?

                SIDNEY
I doubt if you'd be able to reach her.

                DORIS
I can try.

                SIDNEY
You'd have to try awfully hard. She died eight years ago.

                DORIS
You're kidding.

                SIDNEY
No, sometimes I don't kid.

                DORIS
Is there anyone else?

SIDNEY
(*He shakes his head.*)
Just promise me one thing.

DORIS
Sure. What?

SIDNEY
If anything should happen, look after my turtle. He's very sensitive and needs tender loving care.

DORIS
I promise.

SIDNEY
He only eats Macintosh Turtle Food, Special Blend #3. You should write that down. He won't eat anything else. I've tried everything. He likes ground-up flies. Do you have a pencil?

DORIS
I'll remember.

SIDNEY
I'm falling asleep. Don't leave me.

DORIS
I'll be right here.

She leans over and kisses him through her visor. He smiles before falling asleep.

71. CDC OPERATING ROOM.

A team of DOCTORS in the customary space suits are performing the operation on SIDNEY. The operating room is very quiet. The incision is made, the flesh pinned back. All is going smoothly. The DOCTOR spots the growth. He reaches in and finds he can lift it partially out. It is a strange, tabular shape with many filaments running through it. The tube itself is not static but moves slightly, opening and closing.

> DOCTOR
> Strange thing. I wonder what it is.

> ASSISTANT
> Do you suppose that's what was making those sounds?

> DOCTOR
> I have no idea. Do you have the jar ready? I'll cut it out.

> ASSISTANT
> It's coming.

The ASSISTANT steps over to the table and reaches for the jar. He brings it back and shows the DOCTOR that he has it. The DOCTOR nods and takes his knife and reaches down to sever the growth from SIDNEY'S lungs. Just as the knife begins to cut, the tubular form contracts and then expands wide open, letting go with the loudest and most terrifying scream imaginable. The scream is an unexpected shock. The DOCTOR'S hands fly apart and the creature drops back into the body cavity. Two ASSISTANTS drop their instruments and the jar crashes to the floor. The thing is making loud, pathetic crying sounds. It takes a moment for the staff to recover.

> DOCTOR
> God Almighty.

> ASSISTANT
> What is it?

> DOCTOR
> Vocal cords. A giant set of vocal cords. Quick, get another jar, and some clean instruments. Hurry.

They scurry around getting what they need. The DOCTOR reaches in and with one quick slice removes the creature. It continues to emit sounds for a short while, even when placed into the sealed jar. The sounds are strangely human, even moving. It is almost as if the creature is trying to talk.

72. CDC RECOVERY ROOM.

SIDNEY is lying in a bed surrounded by the DOCTOR, DORIS and PARISH.

He looks surprisingly well.

> DOCTOR
> It was the most god-awful thing I've ever heard… or seen. Like from another world.

> SIDNEY
> Well, I'm sure glad I wasn't there.

> DORIS
> Me too.

> PARISH
> So how do you feel?

> SIDNEY
> Wanna know the truth? (*Parish nods.*) Incredible. I mean that. I feel wonderful. Like a whole weight's been lifted out of me.

> DOCTOR
> Six pounds, eight and a half ounces, to be exact.

> SIDNEY
> Wow! It's like I gave birth.

> DORIS
> To a healthy young pair of vocal cords.

PARISH
Now that's what I call an immaculate conception.

DOCTOR
More like an immaculate misconception, wouldn't you say?

SIDNEY
Can I see it?

DOCTOR
Oh, you wouldn't want to see it...

SIDNEY
Sure I would. It's mine, isn't it? Flesh of my flesh. Doctor, tell me the truth, did it look like me?

DOCTOR
Well, I wouldn't say that exactly, but I'd say it had your voice.

SIDNEY
You're kidding? My voice. Poor thing. I've always had the worst voice, I couldn't even sing "Happy Birthday" in tune. Tell me, did it say anything? Like "mama" or "dada" or anything like that?

DOCTOR
Well, I'll tell you, and I'm serious about this, the thing that upset me the most, really, was that I think it was trying to speak. I know that's absurd, but that's the thing that's been haunting me more than anything. I keep wondering if it was my imagination or if it was really true. And what bothers me even more is that I keep wondering what it was trying to say.

PARISH
You know what frightens me the most?

DORIS
What?

PARISH
That this is only the beginning. Something tells me we ain't seen nothin' yet.

73. FLOATING VIRUS. (SUBJECTIVE P.O.V.)

The camera is floating through a busy airport. It moves past ticket counters and security checks, gliding through a baggage X-ray machine and down the long corridor of departure gates. A crowd of travelers moves to the boarding doors of an Eastern Airlines flight. The camera rides after them down the boarding ramp to the plane. The giant face of a stewardess greets the passengers as they move on board. The camera glides toward the rear of the plane. The cabin interior seems cavernous. Another stewardess asks to see a passenger's seat placement. The camera flies into the darkness of her mouth.

74. FLOATING VIRUS. (SUBJECTIVE P.O.V.)

The camera hovers in the center of a football huddle. The faces and helmets above it seem God-like in their size. The huddle disperses and suddenly the camera is overwhelmed by a flurry of movement. Moments later the camera experiences the vastness of the stadium. It rises rapidly and surveys the sight. The force of the wind blows it to the sidelines. It travels along rows of enormous faces. A young boy is about to take a bite of a hot dog. He opens his mouth and the camera enters. Blackness.

75. FLOATING VIRUS. (SUBJECTIVE P.O.V.)

The camera is floating alongside of the FDR Drive in New York City. Boats can be seen on one side, cars on the other. In the distance, a tiny figure is approaching. As it draws closer it becomes more recognizable. It is a runner, jogging. The camera does not move. The jogger approaches rapidly, growing more massive in size as he draws closer. He is breathing heavily and the sound of his breath fills the air. The camera waits. He is sucking air violently. The vastness of his mouth overtakes the screen and the camera is inhaled in an implosive rush into darkness.

76. FLOATING VIRUS. (SUBJECTIVE P.O.V.)

The camera is exploring the surreal landscape of a dentist's office. A middle-aged woman is sitting in the chair. The dentist approaches.

> DENTIST
> Okay, now. Open wide.

The woman opens her mouth and the camera floats in. It watches for a few moments, from the inside, as the dentist works. After a few seconds he stops and hands her a cup of water. For several seconds the camera is engulfed in liquid.

> DENTIST
> Don't swallow. Spit it out.

Suddenly the camera hurls from her mouth, into a sink, and down the drain.

77. CDC SWITCHBOARD.

A team of TELEPHONE OPERATORS is being deluged.

> TELEPHONE OPERATOR #1
> (*Writing down the information she is receiving.*)
> That's Doctor Sanford Milner, Mercy Hospital, Detroit, Michigan. What's the zip on that?

> TELEPHONE OPERATOR #2
> I'll need your area code and phone number.

> TELEPHONE OPERATOR #3
> Someone from the Center will get back to you as quickly as they can. Yes, I realize that it's an emergency. They're all emergencies.

> TELEPHONE OPERATOR #4
> Yes, we realize that. It just started happening all of a sudden. We're working as fast as we can.

> TELEPHONE OPERATOR #5
> I think they will be making a public announcement this evening or tomorrow. But I'm not sure. We're not sure of anything at this point.

> TELEPHONE OPERATOR #6
> Where was that again? Can you spell it? C-h-a-r-l-a-v-o-i-x. How do you pronounce it? Charlavoix? You coulda fooled me.

78. CDC MAP ROOM.

A large world map covers an entire wall in the CDC Map Room. A sizable number of PEOPLE are working with it, placing pins of different colors in many different locations. There appears to be well over five hundred pins on the map, mostly contained to the North American Continent.

BOYS keep running into the room with slips of paper which they give to the people working with the map. The paper is quickly translated into a pin at a particular position on the map. Sitting in the back of the room are PARISH and JENKINS. PARISH has his chin resting in his hands. He seems very concerned as he studies the map before him. JENKINS looks at him. PARISH glances back fleetingly and then turns away.

79. CDC CONFERENCE ROOM.

CDC DEPARTMENT HEADS sit with PARISH and JENKINS.

> JENKINS
> My friend, it has caught up with us. We seem to be in the middle of a full-scale something or another. I'd call it an epidemic except there haven't been any deaths, at least none we can attribute directly to these…

tumors. Listen, let's get this straight. For the time being we're going to call these things... Carl, it was your idea, I think. We're going to call them teratomas. (*Siller looks annoyed.*) Loretta, I know it's not clinically correct but we've got to give them a label.

SILLER
Why don't we make up one?

JENKINS
Loretta, we're dealing with so many unknowns here that I think it would be better to maintain a public stance that gives the impression that we've got some grip on it, some handle. Do you know what I mean? You can't just announce to the world that you haven't the slightest idea what's going on. No one will accept that. So, for public consumption, we're involved in an outbreak of teratoma-like tumors.

FRAMPTON
Can we announce that they're contagious?

JENKINS
I don't know. My thinking is that it's too early to make that public.

SILLER
They're going to find out soon enough. As soon as they get wind of these figures, or even the quarantine requirement.

JENKINS
I'll admit, I'm just stalling for time. But maybe with a full-scale effort to diagnose the outbreak, to observe the patterns, to examine these teratomas, we might come up with something.

ALDERMAN
Like what?

JENKINS
I don't know what. Ideally we'll find an antidote, some sort of immunological response. Hopefully we'll get some idea of what's causing this to happen in the first place.

PARISH
Arthur, we can't afford to run scared. The figures are large but they're not all that overwhelming. Surgery is still effective in removing them and the recovery rate is remarkable in its speed and effectiveness. My feeling is that we convene a national symposium for early next week, get as much material together as we can in the meantime, and make a full-scale presentation to the profession and then the media that same day.

SILLER
You think the media's going to wait?

PARISH
God, I hope so.

80. CDC ENTERANCE.

PARISH is walking out the front door of the Center for Disease Control when he suddenly encounters TONY MAJORS and a CBS camera crew. PARISH keeps walking to his car as the cameras follow.

PARISH
Shit.

MAJORS
Dr. Parish, is it true that a major epidemic has broken out in this country that is being kept under wraps by the CDC?

                          PARISH
          Not true.

                          MAJORS
          Is it true, Dr. Parish, that a strange, tumor-
          like growth is spreading through the
          population at a very rapid rate, afflicting
          large numbers of people?

                          PARISH
          No comment.

                          MAJORS
          Is it true that just last week the CDC
          sent out over eleven million telegrams to
          hospitals and medical personnel warning of
          a potential outbreak?

                          PARISH
          This is all very premature. I have no
          comment.

                          MAJORS
          But you do admit that there is something
          going on?

                          PARISH
          I do not admit anything. This is simply not
          a proper forum for a medical discussion. I
          find your questions poorly informed and
          highly irresponsible. (*He steps into his car.*)
          Good day. (*He drives off.*)

81. RON PARISH'S APARTMENT

A close-up of a television screen shows TONY MAJORS speaking into a microphone while standing in front of the CDC Headquarters.

                    MAJORS
            Although Dr. Parish refuses to confirm
            our findings, the fact remains that doctors
            around the country have been reporting
            to the CDC many instances of this very
            strange and unexplainable outbreak. This is
            Anthony Majors at the Center for Disease
            Control, Atlanta, Georgia.

A commercial begins and PARISH turns the set off. He is fuming.
SYLVIA STRIKER is with him.

                    PARISH
            That goddamn sonofabitch.

                    SYLVIA
            Now what?

The telephone rings.

PARISH nods as if to say "that's what." He goes over to answer it.

                    PARISH
            Hello. Hello, Arthur... Of course I saw it...
            Well, I'm angry too... Yeah, I agree. Well,
            we've got to say something now. We don't
            have any choice. No. No... You want me
            to call a news conference? Shit no, you can
            call it. I don't give a shit who calls it. I don't
            even have to be there. I don't care. Listen,
            Arthur, they grabbed me coming out of the
            building, I did not grab them... Well, listen,
            I think we better coordinate this or we'll
            both be up all night on the telephone. How
            about a news conference at nine o'clock
            tomorrow morning? I can call Howie if you
            want and have him set it up... Okay. That
            sounds good to me... A panel? What kind
            of a panel? You think it's better to have five
            people who don't know anything instead

of one? You or me, it doesn't matter. You know as much as I do and it's your show, so *you* do it... Okay, if you want I'll be glad to be there too. So I'll take care of it with Howie. Right... Okay. Try to get some sleep. Bye. (*He hangs up.*) That guy's too much. He's upset because I was the one on TV. As though I was trying to upstage him or something. Some people... I don't know.

82. CDC AUDITORIUM.

A battery of television cameras are aimed at the CDC Auditorium stage. The lights on the stage are very bright. HOWIE MOORE, CDC Public Relations Director, comes onto the stage.

>HOWIE
>Gentlemen, gentlemen, can I have your attention please. Arthur Jenkins, Director of the CDC will be here in just a minute. He is going to read a prepared announcement. There will not be any questions at this time. He will mention in his announcement the date of a press conference where questions will be entertained.

The PRESS CORPS looks a bit dismayed and begin mumbling among themselves. After a few moments HOWIE MOORE comes back out on the stage.

>HOWIE
>Ladies and Gentlemen of the press, I'd like to present to you Dr. Arthur Jenkins, Director of the Center for Disease Control.

The cameras quickly switch to "on." The REPORTERS stand poised. ARTHUR JENKINS walks over to the microphones. PARISH stands in the wings.

JENKINS
In the last several weeks, we at the Center
for Disease Control have become aware
of a proliferation of a strange, tumor-like
growth, called a teratoma, occurring across
a broad spectrum of individuals over many
parts of the country. These tumors are not
uncommon in and of themselves. We have
known about them for many years. They
have not, to this date, proven deadly and
are surgically removable. What is unusual is
the increase in the number of recent cases.
Six hundred have been reported in the last
several weeks.

A number of reporters are talking among themselves while JENKINS is speaking.

                    REPORTER #1
I don't believe him.

                    REPORTER #2
They're spoon-feeding us.

                    REPORTER #3
You can just tell by the way he's talking that
there's a volcanic story here and they're not
giving us anything.

                    REPORTER #1
My guess is that they don't know what
they're dealing with any better than we do.

                    REPORTER #3
Well damn it! I just wish they would come
out and say it.

                    JENKINS
A full press conference will be held on
Monday, following the symposium. All

questions will be entertained at that time.
Thank you.

There is a great deal of unrest among the REPORTERS. Some of them begin to yell out questions.

> REPORTER #4
> Is it true, Mr. Jenkins, that we are dealing with a virus?

> REPORTER #5
> Are there any preventive measures that the public can take, any precautions against the spread of these teratomas?

> REPORTER #6
> Can the public afford to wait till your symposium?

> REPORTER #1
> What haven't you told us?

HOWIE is backstage conferring with JENKINS and PARISH.

> HOWIE
> I don't think we can leave them like this. They're upset.

> PARISH
> They're scared. It's hard to stay objective when some disease may strike you at any moment, or your kid.

> HOWIE
> I think you've got to go back out there.

> JENKINS
> You go, Ron. You're better at a spontaneous talk than I am.

PARISH walks back on the stage. He is deluged with questions.

> PARISH
> (*Holding up his hands.*)
> Can I have your attention please. (*The reporters quiet down.*) I hear you. I hear what you're saying. But you want answers to questions that we don't have. We are working as fast as we can to find out what's causing these… teratomas, and to find out how to get rid of them without having to resort to surgery. There's no reason for fear. It won't help. If there is a way to prevent these teratomas from occurring we will tell you the moment we find it. Our symposium on Monday will bring together some of the best minds in the country. We already have a very talented staff here at CDC working round the clock. All we can say is that we see no cause for alarm and will do our best to keep the public informed of each new development. If the public has questions, call your doctors. At this point there is nothing else I can say.

He turns and walks quickly off stage. HOWIE and JENKINS meet him.

> HOWIE
> You have just made enemies of every doctor in America. Every drippy nose will be on that phone tonight…

> PARISH
> What could I do? Do you want them all calling here? Good God, every man, woman and child with a cold is going to think he's got it.

> HOWIE
> And maybe they do.

> JENKINS
> God, this is awful. This is just awful.

> PARISH
> Howie, Arthur, I hope you can swim, 'cause I have a feeling we're in over our heads.

83. A SUBURBAN BATHROOM.

An attractive young woman in a bathrobe walks into a bathroom and turns off the water that is filling a tub. She takes off her robe and climbs in gently. The expression on her face indicates that the water is hot. A male voice calls out from the other room.

> MALE VOICE
> How is it?

> WOMAN
> Hot.

> MALE VOICE
> I'm sorry. I thought I had it just right.

> WOMAN
> Oh, that's okay. I just appreciate your doing it for me.

> MALE VOICE
> You can add a little cold water.

> WOMAN
> No. It's fine.

She settles into the tub and lies back. After a few moments she seems a little uncomfortable. She sits up and gently turns on the cold water. She puts her hand under the faucet to splash some on her face when it comes out. She is not at all prepared for the sight of the snake-like creature that emerges as well. She screams when she sees it and jumps hysterically out of the tub. Her HUSBAND runs in and sees her shaking uncontrollably. She can't talk but points him to the tub. There, swimming in the bathwater, is the creature Mr. Robinson had spawned. It moves blindly around the tub.

84. CDC MAXIMUM SECURITY LABORATORY.

The laboratory is bustling with activity. SCIENTISTS and TECHNICIANS are performing all manner of tests in every corner of the complex. It is obviously a day and night operation, judging by the several people sleeping in the corners. DORIS and SIDNEY are among them. They are curled up in each other's arms, A telephone rings and is answered by one of the ASSISTANTS. She walks over to DORIS and shakes her gently by the shoulder. DORIS opens her eyes and is directed to the phone. She looks drowsily at her watch. SIDNEY wakes as well. DORIS rises and goes to the phone. She listens for a moment and then hangs up. She goes over to SIDNEY and whispers in his ear. They both get up and walk to the exit door. The exit procedure is complex, involving passing through four chambers, a change of clothes, a shower and a chemical spray. They pass through them all quickly but thoroughly.

85. PARISH'S OFFICE. NIGHT.

PARISH is sitting at his desk. DORIS and SIDNEY enter.

>   DORIS
> This better be important. I don't go through
> that exit procedure for nothing.

>   PARISH
> It looks like you've been sleeping.

>   SIDNEY
> We figured we'd take two hours a day
> whether we needed it or not.

>   PARISH
> It feels like I haven't seen you in months.

DORIS
More like three days. If you get lonely, you can always come visit. It's a regular beehive down there.

PARISH
Sounds nice. It's been a regular hornets' nest up here... So, I don't suppose there's anything new to report?

DORIS
I can tell you everything it's not, but we're light-years away from knowing what it *is*. Just nothing pans out.

SIDNEY
We must have performed a thousand tests already, no?

DORIS
At least.

PARISH
Not encouraging, huh?

SIDNEY
Nope. When God told Adam to go out and give names to all things, it seems he forgot a few hundred billion or so. There just seems to be so many things in the universe that we don't know what they are.

PARISH
What's he talking about?

DORIS
Oh, he's just been going through this religious revival. Every so often he begins paying homage to the mysteries of the universe.

PARISH
Well, one of those mysteries just arrived here, air freight. (*He reaches down to the floor and picks up a box that has already been opened.*) You ready? (*They nod. He pulls out a bottle with Mr. Robinson's snake inside.*) Surprise!

DORIS
What is it?

PARISH
As far as I can tell it's that… creature from that Mr. Robinson, the one that went down the sewer. (*He pulls some pictures out of his desk drawer and hands them to Doris. She looks, and shows them to Sidney.*) What do you think? Is it the same?

DORIS
Amazing. And it's still alive?

PARISH
As far as I can tell.

SIDNEY
How did they ever…?

PARISH
Came out in a woman's bathtub. (*They all make faces.*) Disgusting, huh? But it has survived.

SIDNEY
It's a miracle.

PARISH
Oh, I don't know if it's a miracle, but it's undoubtedly good fortune.

                    DORIS
It's the first living, surviving tissue we've
had. Maybe the secret's in there. Maybe this
is what we've been looking for.

                    SIDNEY
I tell you, it's a miracle. For anything to
survive the sewers of New York has got
to be a miracle. And to make its way to
Atlanta, that's just not your everyday
happenstance.

                    PARISH
Sidney, I'm looking for a bigger miracle. (*He
hands them the jar.*) See if you two can find
it.

86. JENNIFER CAMPUS' LIVING ROOM.

JENNIFER CAMPUS is sitting in her living room with her husband ARNOLD and an interviewer, PERRY SMITH. SMITH is taking notes in shorthand as JENNIFER speaks.

                    JENNIFER
Well, I've been in the habit of feeling my
breasts, exploring them, you know, for
lumps. I've been doin' it regular for years
now. My sister-in-law had an operation way
back and I wasn't takin' no chances. Well,
about a month ago, I still remember it, it
scared me so, I had just gotten over bein'
sick and I hadn't checked in a day or so.

                    SMITH
When you say sick, what was wrong?

                    JENNIFER
Oh nothin' really. Just a cold. I got a little
dizzy too, I think.

ARNOLD
She couldn't remember things neither for a couple a days.

JENNIFER
Oh *(She waves him off.)* It was nothin'. Just a fever.

SMITH
How high? Do you remember?

JENNIFER
I didn't have no thermometer but it was high. *(She looks to Smith for more questions, but he motions for her to go on.)* Anyway, I just did my normal... massage. You know, I get embarrassed when I talk like this... Oh well, anyway, it was just awful. I went to feel and there wasn't just one lump... They were all over. Just on my left... boob. I was so terrified I threw up.

ARNOLD
All over the dog.

JENNIFER
He was lyin' next to the bed. Arnie took me to the doctor in Springfield next mornin'. He took one little pinch and said he wanted to operate. I've never been so scared in my whole life. Next thing I knew I was on my way to the hospital and before you know it they're wheelin' me in to be operated on. I kept hopin' he could save it. I'm real attached, you know. But he couldn't. He came and talked to me after. He looked pretty petrified himself. After he told me I could understand why.

SMITH
What did he say?

JENNIFER
He told me my breast wasn't filled with lumps at all.

SMITH
No?

JENNIFER
It was filled with eyes.

SMITH
With *what*?

JENNIFER
Eyes. (*She points to her own eyes.*) They was growin' like grapes, he said, all over. Strangest thing ever saw. That's when he called you.

SMITH
And your recovery. How long did that...?

ARNOLD
It was fast. And she didn't complain, nothin'.

JENNIFER
It never hurt, you know? I never felt nothin'. Oh, I miss my breast. I'd be lyin' if I didn't say it. But I don't feel so bad as I always thought my sister-in-law must of felt. But then, she died, and I'm all better.

ARNOLD
Tell him the strangest part.

                    JENNIFER
You mean my eyes? (*He nods.*) Well, I
don't know if this is so important, but I was
gettin' cataracts and now they're gone. But I
don't know if that means nothin'.

87. ALAN GARDNER FAMILY ROOM.

ALAN GARDNER, his WIFE and three CHILDREN are sitting on a comfortable couch in a cozy family room. Interviewer FRANCES TYLER sits across from them.

                    ALAN
So, they gave me six months to live. Well, I'll
tell you, Jesus said you have to lose your life
to have it. Now I know that's true. I've been
born again. I mean, I really have, in more
ways than one. I'd given up hope. I'd given
up everything. I mean, I was only forty-five,
and I was dying. I was inconsolable. (*He
looks at his wife. She smiles back.*) Can you
imagine thinking of losing these kids? Have
you ever seen such beautiful kids? (*Frances
smiles.*) I couldn't believe it was happening
to me. I just couldn't. I would lie in bed and
curse all night, right at the ceiling. When
they took me into that operating room they
said it was probably a waste of time, the
tumor looked so big. But I was reaching out
for anything. Didn't care what it cost. So
they did it and I thank God to this very day
that I told them to go ahead and do it.

                    FRANCES
What did they find?

                    ALAN
I don't know what you'd call it. I think
the papers are calling them… I keep
forgetting… teratomas, I think they are. It

weighed twenty pounds, can you believe it? It was a grizzly thing. It had different things growing in it, like a liver which the doctor said got kind of mixed up with a kidney. They were growing together. You wanna know the strangest thing? It had wings. Strange, huh? It looked as ugly as I used to feel. But I'm a new man, I tell you, I've been reborn.

88. FIFTH AVENUE. A JEWISH TEMPLE.

PERRY SMITH is wandering through the pews in the main sanctuary of the temple. He is following behind ROBINSON, the old man from the 42nd Street hotel. ROBINSON is wearing a janitor's uniform and dusting the pews. He stops occasionally to rearrange the prayer books.

ROBINSON
Sorry it took you so long to find me. I guess this is the last place anyone would ever of thought to look for me. But I've been here about four months now. Kind of felt I needed to make amends, if you know what I mean. So I'm a janitor, nothin' wrong with that. I always had a foul mouth, you know? Every other word was outta the gutter. When that thing came outta me, I don't know, it's like it took a whole part of me with him. I thought about it, you know, and it's funny. It should come outta my mouth and not my ear or some other part of me. You know what I mean? But I tell you, I think it was a blessing, that's what I think. I don't know when I was ever so scared before in all my days as when I felt that thing trying to get out of me. But I'm grateful to it, that little creature. It was like a savior to me. Saved my life… or what little I've got left.

89. CDC COMPUTER CENTER.

PERRY SMITH, FRANCES TYLER and about fourteen other FIELD INTERVIEWERS are filling out long lists of data forms. A crew of computer PROGRAMMERS are taking their information and processing it into the computers. The computers whiz, spin and manipulate the vast input into long sheets of printout information. This information is synthesized and resynthesized. STATISTICIANS type page after page of analysis. Their writings are compiled into folders and bound into booklets.

90. CDC MAXIMUM SECURITY LABORATORY.

DORIS, SIDNEY and a host of SCIENTISTS and TECHNICIANS continue to work at a fevered pace. DORIS is studying a slide under an electron microscope. The expression on her face indicates disappointment.

91. CDC MAP ROOM.

The map is now filled with twice as many pins as it had the last time it was seen. PEOPLE continue adding new pins all the time.

92. CDC SWITCHBOARD.

The CDC switchboard has spread beyond its one room confines with additional hook-ups set up in the hall. All of the OPERATORS are working furiously and MESSAGE BOYS stand by to carry overflow messages to officials with tied up phones. One such message is carried to PARISH.

93. PARISH'S OFFICE.

A YOUNG BOY enters and hands PARISH the phone message. It reads, "I know you're busy when I can't reach you on the phone. We're still praying for a miracle but it looks doubtful by tomorrow. I expect you have the rest of our report. Good luck, Doris and Sidney." PARISH scribbles a quick reply. "Keep the faith! Love, Ron." He hands it to the BOY who turns and runs out quickly. PARISH has a large pile of folders sitting on his desk. One of them is open. He underlines a section with a ruler and then turns to his typewriter and begins typing.

94. CDC ENTRANCE.

A bevy of television cameras, REPORTERS and NEWSPAPERMEN are huddled on the sidewalk as a stream of cars carrying various medical DIGNITARIES arrives at the CDC Headquarters. The cameras cover doctor after doctor as they exit their cars and enter the building. A long, black limousine pulls up and TONY MAJORS and his camera crew rush up to greet it.

                    MAJORS
          Coming out of his car now is Alexi
          Malinofsky, the Director of WHO, the
          United Nation's World Health Organization.
          Dr. Malinofsky, can I ask you a question
          please? Do you think the current outbreak of
          teratoma tumors represents a serious threat to
          the health of the world population?

                    ALEXI
          I certainly hope not.

                    MAJORS
          Does the information you have indicate that
          we are facing a crisis situation?

                    ALEXI
          I have very little information. That is why I
          am here.

                    MAJORS
          As an expert on world health problems, do
          you have any feelings on the way this...
          epidemic is being handled by the Center for
          Disease Control?

                    ALEXI
          I have not yet been informed that it is
          an epidemic and if you don't mind I will
          withhold all comment until the symposium
          has concluded.

He turns and walks into the building.

95. CDC AUDITORIUM.

The auditorium is rapidly filling with important-looking MEN of the medical profession. They sit, not in auditorium chairs, but at long tables. Each seat has its own water pitcher and glass as well as a neatly assembled stack of papers. On the stage, too, is a long table with pitchers, papers and name plaques. The auditorium looks full when JENKINS, PARISH and other CDC DEPARTMENT HEADS enter and take their respective seats. JENKINS takes a gavel and hammers on a wooden block.

> JENKINS
> Ladies and gentlemen of the medical profession, I wish to welcome you and thank you for attending this emergency symposium.

96. CDC LOBBY.

A group of CAMERAMEN are standing around talking.

> CAMERAMAN #1
> They sure do take forever in there.

> CAMERAMAN #2
> You know, I'd feel better if they passed out gas masks. This place gives me the creeps.

> CAMERAMAN #3
> Did you ever see their maximum security labs?

> CAMERAMAN #2
> Nope, and wouldn't care to either.

> CAMERAMAN #3
> We did a story on it once. I tell you, nothing could get out of there even if it wanted to.

CAMERAMAN #4
                    So how did you manage it?

                    CAMERAMAN #3
                    I mean bugs, germs. There's no way for 'em
                    to escape. They take all the air that comes
                    out of there and heat it to five thousand
                    degrees. Everything's airtight and purified.
                    There's nothing to worry about.

Suddenly REPORTER #4 lets out a big sneeze. All heads turn. He smiles comically. There is no response from him to his cohorts.

97. CDC AUDITORIUM.

WENDEL FRAMPTON is seated at a table on the stage, speaking into the microphone. The DELEGATES seem interested in what he is saying.

                         FRAMPTON
                    My point is this. Whatever it is we're dealing
                    with, it's certain that it enters the body's
                    cellular system and begins giving new orders
                    or messages to the cell's reproductive DNA
                    code. How it has gained access to this code
                    is a total mystery. Scientists have been
                    struggling for decades to unlock the secrets
                    of DNA with little real success. And here
                    we have some unknown quantity invading
                    the body, entering the cells and ordering
                    them to reproduce at an extraordinary rate
                    of acceleration, much faster than ordinary
                    tissue growth.

98. MAXIMUM SECURITY LABORATORY.

A slide of cellular tissue appears on the screen, DORIS lifts her head up from the microscope. There is a strange but interested look on her face. She adjusts the magnification and continues looking.

99. CDC AUDITORIUM.

PARISH is addressing the MEMBERS of the symposium.

> PARISH
> We know that viruses have the capacity to enter a cell and alter the cellular machinery for their own needs. The cell loses its normal physical characteristics and functions, and participates in the life cycle of the virus. The virus does not replicate unless it is inside a cell. It needs a host for its own growth. Viral forms are therefore a logical possibility and the likely object of our search. There are important questions to be asked, however. How do these viruses know how to initiate such sophisticated cellular growth, and why doesn't the body launch an all-out immunological defense against them? What are the mechanisms involved here? What are the attractions?

100. CDC CAFETERIA.

Two COUNTERGIRLS are talking.

> GIRL #1
> Your boyfriend's here again. I saw him in the lobby.

> GIRL #2
> I did too.

> GIRL #1
> Did you watch him on the news the other night?

> GIRL #2
> *(Nodding her head shyly.)*
> Uh-huh. He's on a lot.

> GIRL #1
> What'll you do if he invites you out for dinner again?

> GIRL #2
> Blush, probably. That's what I always do. Besides, he doesn't really mean it. He's just flirting.

> GIRL #1
> Well, I sure wish he'd flirt with me. I sure do.

101. CDC AUDITORIUM

> STILLER
> Somehow, the bodies immunological system is being tricked by these viral forms. The body does not see them for what they are. It seems, in fact, as though they are *welcomed* into the body. The body actually appears to cooperate with them by numbing the nerve tissue surrounding the teratoma growth.

102. MAXIMUM SECURITY LABORATORY.

DORIS takes her head away from the electron microscope and stares at the wall for a few moments.

> DORIS
> Sidney, do me a favor. Would you set up the video hook-up for the microscope?

> SIDNEY
> What do you see?

> DORIS
> I'm not sure yet. I just want to record some pictures.

SIDNEY
Sure. Be glad to.

103. CDC AUDITORIUM.

RONALD PARISH is addressing the symposium again.

PARISH
I think, from the review of the statistical evidence, several conclusions are possible. It is apparent to us now that what we are witnessing exhibits a structured pattern of development and is random in its occurrence, as we had initially expected. The teratoma forms have evolved in the fairly short period of five months, from primitive, almost prehistoric forms to sophisticated, human-like development. A fascinating observation is that this growth occurs across wide territorial distances at an unusual rate and without significant duplication. This indicates that an advance in one area is somehow communicated to a teratoma growing in another. This is a most unusual discovery and one of the most confusing. One concept that's been used to describe this pattern was suggested by Dr. Raymond: experimentation. The question here is – and I know we've posed a lot of questions here today – what is it that is doing this experimenting? And what is it trying to create? I guess the focal question of this whole symposium boils down to this: should we assume, dare to assume, that what we are confronted with here is... intelligent?

There is a fairly strong ripple of response throughout the auditorium. An older man in the back of the auditorium stands up.

                    MAN
Don't you think you are making some
rather outlandish assumptions?

                    PARISH
Yes, but in response to rather outlandish
circumstances.

                ANOTHER MAN
Does assuming the virus is intelligent have
any medical value?

                    PARISH
To the extent that it helps us track it
down, yes. A detective has a better chance
of finding a criminal when he knows
something about him. Intelligence operates
normally within certain rational parameters.
It is easier to predict or outmaneuver than
irrational behavior.

                    JENKINS
I would like to interrupt this if I may.
However important this debate might be,
our primary responsibility at this time is to
make recommendations to Congress and
the public regarding an immediate national
response to the situation. It seems to me
that our alternatives exist between two
polarities. We are faced with a contagious
disease, nowhere near the magnitude or
number scope of an influenza epidemic,
but still obviously of great seriousness. We
can proceed either by taking no action at all
at this time or by supporting a nationwide
restriction on public assembly. This
would involve closing schools, churches,
restaurants, places of mass entertainment.
Vital arteries such as mass communication
and places of business would be left open.

Protective surgical masks should probably
be mandatory if this disease continues
to spread. Our recommendation at this
time, however, is to wait and see, with the
clear understanding that broad emergency
measures be ready if the situation warrants
it.

104. TELEVISION.

The following television program is seen on several different television screens as the program continues. It begins in a bar, proceeds to a family den, continues on a bank of televisions in the appliance section of a department store and concludes on PARISH'S television in his apartment. It is a news program already in progress.

>   ANCHORMAN
> Reaction to today's announcement was
> immediate and ranged from anger to fear, as
> Lila Phillips reports.

The image changes to LILA PHILLIPS on the steps of the Capitol Building in Washington DC.

>   PHILLIPS
> Congressional response to today's
> symposium in Atlanta can best be described
> as heated. Congressman Winsten of Illinois
> called for the dismissal of Arthur Jenkins,
> Director of the Center for Disease Control,
> and Representative Hodgkiss of Missouri
> went even further.

The scene changes to REPRESENTATIVE HODGKISS standing before a battery of microphones.

>   HODGKISS
> I think the American People have the right
> to know what is causing this terrifying
> disease. We will not be hoodwinked by

clever phrases like "intelligent viruses." Who do they think we are? We cannot tolerate a situation of this kind. Our medical community is the richest in the world. It is paid to give us answers, competent answers. And let me assert that I believe that we are talking about a question of competency. Or, should I say, the lack of it. I am outraged by the entire handling of this affair and promise to recommend that a congressional inquiry into the matter be instituted at once.

The scene changes to people mingling around the REPORTER in downtown Washington.

PHILLIPS
Washington's reaction was not limited to Congress. People on the street had their feelings too.

The scene changes to interviews with four different people.

MAN
I don't like it. I don't sleep at night. I keep feelin' stuff inside me. I don't know if it's real or not. I can't get an appointment with my doctor for over two months and you gotta wait at the hospital for twenty hours, I hear, before they can see you. I think it's a disgrace.

WOMAN
Why don't they give us shots? Why don't they do nothin'? This is America. This kinda thing's not supposed to happen in America.

WOMAN
(*Wearing a surgical mask.*)
I think wearing a mask is just a sensible response to the problem. They wear them in

hospitals so they don't spread germs, so why shouldn't I wear them to keep from getting them? My entire family's been wearing them for a week now. I've also decided to keep my children home from school until I understand more about what this is. I don't believe in taking chances.

MAN

One of the fellows at work has a friend whose wife got it... one of these... teratoma things. The way he described it I couldn't imagine anything more awful. I think I'd rather die than have something like that growing inside me. Just talking about it gives me the shivers. I can't believe that medical science doesn't have a cure for it. But I guess they're still working on cancer too. I just hope this one doesn't take so long, or we'll all be walking around with these. (*He shudders*). I don't even want to think about it.

The scene changes to hospital interiors.

PHILLIPS

Hospitals around the country have set up intensive care isolation wards. Many of them are already full. This is causing massive problems for the hospitals, as Dr. Robert Elfstron, Director of the Martin Luther King Memorial Hospital, told us.

DR. ELISTROM

The tragedy is that we don't know what we're looking for. Everybody with a cold or a swelling or just general discomfort is coming to us. In some instances, it looks like we might have something. Often we just can't tell. When it looks serious, we keep them but often something that looks serious isn't and someone with a running nose has got it in 'em. It's all terribly confusing, I'll tell you.

LILA PHILLIPS is standing on the steps leading to a large hospital.

> PHILLIPS
> One of the stranger stories related to this teratoma outbreak has occurred in hospitals catering to middle- and upper-class families, as Dr. Peter Johnson of the Mount Carmel Hospital in Greenville Heights told me.

JOHNSON appears on camera.

> JOHNSON
> In the past week individuals, even some families, have approached me about moving into our isolation wards. I took it as a joke at first but I've had offers of up to $100,000 to let people stay there. And, you know, on a certain level that is very tempting. We could make a down payment on some very useful equipment with that kind of money. The interesting thing is that I've heard from doctors all over the country who say they have the same situation, the same kinds of offers. I think that must give you some idea how scared a lot of people are by this thing.

LILA PHILLIPS is standing on the steps of the Capitol Building again. She takes a surgical mask out of her pocket and ties it around her mouth.

> PHILLIPS
> It may look strange, but its cheaper than a gas mask and probably as effective. This is Lila Phillips at the Capitol in Washington D.C.

A hand reaches out and turns off the television. PARISH steps back and looks at SYLVIA. She is sitting on the couch in his living room.

> PARISH
> Sylvia, my love, you have just seen shit hit a fan. (*The telephone rings.*) What perfect timing. I should have had money on it. (*He lifts the phone and speaks without listening to find out who it is.*) Hello, Arthur, I just saw it too. (*He looks confused.*) Who? Sidney? Sidney! I wasn't expecting you. What's up? What? What do you mean? You're kidding? Of course. I'll be right there. (*He hangs up the phone.*) They found something.

105. MAXIMUM SECURITY LABORATORY.

The last set of doors in the airlock entry system to the laboratory opens. PARISH enters. SIDNEY and DORIS are standing by the electron microscope. Several other TECHNICIANS and ASSISTANTS are working in the room as well. DORIS looks over to PARISH.

> DORIS
> I think we found it. (*Parish is wide-eyed.*) But if we have, it is so incredible that I don't know what to say. (*She pauses.*)

> PARISH
> Don't leave me hanging like that.

> DORIS
> I'm serious. I don't know how to tell you. Maybe it's better if you just call the men in white coats and let them take me away right now. It would make it a lot easier on me.

> PARISH
> Would you stop being so dramatic and just tell me!

DORIS
Sidney, would you tell him?

SIDNEY
I don't believe it either.

DORIS
Well, let me put it this way. We have either discovered a new viral form or we have spotted a flying saucer.

PARISH
(*Disbelieving.*)
A *what*?

DORIS
A flying saucer. I'm serious. I was studying some tissue from the top of the head of that Robinson creature. I was using the electron microscope at full magnification. Suddenly I noticed a set of cells with a streak moving through them. I decided to trace it. It took about six hours but I found it. It was minute but absolutely saucer-like in shape.

SIDNEY
And it moved like a flying saucer.

PARISH
And how does a flying saucer move?

SIDNEY
Oh, you know. You always hear reports about how they fly at these fast speeds but still can make right turns and reverse themselves without slowing down. That's how it moved.

PARISH
I don't believe it. It sounds too fantastic.

                    DORIS
I made a video tape. I think you should see
it.

                    PARISH
You're damn right I should see it.

                    DORIS
       (*Going over to turn on the machine.*)
Remember, it's still small. We can't get it any
bigger.

She turns on the tape. The video image is tracing a liquid trail through a cellular landscape. After about ten seconds we see the tail. PARISH moves into the picture screen. He studies the image closely. The shape he is staring at is unquestionably saucer-like. It moves rapidly through the space of the cell. The movements have a certain mechanical look to them.

                    PARISH
It's amazing.

                    SIDNEY
And notice something else. How it doesn't
leave the area of the screen.

                    PARISH
Uh-huh.

                    SIDNEY
I think it knows we're looking at it.

106. JENKINS OFFICE. NIGHT.

JENKINS, PARISH, DORIS and SIDNEY are sitting informally on the couch and floor.

                    JENKINS
What would you call it? An invasion from
outer space?

DORIS
Well, you can hardly call it "outer" space.

JENKINS
Inner space, then?

DORIS
But what does that mean?

JENKINS
Could it just come from right here? (*He waves his hand in the air.*)

DORIS
What's "right here," really? I mean, look at your own hand. To a creature that's small enough, your hand could be a universe. The molecules could be stars, for all we know.

SIDNEY
I don't think we should get off the track. It's possible that it is just a virus with an unusual shape. Some viruses look like rocket ships. We never stopped to wonder about them.

DORIS
Maybe we should.

PARISH
Okay. I think we're getting a little too far out here. Let's get back down to earth.

JENKINS
Could it have come in on the space probes, with the astronauts? Even with all the precautions?

SIDNEY
Maybe it didn't come in at all. Maybe it's always been here.

JENKINS
But why wouldn't we have known...
before?

SIDNEY
Cancer's been around for centuries. How come we're only beginning to discover it now?

DORIS
The environment. Pollution.

JENKINS
(*Grasping for straws.*)
Do you think...?

PARISH
Who knows what to think.

SIDNEY
You know what's interesting? In the movie *The War of the Worlds* – did you ever see it? It's one of my favorites. There's an invasion from Mars and what kills the Martian invaders? Viruses. Now we have viruses becoming invaders and growing these creatures. Don't you find that interesting?

JENKINS
I hate science fiction.

SIDNEY
I have a feeling you better get used to it. Something tells me we're living it.

Suddenly a siren goes off, followed by a series of loud bells.

JENKINS
(*Grasping his heart.*)
My God. What's that?

PARISH, DORIS and SIDNEY are already up and heading to the door.

>   PARISH
> Maximum security lab. Emergency.

107. MAXIMUM SECURITY LABORATORY. EXTERIOR.

A crowd of people is assembled outside a special viewing window into the Maximum Security Lab. PARISH, DORIS and SIDNEY come running. Four sleepy SECURITY GUARDS are standing there as well. They are all looking inside.

>   PARISH
> What's happening?

They point through the window. Standing outside, along with several space-suited TECHNICIANS, is a MAN in street clothes held by two TECHNICIANS. He doesn't appear to be struggling. Another TECHNICIAN raises his arms to indicate that he doesn't know what is going on.

>   PARISH
> Where's the intercom? (*One of the security
> guards goes to show him.*) Where were you
> when he got in?

>   GUARD
> We never had nothing like this happen
> before. Just took us by surprise.

>   PARISH
> You're paid not to be surprised. (*He takes
> hold of the intercom.*) Hello in there. Do
> you hear me?

>   MALE VOICE
> We hear you.

>   PARISH
> Who's speaking?

TIM
(*Waving his hand.*)
It's me Ron, Timothy.

PARISH
Tim, what's going on?

TIM
You got me. This guy just walked in here. We grabbed hold of him as soon as we saw him but he doesn't seem to be struggling or anything.

PARISH
Who are you?

HEDGES
Carrol Hedges is my name and I can explain everything, so there's nothing to get excited about.

PARISH
Well, what the hell are you doing in there? Do you realize it's a maximum security installation? That you've put yourself in imminent danger?

HEDGES
Yes, I do. I'm sorry I had to do it this way but I realized if I was going to be of any help to you I'd have to act pretty quickly. I've been trying to get through to you for two weeks, ever since those telegrams went out. It has just been impossible.

PARISH
What are you doing here? What is this all about?

HEDGES

I think I can help you. I don't know if you've heard of me before but there have been a number of studies done on me that have been published in several medical journals, and *Psychology Today* did a story not too long ago.

PARISH

Who are you? What are you talking about?

HEDGES

I've been working for the last several years with bio-feedback training. I am, I think, without boasting, probably the foremost practitioner of bio-feedback control in the country.

PARISH

What does that have to do with anything?

HEDGES

It means that I can control, to a great degree, my autonomic nervous system. I can control my heartbeat, I can consciously fight off germ infection and prevent colds, I can flush blood to any part of my body at will. For example, if one of you kind gentlemen here will watch, I will cause my left earlobe to blush. (*He closes his eyes and concentrates. After a few seconds his left earlobe is turning bright red. Tim looks at it and nods his head, smiling.*) You see, I just directed the blood to flow there.

PARISH

Mr. Hedges, this is not a circus audition.

HEDGES
You're absolutely right and I do not mean to
take advantage of your busy time. But I do
think I can be of invaluable service to you.
If these creatures of yours are intelligent, as
the newspapers announced today, I think
I stand a fair chance of communicating
with them – probably a fairer chance than
any of you. You see I can bring my own
intelligence into very minute parts of my
body and control its function. I believe I
can contact these viral forms and either find
out what they're about or simply how to
destroy them. I know you will think this is a
crazy scheme and I know you would never
have consented to it had you had time to
think about it. The fact is, however, that the
deed is done. I am already overexposed and
highly contagious. All I ask now is that you
put me somewhere and let me go to work.
Viruses are small, you know, and it may take
me a while to find it, let alone make contact.

             PARISH
I don't believe this. This place is feeling
more and more like a lunatic asylum. What
am I going to do with this guy?

             DORIS
Why not set up a bed, upstairs, in Isolation,
and just see what happens?

             PARISH
But it's like blackmail. I don't like it.

             HEDGE
It's not blackmail. You could send me away.
I've already gotten what I came for. I can
feel it in me already. The only thing is that if
I have any significant developments I hope

I'll be able to reach you more quickly than I was during the last two weeks.

SIDNEY
He's got a point. I think we should keep him.

PARISH
All right. Enough of this. Transfer him to the Space Recovery Station. At least it's furnished and well-equipped. (*He turns to the guards.*) And you, you are in dire trouble. If anything like this ever happens again, if there's so much as a single visitor walking through the halls without a name tag, that's it. And I mean it. Now one of you better track down a dossier on this guy. All I need is to find out he's a Soviet agent or some radical terrorist or something. (*He motions for Doris and Sidney to follow him. They walk to a stairwell.*) Listen, I need to get a good night's sleep. I just can't handle any more today. I think, though, we should meet privately first thing in the morning and pursue this science fiction development and find hopefully some logical solution.

SIDNEY
We can call out the Marines.

PARISH
Very funny.

108. PARISH'S APARTMENT.

A telephone rings. The room is very dark. A hand reaches out and takes hold of the receiver on the night stand next to the bed.

SYLVIA
Hello? Okay, thank you. (*She hangs up, gropes around the nightstand for the remote control TV unit, finds it, and flicks it on.*)

PARISH
Who was that?

SYLVIA
Dunno. Just said to turn the TV on right away.

PARISH
What's on?

SYLVIA
Didn't say.

PARISH
What time is it?

SYLVIA
Dunno.

The light of the TV begins to fill the room. PARISH forces his head up on the pillow. The TV settles into a picture. SYLVIA lays back down. It is a morning news show. The image cuts to the TV screen.

HOST
The headline that little boys dreamed of as children and adults learned to grow cynical about has this morning become a reality. (*He holds up a copy of the* New York Daily News *with its giant headline: EARTH INVADED FROM OUTER SPACE. He reads it out loud.*)

PARISH
(*Jumping out of bed.*)
Goddamn it! How did that happen?

                                HOST
The truth of the matter is that it may not
be an invasion in the traditional sense of
the word. It may not even be an invasion
at all. What we are dealing with is micro-
organisms, virus-like, invisible to the human
eye, which under extreme magnification
happen to look like flying saucers.
According to Arthur Jenkins, Director of
the National Center for Disease Control in
Atlanta, they may be the cause of the strange
teratoma outbreak afflicting the country.
More on all of this now from Tony Majors,
in Atlanta.

                               PARISH
I don't believe it. Why would he do such a
stupid thing? I just don't believe it.

                               SYLVIA
I'll bet he was just afraid of losing his job.

                               PARISH
Well, now he can bet on it. Oh God, what
has he done?

109. PONCE DE LEON DRIVE. ATLANTA.

PARISH is driving into work. The roads are crowded. He is listening to
the radio.

                               RADIO
The National Guard has been called out in
Detroit to quell a riot which began nearly
an hour ago. There seems to be no initial
incident responsible for the rioting although
some people claim that it is related to the
scare story out of Atlanta this morning
about an invasion from outer space. A focal
point for the rioting is said to be the New

Grace Hospital. While it is in the center of a
ghetto area, it is also known to contain one
of the largest isolation wards for victims
of the teratoma disease now crippling the
country.

PARISH
Crippling? Bullshit. (*He flicks the radio off.*)

As PARISH approaches the Center he notices large CROWDS and military road blocks. His car pulls up to one of the barricades. He is stopped by several SOLDIERS.

SOLDIER
I'm sorry, but there is no through traffic
allowed. You'll have to detour.

PARISH
Goddamn it! I work at the Center.

SOLDIER
I'm sorry. We're not allowed to let anyone
through.

PARISH
(*Pulling out his wallet
and identification badge.*)
I'm in charge of the Virology Department. I
need to get to my office.

SOLDIER
I'm sorry but our orders…

PARISH
I don't give a damn about your orders!

The SOLDIER motions for another SOLDIER to come over.

SOLDIER #2
What's your problem here?

> PARISH
> Listen, I'm one of the people in charge of
> the teratoma program. I must get to my
> office. (*He hands him his identification.*)

The SOLDIER takes the identification over to a jeep and radios ahead. CROWDS of people are milling around the barricades, some still wearing nightclothes. There is a lot of talking and yelling among them. The SOLDIER comes back. He hands PARISH his wallet.

> SOLDIER #2
> Okay. Let him through.

PARISH drives past the barricade and on toward the Center two blocks down the road. The Center is surrounded by military hardware, tanks, guns, jeeps and large numbers of PERSONNEL. Helicopters are circling overhead. PARISH looks at it all in disbelief. He reaches down beneath his dashboard and turns on his CB radio. The flurry of transmissions discussing the CDC as the center of a military operation is amusing and absurd to him. He reaches another checkpoint and turns off the radio.

> SOLDIER #3
> Dr. Ronald Parish? (*Parish hands him his
> I.D.*) Okay, go ahead.

110. CDC LOBBY.

The CDC lobby looks like a military headquarters. A woman behind the reception desk greets PARISH as he enters.

> RECEPTIONIST
> Good morning, Dr. Parish. Exciting, isn't
> it? (*He nods and begins heading toward
> his office.*) Oh no, you'll have to wait.
> They're not letting anyone go anywhere by
> themselves. (*She types a label on a small card
> and hands it to an M.P. as he approaches.*)

M.P.
(*Looking at the label.*)
Dr. Parish, would you follow me please?

He leads PARISH to a special booth and asks him to step inside. His photograph is taken and immediately fixed onto his label. The M.P. pins the label onto his jacket. Taking a clipboard the M.P. looks down at it and then addresses PARISH.

M.P.
Doctor Parish, you are scheduled for a debriefing upon arrival. Won't you come with me please?

111. CDC HALLWAYS.

The M.P. leads PARISH down a series of hallways. He passes a number of cohorts, all being escorted by M.P.s. They look at each other and shake their heads. PARISH is led to a private office.

M.P.
You will be meeting with Major General Thomas Piedmont.

The M.P. opens the door. The GENERAL is sitting behind a desk.

112. GENERAL'S OFFICE.

The GENERAL nods to PARISH.

GENERAL
Come in. You are?

PARISH
Dr. Ronald Parish, Virology.

GENERAL
Piedmont. Pentagon. Sit down, please.
(*He leafs through a file on his desk and pulls out a small looseleaf binder. He reads*

through it quickly.) Dr. Parish, our orders for the time being are "business as usual," or at least as usual as they can be under the circumstances. A military medical team is being assembled now and will be reporting here for duty within 24 hours. Our immediate intention is not to interfere with your work but to train our personnel to be able to expand the base of operations here and to set up further research under the auspices of the military at various installations around the country. A team of "specialists" will be arriving this afternoon and we have scheduled a meeting with both them and your staff for three o'clock. I hope that is satisfactory.

PARISH nods his head. The GENERAL rises. The M.P. is waiting for PARISH when he opens the door.

113. PARISH'S OFFICE.

PARISH is sitting at his desk. His STAFF is sitting at his feet, sprawled all over the carpet. They look exhausted. DORIS and SIDNEY are sitting together on the couch.

>   PARISH
> Anyone see Jenkins?

>   DORIS
> They took him to Washington this
> morning.

>   PARISH
> How did he look?

>   DORIS
> Wasted. I don't think he knew what he was
> doing.

SIDNEY
He certainly had no idea of the impact...

JOHN
Who could have?

PARISH
They're going to cut his head off. Who did he talk to? Do you have any idea?

DORIS
I saw Tony Majors on the elevator last night, after you left.

PARISH
That explains it. (*Parish stops talking but is fuming inside.*)

DEBORAH
I hear they may set up a barracks for us here, if things get bad.

JOHN
I think that's just a rumor.

DORIS
God, I hope so.

GEORGE
What about our work? Do you think we'll continue?

PARISH
Who else have they got?

SIDNEY
That's a frightening question.

> DORIS
> They took the video tape this morning. I think they flew it to the Pentagon.

> PARISH
> Why didn't anyone call me?

> DORIS
> They wouldn't let us make any calls.

> PARISH
> What about the field representatives? Has anything been done? Was anyone notified?

Doris shrugs her shoulders. No one else seems to know. Parish looks disgusted. He pulls an old cigar out of his desk drawer and rips off the cellophane. He reaches for a pack of matches and strikes one.

114. HOSPITAL. NASHVILLE, TENNESSEE.

Flames are shooting out of a ten-story hospital. Many fire trucks are fighting the blaze. A local Nashville news CREW is covering it. PEOPLE are screaming and jumping out of windows. The on-camera REPORTER is speaking into a microphone. His voice throbs with emotion.

> REPORTER
> Oh, the horror of it! It's a terrible blaze. The worst fire in Nashville history. Already forty dead and hundreds still trapped inside. It's just awful. People are hanging from the window ledges and firemen can't get close enough to the building to catch them when they jump. (*Suddenly the reporter is interrupted as someone hands him a piece of paper. He stops to read it. He says, "Oh, my God," as he reads it. Then he turns to the camera.*) Ladies and gentlemen, this is a copy of a message called into the station just minutes ago. It reads: "This fire is only the beginning. It is the work of God-fearing

Christians doing the work of the Lord and
purging the world of the creatures of the
Devil." It is signed "Warriors for God, the
Christian Underground." *(He does not
speak again. The camera focuses on the
blaze.)*

115. SMALL COUNTRY HOUSE, SOUTHERN GEORGIA. NIGHT.

Twelve MEN wearing gas masks and carrying torches approach a small house. They do not stop at the door but kick it down and storm into the house. Suddenly there is screaming. A black MAN is dragged out of the house as a WOMAN and two CHILDREN run after him. They are hardly out of the house when it is set on fire.

WOMAN
He don't have it! He don't have nothin'! He got a goiter on his neck. Two years now. He don't have the sickness. He don't have it!

When she reaches the mob she finds her husband hanging from a tree, dead. She sees him and just stands there.

116. X-RAY VAN.

A mobile X-ray van is parked in the parking lot of a suburban shopping center. A line winds its way to the van. PEOPLE are wearing all sorts of makeshift nose and mouth coverings from handkerchiefs to gas masks.

117. CDC MAP ROOM.

The map is completely overrun with pins and is no longer being used. Television monitors and computer hook-ups have replaced it. TECHNICIANS in army uniforms type instructions into computer keyboards and the screens print out the names of states, counties, cities, wards, and names of affected individuals.

118. PARISH'S OFFICE.

PARISH is sitting in his office talking to GENERAL DAVID WEBBER. PARISH is in military fatigues.

> PARISH
> General, you want fast and easy answers. Well, we don't have them. Miracle cures are the exception, not the rule, in medical history. Cures take time.

> WEBBER
> Something we don't have.

> PARISH
> Admit it. The army cannot do battle with a virus.

> WEBBER
> An alien... virus.

> PARISH
> That doesn't make it any more combatable. You can't use your tanks. You can't pull out your atomic warheads. We're doing everything that can be done.

> WEBBER
> What about the new serum?

> PARISH
> It's insane. It could kill more people than the virus has infected, and the virus hasn't killed a soul. Somebody's got to remember that. *People* are killing people out there. Not the virus.

> WEBBER
> We've discovered eighteen of these flying saucers so far. I think it's time you stopped

referring to them as viruses. We are under
attack, and we have no defenses.

PARISH
Well, complain to God then. He's the one
who built this fortress. (*He hits his chest.*)
Maybe there are some things we're supposed
to be vulnerable to.

WEBBER
That's not a very professional outlook.

PARISH
What do you want from me? I'm human.
We're trying everything we know. At this
point I don't think it'll hurt to pray. Let's
pray that this thing just runs its course.
That's what we should pray for.

119. SPACE RECOVERY STATION.

SIDNEY is visiting HEDGES is the Space Recovery Station. SIDNEY is dressed in a space suit.

SIDNEY
We're set for tomorrow. Got a full staff
arranged. And that's no easy feat these days.
How do you feel?

HEDGES
Fine, really. The only problem I have is that
numbness barrier. It's almost impossible to
feel through it. But I'm just going to dive in.
I feel confident.

SIDNEY
The report says it's grown as big as a
cantaloupe.

HEDGES
At least. I can feel it moving in there. (*He taps his right side.*) It's a very complex thing that's growing. I can feel all sorts of tissue transformations. The strangest thing is that I can feel it growing brain tissue. It has a very distinct feel.

SIDNEY
I'll bet. Tell me Hedges, do you really think you can make contact?

HEDGES
I wouldn't have put myself through it if I didn't.

SIDNEY
It doesn't frighten you?

HEDGES
The most frightened I've ever been was the first time I tried to feel into my heart. It's not like imagination, you know. Your mind really travels there. An amazing thing, the mind. I could feel the heart forming around me. It grew larger and larger. You know, when you focus the mind to the size of an atom, the body seems awfully big. There are four billion cells in a drop of blood. Imagine getting lost in there. That's what scared me. I couldn't remember how to get out. It's like another world. But I always manage, you see. I always get back, so I don't bother getting frightened any more. Don't worry about me tomorrow. I'll find the secret to these things if it kills me.

120. SPACE RECOVERY STATION.

A large machine monitoring body function is hooked up to HEDGES. A team of ATTENDANTS is standing around him dressed in space suits. DORIS and SIDNEY are among them. The machine is reading brain waves, heart function and breathing, on separate screens. HEDGES is lying on his back. He looks very relaxed and there is the hint of a smile on his face. Wires are attached all over his body.

          SIDNEY
          (*To Doris.*)
You know, he thinks we're crazy for monitoring him like this. I think he just wanted someone around to hold his hand.

          DORIS
But what if something should go wrong?

          SIDNEY
He doesn't believe that could happen.

          DORIS
How long is it now?

          SIDNEY
Twenty-two minutes.

          DORIS
He's hardly breathing. It's like a trance.

          SIDNEY
I think he's asleep.

          DORIS
How do we know if he's found it?

          SIDNEY
Maybe he'll telephone. (*Suddenly there is a ringing sound.*) That may be him now.

The needles are fluctuating on all the machines. HEDGES is breathing wildly. His eyelids are fluttering. His body begins shaking violently.

>   DORIS
> My God somebody do something!

The TECHNICIANS rush a cardiac unit to his side and begin administering oxygen. The terminals of the cardiac machine are placed on his chest. The monitoring machines indicate a sudden cessation of all life energies. The TECHNICIANS are shocked.

>   TECHNICIAN
> Impossible. People don't die that fast.

>   DORIS
> Die?

>   TECHNICIAN
> He's dead.

The TECHNICIANS attempt to revive his heart but with no success. The atmosphere is one of chaos and panic. Suddenly, HEDGES opens his eyes. The heart monitor registers a total revival. Breathing is normal. Only the brain monitor shows no activity. HEDGES seems conscious but in a state of shock. There is a fearful expression on his face.

121. OPERATING ROOM.

HEDGES' body, encased in a plastic container, is rushed into the operating room. SURGEONS in space suits enter quickly and prepare the body for surgery. The operation commences rapidly and progresses speedily. The SURGEONS work with an elegant detachment. The camera focuses on the detail of the operation. Layer by layer the SURGEONS cut their way into the body cavity. Each layer reveals another layer below it. A SURGEON moves his hands through the inner organs, parting them and searching for the tumor. He and the camera discover it at the same time. Moving aside the stomach he uncovers a head. Its eyes are open and staring at the SURGEON. The SURGEON gasps. It is HEDGES' head, an exact duplicate, growing inside him. The head appears to be alive. It moves and watches the SURGEON and his team of ASSISTANTS. Its mouth is moving and it seems to be trying to speak. Suddenly a voice emerges. Its speech seems imbecilic, unable to formulate itself in a coherent fashion. There is a look of pain and frustration on the face as it attempts to communicate. The SURGEONS stare at it in horror. They cannot move. Suddenly one of the SURGEONS speaks.

                     SURGEON #1
Cut it out.

                     SURGEON #2
I can't.

                     SURGEON #3
It's trying to say something.

                     SURGEON #1
It's horrible.

                     SURGEON #2
It's trying to speak.

                     SURGEON #
Give me the knife. I'll do it.

He takes the knife from SURGEON #1. He reaches into the body cavity. The head looks at him in horror. It begins to shriek, trying furiously to form a ward. The SURGEON backs off.

                     SURGEON #2
I can't do it. God Almighty.

                     SURGEON #1
I can't stand it.

SURGEON #1 grabs the knife back from SURGEON #2 and reaches back into the body. The head looks terrified. Its eyes are wide open. The camera backs away as the SURGEON cuts. There is a sudden gush of blood onto his robe and a piercing, sorrowful cry. Then all is silent. At the same time the machine monitoring HEDGES' brain function returns to normal activity. All his vital signs are healthy. The SURGEONS look at each other with shocked surprise. One of the ATTENDANTS holds up the head to place it in a jar. He stops to look at it. Its lips are still moving. Suddenly words form in a faint whisper, "I... come... I... come... to..." And then it dies.

                    SURGEON #1
          Amazing. God-awful amazing.

122. RECOVERY ROOM.

PARISH, DORIS, SIDNEY, several SURGEONS and MILITARY PERSONNEL are standing next to HEDGES. He is lying weakly in his bed. Everyone is dressed in military garb. HEDGES is speaking.

                    HEDGES
          It took over control of my brain. I was
          powerless. I couldn't see it but I could feel
          its presence. It had a vast intelligence. There
          was nothing I could do in the face of it. It
          wasn't human. It was far superior to human.
          In some ways it felt more like spirit than
          matter. It was a humbling experience

                    GENERAL WEBBER
          Can it be destroyed? That's the important
          question.

                    HEDGES
          I don't see that as relevant.

                    GENERAL WEBBER
          It is an alien force.

                    HEDGES
          It was trying to tell us something.

                    GENERAL WEBBER
          It is creating monsters.

> HEDGES
> But we do not know to what end. All I can tell you from my brief experience is that if this force wishes to take over our planet, to dominate human life, there is very little we will be able to do about it. It is smarter than we are.

123. CDC MAP ROOM.

Two WOMEN, following lists attached to clipboards that they are carrying, extract pins from the map and drop them into buckets appropriate to their colors. About eighty pins are removed.

124. CDC SWITCHBOARD.

The camera pans along the banks of TELEPHONE OPERATORS. Only three of them are on the telephone. OTHERS are staring into space or reading newspapers. They are all wearing army fatigues.

> OPERATOR #1
> They've ended the martial law in Los Angeles. There hasn't been a single incident in a week.

> OPERATOR #2
> Does it say when their last outbreak was?

> OPERATOR #1
> Last reported case in a hospital was ten days ago.

> OPERATOR #3
> That's because they transferred all the teratoma cases to those concentration camps.

> OPERATOR #1
> They should have done that all over. As soon as they discovered a case, ship them to a concentration camp.

> OPERATOR #2
> Yeah, but they already had all those camps out West from World War II. That's where they kept the Japanese. Where could you put all the people from around here?

> OPERATOR #1
> You could have locked 'em up in zoos for all I care.

> OPERATOR #2
> That's a nice humane attitude.

> OPERATOR #1
> Well, if it wasn't for all those people with teratomas I wouldn't be wearing these dumb clothes and I wouldn't have been forced to stay in this hole for five weeks. I tell you, I'm goin' absolutely bananas.

> OPERATOR #3
> What can you do? It was a national emergency. We've been sitting here for the good of the country.

> OPERATOR #1
> My ass!

125. CDC CAFETERIA.

SIDNEY, DORIS and HEDGES are having lunch. They, and everyone else in the room, are wearing surplus army garb.

> SIDNEY
> From all I can tell they're improving on us.

> HEDGES
> How so?

SIDNEY
All the recent specimens have shown a remarkable refinement. The brain cells in your own... what should I call it?

HEDGES
You can call it my head. I'm not sensitive.

SIDNEY
Okay. The tissues I examined from your brain cells had a much more elastic chemical bonding than any human brain tissue I've ever seen. It had a range of adaptability that we just don't have. And then there's that tissue that came in from Alaska.

HEDGES
What tissue is that?

DORIS
You haven't seen it?

HEDGES
Well, I'm not exactly on the staff, you know.

SIDNEY
Oh, you've got to see it. It's pretty remarkable.

DORIS
Beautiful, really. Come on. Let's go show him.

126. MAXIMUM SECURITY LAB. EXTERIOR.

SIDNEY and HEDGES are standing outside the window looking into the Maximum Security Lab. DORIS is inside. She takes a jar off of a shelf and brings it to the window.

                    SIDNEY
          Just look at this.

DORIS unwraps a towel from around the jar. The flesh floating inside it is glowing.

                    SIDNEY
          It's luminescent.

                    HEDGES
          Very lovely.

                    SIDNEY
          And not of this world.

                    HEDGES
          It glows a little like those fish you see in
          National Geographic. You know, the ones
          that glow in the dark. They come from
          the blackest parts of the ocean. Doesn't it
          remind you of them?

                    SIDNEY
          Uh-huh, a little.

                    HEDGES
          Maybe we're dealing with creatures from
          a very dark place. I wonder sometimes
          if we're not dealing with some kind of
          demonic force. It seems to me that these
          teratomas feed on our poisons.

                    SIDNEY
          How do you mean?

                    HEDGES
          Well, I've had the most curious sensations
          since my operation.

Suddenly, DORIS knocks on the glass. She mouths a word though the glass. "Enough?" SIDNEY nods back "yes." She wraps up the bottle and puts it back on the shelf.

SIDNEY
What kind of sensations?

HEDGES
Well, I've been feeling deeply throughout my whole body, into places I'm very familiar with, and they haven't felt the same. What I realized only yesterday was that I felt very clean inside. And then it dawned on me. My glands, my organs, even my blood, had been purged, cleansed of their impurities. And I hypothesized that my tumor, my head, had used these poisons in my system to grow, to build itself.

SIDNEY
Huh, that's very interesting. I had a very similar response after my operation. I felt especially good inside. I figured it was just because this thing was out of me. I even found myself praying and thanking God, and I don't even believe in God.

HEDGES
It just cleaned you out.

SIDNEY
I don't know how to respond to that. On the one hand it's great that something could consume that crap in you but on the other hand, what is it using it for? What is it trying to create?

HEDGES
My guess is that we will simply have to wait and find out. And I have no doubt that we

will. Nothing goes to all this effort without some purpose, without some grand design. My guess is that we'll know soon enough.

127. CDC AUDITORIUM.

The auditorium is rapidly filling with PEOPLE from all over the CDC. They are sitting in the aisles and lining the walls. Television cameras are positioned against the back wall. The similarity of dress gives a strange, proletarian look to the proceedings. HOWIE MOORE from CDC public relations approaches a microphone on the stage. The auditorium quiets.

>   HOWIE
> Can I have your attention please. Quiet please. Thank you. As you have all probably gathered, we are about to hear a very important announcement. This announcement is going to be carried nationwide. (*He pauses as someone whispers something to him from off stage.*) Worldwide, that is, in just one and a half minutes. It is requested, therefore, that because of the large viewing public, a sense of decorum be maintained. I would now like to introduce to you a man you have all seen around here a lot in the last six weeks, General David Webber.

GENERAL WEBBER walks to the microphone. He looks at everyone in the auditorium and smiles nervously. After a moment of awkward silence, he speaks casually into the microphone.

>   WEBBER
> We have to wait until I get my cue from the boys in the booth up there, so everyone just relax for a minute, if you can. I figure you already have some inkling of what I'm going to say. I've been here long enough to know that nothing stays private very long

here, even confidential announcements like this. It'll just be a few more seconds. *(He rocks nervously back and forth on his heels. The camera studies the faces in the auditorium. They all appear apprehensive. Suddenly the signal comes from the back. The camera's red lights turn on.)* My name is General David Webber. I am currently in charge of operations at the National Center for Disease Control in Atlanta, Georgia. I have been asked today by the President of the United States to make the following announcement. For the last two weeks there have been no reported cases of teratoma tumors in the United States or to the best of our knowledge, anywhere else in the world. The cessation of cases follows a rapid decline in the spreading of the... infection over the last month. Although saucer-like formations have been reported and documented in teratoma tissue, the final consensus is that we are dealing with a viral form and not an extra-terrestrial invasion. No studies have found any evidence to support the invasion theory. An assembly of top scientists from around the world, in special meetings this morning, has concluded that the virus has run its course, that the teratoma infectious spread has been contained and is now over. The President has asked me to announce that the state of emergency that has been in effect for the last six weeks is officially ended.

128. FLOATING VIRUS. (SUBJECTIVE P.O.V.)

The camera is floating in a cloud bank and observing a sunset as the very fabric of the cloud changes colors. It is a dazzling display. High overhead the first stars are beginning to appear in a darkening sky. Below, the farmland radiates the brilliance of the setting sun. The camera begins to drop to the earth flying quietly over the rooftops of barns and farmhouses. The camera slows and hovers over a small and badly painted house. A young GIRL in a cotton dress is standing behind the house trying to urge a baby calf to follow her to the barn. The camera drops down close to her and the more gigantic her image becomes the more beautiful she appears. The camera circles around her, examining her from every angle, flying through her hair, gliding through her fingers. It is a very sensuous exploration. The GIRL tries to lift the calf but does not have the strength. She tugs on the rope around its neck but the calf is stubborn and the GIRL falls to the ground. The camera moves slowly down the floral pattern on her dress. It reaches the hem as the GIRL stands up. Suddenly the camera is beneath her. The sunlight pours through the cotton fabric as though through the window draperies of a country cottage. Her legs reflect the golden glow. The camera rises slowly up the thighs, into a tangled forest of pubic hairs and into the darkness within her.

129. SIDNEY PIERCE'S APARTMENT.

PARISH, SILVIA, DORIS and SIDNEY are sitting at a dinner table in SIDNEY'S apartment, eating.

>   SIDNEY
> I feel frustrated, that's how I feel. It's like
> reading a good book and then discovering
> that someone has used the last three pages
> to start the campfire. It can't be over. It just
> can't be.

>   SYLVIA
> Could you pass the salt please?

DORIS reaches for the salt but doesn't find any. Everyone looks. SIDNEY blushes.

>   SIDNEY
> I happen to be on a low sodium intake diet.

PARISH
With all your diets and allergies, I'm surprised you can handle food. Doris, I would have expected you to have converted him by now.

DORIS
To what, humanity? I'm working at it.

SIDNEY
She got me to use Tabasco sauce. I never used to use that before.

PARISH
Thank God, there's still hope.

DORIS
I would have gotten salt when I went shopping, but whoever thinks you need salt? You always have salt. It'll take us a while to get readjusted. What else can I say?

They continue eating.

SIDNEY
So, you're not frustrated? It doesn't bother you that it's over and it didn't end?

PARISH
Not at all… because it's not over.

SIDNEY
It's not over? What do you mean it's not over? What kind of inside dope do you have?

PARISH
Let's wait till we finish dinner. No need to spoil a good meal.

SIDNEY is curious but hesitates to ask anything more. He simply stops eating and stares at PARISH. DORIS and SYLVIA seem very curious too but continue eating.

                    SIDNEY
You've already spoiled it. Tell me.

                    PARISH
When we're done. Over coffee. It's just a theory and doesn't go well with roast beef.

130. SIDNEY PIERCE'S APARTMENT. LATER.

DORIS is pouring coffee for everyone. They are sitting in the living room.

                    PARISH
It feels good to be free again, doesn't it?

                    DORIS
Delicious.

                    SYLVIA
Pass the sugar please,

DORIS reaches for the sugar. SIDNEY blushes.

                    SIDNEY
I'm embarrassed.

                    PARISH
You should be.

                    SIDNEY
Sugar's not good for you.

                    PARISH
Neither is coffee. But it doesn't keep me from drinking it.

SIDNEY
I have some Ovaltine. It's pretty sweet.
Maybe you could add that...

SYLVIA
That's okay. I'll just take cream. You do have...?

SIDNEY
How about buttermilk? (*He laughs.*) No, I'm joking... I think we have cream.

DORIS
(*Picking up a pitcher.*)
Of course we do. (*She pours it for Sylvia.*)

SIDNEY
So now that I have indigestion, and before I get insomnia, will you tell us about your theory?

PARISH
Well, if you're really interested. (*Sidney gives him a dirty look.*) Okay. I've just been puzzling things together, that's all, and I've come up with some rather interesting discoveries.

DORIS
Such as?

PARISH
That the teratomas have grown in virtually every part of the human body except one. We've found them in the rear end, the thigh, the neck, the bladder, the intestines and the lungs. You name it. They've grown everywhere... except the uterus. I've gone over every list, I've done computer checks, and the only thing I keep being shown is

that teratomas have grown in every part of the human body except where babies grow. And I find that pretty incredible.

DORIS
That is incredible. But what does it mean?

PARISH
There are two ways of looking at it. Either the virus just happened to overlook it, or it consciously, purposely avoided growing there. My question is, what happens when this intelligence discovers the uterus or decides that it is time to enter it?

SYLVIA
But they're gone. It's all over.

PARISH
My guess is that we'll know if that's true... in nine months.

DORIS
What are you saying?

PARISH
That it's going to give birth.

SIDNEY
(*His mouth wide open.*)
Amazing.

PARISH
I've been thinking a lot about this. Did you realize that a child, an embryo, is the only intruder a body allows into itself without trying to destroy it? Somehow it instructs the body that it is friendly, and the body not only accepts it, but serves it and gives it nourishment. My thinking is that this virus

has invaded our bodies by communicating
the same message. Using that secret, this...
intelligence has been experimenting with
human life forms and now – of course this
is only a guess – I think it will attempt
to synthesize all of this experimentation
into a natural birth. I would even go so
far as to say, judging by some of the more
recent examples of its experimenting, like
the luminescent skin, that it may produce
something more than natural... more
supernatural. This may all sound off the wall
to you but I'll bet my bottom dollar that it's
not over yet. If you want my guess, I think
it's just the beginning.

DORIS
So now that you've scared us all to death,
what are we supposed to do about it? Wait
till it grows up?

PARISH
I think we better be on the lookout for
strange or unusual births.

SIDNEY
But what if it isn't strange? What if it's...
normal? How would we ever know?

PARISH
It may be that we never will.

DORIS
So what do you propose?

PARISH
All I can say is that we're damned lucky that
we've got the CDC. It's our umbrella. We're
simply going to initiate a national study on
birth problems and birth defects. We'll have

every hospital and obstetrician in America
doing the looking for us. We'll use the
research staff to do the fieldwork. They'll
know what to look for. And we'll keep it all
hush-hush. What do you think? Have we
got a chance?

SIDNEY
Time will tell. But I'll tell you one thing, I'd
try not to eat any eggs next... (*he counts to
himself on his fingers and stops when they
reach nine*) December because you may end
up with them all over your face.

131. HOSPITAL DELIVERY ROOM.

A baby is born. The DOCTOR looks at it and smiles. It is healthy. He carries it to its MOTHER. She beams.

132. HOSPITAL INCUBATION ROOM.

The camera tracks across a row of incubators and their INHABITANTS. NURSES are caring for them.

133. DOCTORS OFFICE.

JENNIFER CAMPUS, CDC researcher, is sitting in a doctor's office interviewing the DOCTOR. He shakes his head "no" to a rapid barrage of questions. The scene, however, is silent and only the "no's" are understood.

134. PEDIATRIC WARD. CHILDREN'S HOSPITAL.

PERRY SMITH, CDC researcher, is touring a ward for children suffering from birth defects. The camera does not dwell on the children but observes SMITH'S professional and emotional responses.

135. PARISH'S OFFICE

PARISH is sitting at his desk examining photographs and medical reports. He scans them quickly and tosses them onto a large stack. He has a discouraged look on his face.

136. BIRTH MONTAGE.

A sequence of births occurs focusing primarily on close-ups of INFANTS' faces, MOTHERS' faces, FATHERS' faces, DOCTORS' faces, and NURSES' faces. Intercut with these joyful images are shots of PARISH and his COHORTS anxiously trying to track down a single birth. The magnitude and complexity of the search are sketched in the interplay of faces.

137. CDC HALLWAY LEADING TO THE LOBBY.

PARISH, DORIS and SIDNEY are walking down the hall, talking. Their pace is leisurely. They are putting on their coats.

          DORIS
          (*To Parish.*)
Disappointed?

          PARISH
Sure.

          DORIS
No hope at all, huh?

          PARISH
Nope. It's been nine months. I'd need a miracle at this point.

          SIDNEY
Maybe it'll be a ten-month baby.

          PARISH
Or an eleven- or twelve-month one, right? Sure, in some bizarre way. I guess that's

always possible. But it's not what I expected, not what I was looking for. Oh well, I guess it was over. I probably should be grateful. God knows what it might have been. Maybe it's better that we never know. (*He opens the door.*) Jesus, look at all that snow. Well, take it easy guys. See you Monday.

                SIDNEY
Take it easy, Ron. Listen, if you get lonely with Sylvia away, give us a call. We'll go to the movies or something. Bye-bye.

138. SIDNEY'S APARTMENT.

SIDNEY and DORIS are lying together on the couch listening to Mozart's *Magic Flute*. Suddenly the phone rings. SIDNEY doesn't look too interested in answering it, but DORIS pushes him.

                SIDNEY
A hundred to one it's my mother.

                DORIS
You're on.

                SIDNEY
Hello? Oh, hi Ron. That was fast. Couldn't bear to be away from us, huh? No, I'm not disappointed. I was just expecting a call from heaven, but you'll do... My mother, that's who. I'm beginning to think she doesn't love me anymore. What's on your mind, Ron?... Really? What do you think? Yeah sure, I'm game. Let me check with Doris. (*He turns to Doris.*) Ron's come up with something, some kind of lead, about a three-hour drive south. He wants us to go. What do you say?

> DORIS
> What kind of a lead?

> SIDNEY
> (*Into the phone.*)
> What kind of a lead?... He said he'll tell us in the car.

> DORIS
> And what if we're not interested?

> SIDNEY
> Did you hear her? Yeah, okay. (*To Doris.*) He says that's perfectly all right. He understands. But don't come back to work on Monday. (*To Parish.*) How soon before you'll be here? Okay, we'll be downstairs. Right. Okay, I'll tell her. See you soon. (*He hangs up.*) He said to make a thermos of coffee and to dress warmly because his car heater's acting up. This should be a lot of fun.

139. SIDNEY'S APARTMENT BUILDING. EXTERIOR. NIGHT.

PARISH'S car pulls up in front of Sidney's apartment. The horn honks and SIDNEY and DORIS hurry down the front stairs and hop in.

140. PARISH'S CAR. INTERIOR. NIGHT.

PARISH, DORIS and SIDNEY are huddled close together in the front seat of the car.

> PARISH
> I'm telling you from the start, it's a long shot, but it's a tempting long shot. I got a call from a Dr. Monroe. They put it through from the switchboard at the Center. He said he was calling from a small town called Silversprings, near the state line, just north

of Florida on U.S. 75 He told me that about eight months ago, he saw a girl named Mary Ellen Rogers. Said she couldn't have been more than twelve years old. She wasn't feeling right, he said. He did tests and found that she was pregnant. The little girl denied ever sleeping with a boy. According to the doctor, she acted as though she didn't even know such things were done. He said he found it hard to believe she didn't know what was going on. When he told the mother, she supposedly started yelling and screaming and threatening to beat her daughter within an inch of her life. When she calmed down, the poor girl backed into a corner, he said, while the mother asked him if it was possible to get pregnant if you've never had your period. The little girl kept insisting that she never had. Anyway, to make a long story short, the doctor said he pretty much forgot all about it until the other day. The mother came to his office to ask if her daughter had been by to see him. Said she hadn't seen her in a week and feared she had run away to have the baby, since the mother wanted to put it up for adoption right away and the girl was insisting that she wanted to keep it. She kept insisting, according to the mother, that she *had* to keep it, because it wasn't hers, because it came from another world. He said the mother said it with a straight face and that he couldn't stop thinking about it for two days before he decided to call me. He figures the baby will be born any time now and if we come down he'll try to find it for us.

SIDNEY

Yep, I'd call that a long shot, going for an Olympic gold medal.

                        PARISH
What about her thinking the baby was from
another world?

                        DORIS
If I was twelve years old and having a baby,
I'd probably think that too.

                        PARISH
Well, we can always turn back.

                        SIDNEY
Hell no! It may be a long shot, but it's the
only game in town.

141. PARISH'S CAR. HIGHWAY. LATER.

DORIS is sleeping. SIDNEY appears to be on the way out. PARISH reaches down for his C.B. and turns it on. The static on the air waves wakes DORIS up and jars SIDNEY back to consciousness.

                        PARISH
Breaker one nine, I need a northbound 85.
Breaker one nine, I need a northbound 85.

                        VOICE
You've got a southbound 85. What's your
handle?

                        PARISH
You got the Surgeon General here.

                        VOICE
You got the Rising Star. What's your ten-
twenty, good buddy?

                        PARISH
Five miles out of Newcastle.

                    VOICE
You must be pretty close. Whatcha drivin?

                    PARISH
Powder blue Chevy, '74.

                    VOICE
Okay, you just passed me. I'm right on your
back door, good buddy. Where you headin'?

                    PARISH
You got a ten-twenty on Silversprings?

                    VOICE
Ten Roger. It's home port. Why don't I take
the front door and you can follow me home.

                    PARISH
We're searchin' for a Dr. Horace Monroe in
Silversprings. 1830 Washington Street.

                    VOICE
Ten four. I'll take you right home.

                    PARISH
Ten Roger. Thank you, good buddy.

                    SIDNEY
What was that all about?

                    PARISH
We just found a guardian angel. He's going
to take us to Dr. Monroe's front door.

A red pickup truck pulls alongside Parish's car. The driver waves hello and pulls up into the lane ahead.

142. DR. MONROE'S RESIDENCE. EXTERIOR.

PARISH, SIDNEY and DORIS are standing on the porch of an old house and knocking at the door. An old WOMAN answers and motions them to come in.

143. DR. MONROE'S RESIDENCE. INTERIOR.

The group stands in the MONROE entrance hall. MRS. MONROE is talking to them.

>   MRS. MONROE
> The doctor asked me to apologize to you
> but he was called away on an emergency
> delivery in Connorsville and didn't think
> he'd get back in time to see you. He said I
> should give you directions to the Rogers
> home. He thought the mother could help
> you. I should warn you though, she's not a
> real friendly type. I wish you luck.

144. THE ROGERS HOUSE. EXTERIOR.

PARISH'S car pulls into the driveway of a small country farm. There are no lights on. PARISH takes a flashlight out of his glove compartment and they all walk together up to the front door. They begin knocking. At first there is no answer, but then they hear a voice calling from inside.

>   VOICE
> Okay, I'm comin', I'm comin'.

A scrawny, mean looking-middle-aged, WOMAN appears at the door. She looks through the window in the door but doesn't open it.

>   PARISH
> Hello there. We're looking for a Mrs.
> Rogers.

>   VOICE
> You've found her.

PARISH
Can we speak to you a minute?

VOICE
'Bout what?

PARISH
It's about your daughter, Mrs. Rogers, Mary Ellen.

VOICE
She's no daughter of mine. I got nothin' to say about her.

PARISH
We hear she's about to have a baby.

VOICE
You go ask Joe Brodie about that. I got nothin' to say. That's his responsibility now. I don't want nothin' to do with none of 'em.

PARISH
Who's Joe Brodie? Where can I find him?

VOICE
I got nothin' more to say to you.

She backs away from the window. They stand there for a moment and then walk back to the car.

DORIS
It feels like a wild goose chase.

PARISH
What have we got to lose?

They get back into their car.

145. SUNOCO GAS STATION.

The car pulls into the station. An ATTENDANT comes out and approaches PARISH.

                    ATTENDANT
          What can I do for you?

                    PARISH
          We're looking for someone named Joe
          Brodie. Did you ever hear of him?

                    ATTENDANT
          You mean Jacob Brodie's boy?

                    PARISH
          I don't know.

                    ATTENDANT
          Well, they got a kid named Joe. About
          twelve or thirteen.

                    PARISH
          I guess that's him. Where can I find him?

                    ATTENDANT
          Real close. See that light down there? Just
          make a left. Go three blocks, make a right,
          and they're the last house on the block, at
          the dead end. You can't miss it.

                    PARISH
          Thanks a lot.

                    ATTENDANT
          My pleasure.

The car pulls out.

                    SIDNEY
Dead end, huh? This gets more encouraging
all the time. I tell you, after seein' all these
people, I don't know if I want to find any
baby.

146. BRODIE HOUSE. INTERIOR.

MRS. BRODIE walks to the door and opens it. PARISH, DORIS and SIDNEY are standing there. She seems surprised and afraid when she sees them.

                    MRS. BRODIE
Can I help you?

                    PARISH
We're looking for Joe Brodie.

                    MRS. BRODIE
For Joe?

                    MR. BRODIE
Who is it Thelma? (*He walks into the room.*)

                    MRS. BRODIE
People looking for Joe.

                    MR. BRODIE
What do you want with Joe?

                    PARISH
We'd like to talk to him. About Mary Ellen
Rogers.

                    MR. BRODIE
About Mary Ellen? Somethin' strange is
sure going on here. Mary Ellen Rogers
moved to her grandma's, I was told, before
the school year. We haven't seen her in six,
eight months at least.

PARISH
Mrs. Rogers told us to see Joe…

MR. BRODIE
You gotta understand, she's a crazy woman. You can't believe hardly anything she says.

PARISH
She says Joe and Mary Ellen…

MR. BRODIE
I told you, you're makin' a mistake to believe anything that comes out of her mouth. My boy Joe had nothin' to do with that girl. He's an honest, God-fearin' boy who don't do wrong by nobody.

PARISH
Is he home now? If we could just talk to him.

MR. BRODIE
He's at the gym. Basketball practice.

PARISH
Isn't it awfully late?

MR. BRODIE
Listen, I told you…

The front door flies open and a YOUNG BOY comes charging in. He is breathing heavily. He has a strange expression on his face and blood on his coat. His MOTHER screams and grabs him. EVERYONE seems shocked.

JOE
It's Mary Ellen. She just had a baby. It ain't human. I never seen nothin' like it. You gotta come, fast. You won't believe your eyes.

> MR. BRODIE
> Where you been?

> JOE
> Down by the old barn. Come on, you gotta hurry. That's where Mary Ellen's been.

> MRS. BRODIE
> You been seein' her?

> JOE
> Don't got time to talk. Come on, quick!

> PARISH
> You can go in our car.

> JOE
> Who are these people?

> PARISH
> We came to see the baby.

> JOE
> How'd you know?

> PARISH
> We've been waiting for it.

> JOE
> You won't believe your own eyes. Hurry, let's go!

> MRS. BRODIE
> (*Angry.*)
> Joseph!

> JOE
> Mama, bring some blankets. And hurry. Mary Ellen's waitin'.

147. PARISH'S CAR.

DORIS and SIDNEY hop into the back seat. JOE jumps up front.

> PARISH
> Shall we wait for your father?

> JOE
> He knows where it is. Let's get goin'. Just go straight till I say turn.

The car squeals out from the driveway and speeds dizzily down the road.

> PARISH
> What's it like? Tell us what it's like?

> JOE
> From another world, you'll see. I can't describe it. (*Suddenly he begins crying, sobbing. Doris strokes his hair.*) People think it's my baby, But I didn't do nothin'. It's nobody's baby. Oh, God. (*He starts crying again.*) Turn here. Go straight down the road till the end. I tell you, you won't believe it. (*He cries.*)

The car races down the dark, tree-lined road as the bare winter branches flash by. Suddenly they are at the end of the road and the car brakes to a halt. JOE jumps out and starts running into the woods. He motions for everyone to follow him. PARISH grabs the flashlight and gets out too. DORIS and SIDNEY are behind him. They run after JOE into the woods.

148. WOODS.

The flashlight shines on the tree trunks and barely illuminates. JOE running ahead of them. The camera tracks quickly with them. There is a sense of continuing speed and urgency. JOB begins yelling.

> JOE
> We're here Mary Ellen. We're here.

Headlights from MR. BRODIE'S car light the woods behind them, casting tall, eerie shadows on the trees as they run. In the distance, they see an old barn. JOE stops just outside the door. He waits for PARISH and his friends to meet him. They are all breathing very heavily and they stop a moment to slow down. JOE nods to everyone that it's all right to enter, and opens the door.

149. BARN INTERIOR.

The barn door opens slowly. In a corner stall, lit only by a kerosene lamp, is MARY ELLEN. The barn is filled with shadows that wrap around the ceiling as the group approaches. JOE goes to her first and sits down at her side. She reaches out and silently takes his hand. In her arms she holds the baby, covered completely in a blanket. She has a strange look in her eyes. It is frightening and compelling. PARISH, DORIS and SIDNEY draw near. Their faces are filled with fear and unknowing. There is a strange sound in the barn. It is familiar, like a ringing in the ears, but more intense. It grows louder as they approach. It becomes deafening. PARISH, DORIS and SIDNEY are aware of it and uncomfortable. Their eyes seem to search for its source but cannot find it. The shadows in the room continually alter the space, wiping away the hard edges of the barn and creating at moments a room without form, without boundaries. PARISH moves hesitantly through the darkness of this uncharted space. SIDNEY and DORIS follow. They take a few steps. At this distance, MARY ELLEN is recognizable as the young girl in the cotton dress. She smiles at them sweetly as they approach. The sound grows to a new intensity, like the roar of a hundred waterfalls. There is a feeling of great energy in the room. PARISH seems to be fighting for the strength to speak. It is difficult for him to produce the words. Slowly they form on his lips.

> PARISH
> We have come to see your baby.

> MARY ELLEN
> (*Softly.*)
> I know. He told me you would come.

PARISH

He told you...?

MARY ELLEN

You have been observing his arrival for a long time. You are here now as witnesses to his birth.

PARISH, DORIS and SIDNEY stare at the girl in disbelief. Suddenly the barn door opens and MR. and MRS. BRODIE enter. JOE runs to them and takes the blankets from his mother's arms. She puts her hands to her ears as she experiences the strange roar that fills the room. It is now like wind and thunder. MR. BRODIE stands motionless in the shadows. JOE lays the blanket out in front of MARY ELLEN. Quietly and with great gentleness, she lays the baby bundle down upon it. Slowly, she begins to unwrap the blanket. The thundering sound booms still louder and suddenly breaks into a chorus of trumpets and voices, an unearthly choir of a thousand sounds. As the blanket unfold, a light begins to radiate from within it. It is hardly open and already dazzling. It is hard to look directly at it. PARISH, DORIS and SIDNEY squint. The last sheath of the blanket is drawn back. Resting in the center is a large oval shape. It is glowing. From a distance it looks like an egg without a shell. PARISH steps closer. SIDNEY and DORIS follow. JOE takes a thermos and a cloth and hands them to MARY ELLEN. With great delicacy, she removes the top of the thermos and pours some water onto her wrist. Satisfied with its temperature, she moistens the cloth and then begins to wipe the strange thing lying before her. Suddenly it begins to respond to her cleansing and moves in an unexpected way. Layer upon layer of its surface begin to unfold and slowly extend outward. PARISH stares in amazement as a pair of golden wings take shape before him. They unfold like the wings of a newborn chick. They are glowing. Fully extended, they reach a span of four feet, MARY ELLEN leans down and lifts the winged being to her. She presses it lovingly to her tiny breasts. Slowly she turns it around for all to admire. PARISH, DORIS and SIDNEY gasp in astonishment. Suspended before them is a winged CHILD, an angel. The camera moves slowly toward it. Brilliant light emanates from his body and fills all the space before it. Suddenly the INFANT smiles. It is a smile of such tenderness and love that his entire body glows brighter as it appears upon his face. Slowly, he begins to move his lips. It seems he is trying to speak. The choir of voices grows quiet as his first words are heard. His voice is male and female.

                    CHILD
            (*Speaking softly, with
            conscious deliberation.*)
        Behold and rejoice, for I am born. Spirit is
        made flesh.

PARISH, DORIS and SIDNEY stare in amazement. Their eyes are filled with awe and wonder. MRS. BRODIE peers at him from the shadows. MR. BRODIE backs against the wall.

                    CHILD
        Your people have known great trials to
        prepare for my birth. Your reward will be
        great, for I come in peace and love.

MARY ELLEN strokes his head. His wings stretch out from his back and gently sway in the cool air. She rubs his brow and his wings close softly behind him. He coos for a moment like a newborn child. JOE reaches out and takes the infant's hand. Tiny fingers close around it. JOE bends over and kisses the hand. The BABY smiles again and the room fills with light. Suddenly the wings unfold. The CHILD'S eyes glow brightly and he begins to speak again.

                    CHILD
        I come to prepare the way for a greater birth
        than mine. I come as a servant to Him, and
        to you. Take care of your child and he shall
        care for you and all your children. Now I
        must sleep.

His eyes begin to close and his wings fold quietly behind him. MARY ELLEN holds him to her with great happiness and love. PARISH, DORIS and SIDNEY are kneeling before him. Their mouths are wide open. Their eyes are filled with tears. MARY ELLEN lowers the INFANT to the blanket. His body is rosy red and radiant. His tiny feet kick in the air and his hands reach up and play with the empty space around them. MARY ELLEN strokes his belly and he laughs sweetly. Slowly, she folds the blanket over his naked body and pins it together with a safety pin. She draws back to admire the BABY as he begins to float silently off to sleep. It is with unexpected suddenness that a pitchfork comes slashing through the air and slices into the sleeping CHILD. MR. BRODIE screams as he plunges it in again. JOE jumps up and lurches at his father, wrenching him away and throwing him to the floor. MARY ELLEN recoils in horror and then falls upon the tiny BABY. The blanket is staining quickly with blood. She screams. Furiously she pulls the blanket apart and stares in horror at the sight of its wounded body. The light around the BABY is glowing sporadically, dimming and then bursting brightly through the room. Gradually it grows fainter and does not revive. A great sadness and confusion appear in the CHILD'S eyes. The strange buzzing sound shrieks through the barn like a million wild bees. As the light coming from the CHILD begins to die, the sound, too, begins to fade. PARISH and SIDNEY are with JOE, holding his father. He does not struggle. There is a look of madness on his face, a demonic glare in his eyes. MRS. BRODIE huddles in a corner, not moving. DORIS stares at the dying CHILD, unable to move. MARY ELLEN cuddles the BABY in her arms and rocks him back and forth. Tears are pouring from her eyes. The room darkens quickly. The CHILD'S mouth begins to move. He tries to speak but his voice is weak. MARY ELLEN leans close to him, her ear close to his mouth.

>CHILD
>(*Whispering with difficulty.*)
>I will come... again.

Suddenly his eyes close and his light expires. His wings hang loosely from his back. The barn grows dark. The shadows envelope the walls. MARY ELLEN looks sorrowfully at his little body.

>MARY ELLEN
>(*Whispering to her dead child.*)
>When?

An unearthly silence fills the barn. MR. BRODIE'S eyes slash wildly through the shadows and then retreat into some inner world. A terrible stillness overwhelms the screen.

Secrets of the Astral Plane

EXT. – RUSSIAN VILLAGE – NIGHT.

It is nightfall. Byzantine domes and church spires are silhouetted against the last rays of a blazing sunset.

Super-imposed in white letters over the silhouette: "KUNTSEVO, U.S.S.R – AUGUST, 1936."

The sound of cars racing can be heard in the distance.

CUT ON THE SOUND OF TIRES SCREECHING TO:
A convoy of four black Soviet sedans hurling down the dark streets of a small village. A peasant family, caught in the glare of the headlights, jumps to the curb as the cars speed by.

INT. – SEDAN CAR – NIGHT.

Sitting in the back seat of the lead car is LAVRENTI PAVLOVICH BERIA, the head of the Cheka, the Soviet secret police. He appears grim and motionless as the car swerves down the narrow streets.

EXT. – VILLAGE STREETS – NIGHT.

Buildings and faces, caught in the blinding headlights, flash white and blur into shadow.

A huge statue of Joseph Stalin emerges from the darkness, a towering figure outlined by the lights of the approaching cars.

The cars stop at the base of the monument. People walking nearby scurry away.

Car doors open. Men in dark suits jump out.

The hammer and sickle insignia in BERIA'S lapel glimmers as he steps from the car.

BERIA walks in front of the headlights, casting an ominous shadow over Stalin's statue.

DISSOLVE TO:
INT. – SMALL THEATER – NIGHT.

VLADIMIR ABLOGIN, a dark-haired man with intense black eyes, is sitting motionless in a backstage dressing room. He appears to be in a trance. Suddenly his eyes blink and he snaps out of it. He turns to an attractive young WOMAN standing nervously beside him.

>   ABLOGIN
> They're coming. We have little time.

The WOMAN, a tall, blonde-haired beauty, is frightened. She stares at ABLOGIN, her face full of confusion. There is a sudden knock at the door. Her body tenses.

>   STAGE MANAGER (O.S.)
> Five minutes till curtain.

The camera holds on the WOMAN'S face and observes the panic growing inside her.

EXT. – THEATER – NIGHT.

A gaudy theater poster shows ABLOGIN dressed in a turban and black robes. He is a famous mentalist. The WOMAN, his assistant, poses beside him.

Russian workers pass in front of the poster, lining up to buy tickets for the performance.

We hear the sound of boots approaching. Several PEOPLE standing in line turn to look. A WOMAN gasps. The line parts and people step back. BERIA'S hammer and sickle insignia moves toward the camera and overwhelms the screen.

INT. – DRESSING ROOM – NIGHT.

We see a photo of ABLOGIN and his young female ASSISTANT sitting beneath a tree holding hands. It is obvious that they are not only cohorts but lovers. Slowly the photograph rises out of its silver frame and slides discretely into the young WOMAN'S blouse.

There is a knock at the door. The STAGE MANAGER enters excitedly.

> STAGE MANAGER
> We have an unexpected guest. Beria is here.
> (*The WOMAN freezes.*) I have given him
> my best seats.

> ABLOGIN
> He did not come for the show.

> STAGE MANAGER
> (*Not understanding.*)
> Curtain is in one minute.

The young WOMAN turns to ABLOGIN.

> WOMAN
> Come with me!

> ABLOGIN
> No. My destiny is here. It would be foolish
> to run.

> WOMAN
> (*Tearfully.*)
> Vladimir!

ABLOGIN reaches for her waist and gently pulls her toward him. They kiss passionately. Then ABLOGIN steps back.

> ABLOGIN
> Hurry. (*Her eyes hold on his face.*) We are
> one soul. We can never be apart.

With heartbreaking tenderness, she turns and hurries from the room. ABLOGIN listens to her footsteps as she moves down the hall and out the stage door.

CUT ON THE SOUND OF THE STAGE DOOR SLAMMING TO:
The sudden roll of a drum as a tiny band in the theater begins to play.

INT. – AUDITORIUM – NIGHT.

The stage lights come up and the curtain rises, revealing ABLOGIN in his turban and robes. The audience applauds.

EXT. – THEATER – NIGHT.

A number of BERIA'S MEN spread out around the perimeter of the theater. They take up posts at every exit. Laughter can be heard erupting inside.

CUT BACK TO:
INT. – AUDITORIUM – NIGHT.

ABLOGIN is naming the contents of a woman's satchel as her astonished husband produces each item mentioned.

> ABLOGIN
> In a green coin purse you will find, let me see... (*He closes his eyes.*) Two rubles... three kopeks.

The husband takes out the purse, opens it, and counts the money. It is exactly as ABLOGIN had said. The audience bursts into applause.

> HUSBAND
> (*Amazed, he turns to his wife.*)
> Where did you get this money?

His wife blushes and looks away. The audience laughs.

> ABLOGIN
> From your pants pocket.

The woman gasps at the disclosure but nods her head.

>   WIFE
> It's true. He was drunk. How did you
> know?

The crowd roars with laughter.

>   ABLOGIN
> There is nothing hidden from the great
> Ablogin.

The audience cheers. BERIA sits silently watching. A large, heavyset man mounts the stage. He seems awkward and embarrassed.

>   ABLOGIN
> Come now. I'm not going to hurt you. (*The audience laughs.*) What's your name?

>   MAN
> Ivan... Kozyrev.

>   ABLOGIN
> Ivan... a pleasure to meet you. You know who I am?

>   MAN
> Of course.

>   ABLOGIN
> Who?

>   MAN
> Who? You are Ablogin.

>   ABLOGIN
> You're sure?

>   MAN
> Yes. I think so.

ABLOGIN
You don't know?

MAN
I know. You are Ablogin.

ABLOGIN smiles. Then his eyes close and he enters a trance. The audience watches intently. They seem to know what's going to happen. The MAN stands uncomfortably, not sure what to do. Suddenly ABLOGIN opens his eyes and an immediate change overcomes the MAN. For a moment he seems confused and then suddenly there are tears in his eyes. A hush falls over the audience.

MAN
(*Reaching out to Ablogin.*)
Mama! Mama! It's me, Ivan. Don't you know me?

ABLOGIN
Ivan.

MAN
(*Sobbing.*)
Mama! Mama!

The MAN reaches out and hugs ABLOGIN.

The audience watches in amazement. After a moment ABLOGIN nods his head and breaks the trance. Instantly the MAN recoils, stunned to find himself on a stage. He wipes the tears streaming from his eyes and stares at ABLOGIN in confusion. ABLOGIN smiles. The small band hits a triumphant chord and the audience bursts into laughter and applause.

ABLOGIN
Thank you, Ivan. You can sit down.

Still dazed, the MAN begins walking to the back of the stage. ABLOGIN motions for someone from the audience to help guide him back to his seat. As the MAN is led down the steps, ABLOGIN glances into the wings. BERIA'S MEN are preparing their assault.

                        ABLOGIN
            I want another volunteer.

MANY hands rise and ABLOGIN picks one. A young WOMAN jumps up and heads toward the stage. ABLOGIN closes his eyes. The WOMAN mounts the stage and approaches him. Suddenly a huge TIGER leaps at her from where ABLOGIN stood. Half the audience jumps. She screams and runs back down the stairs. Then, just as quickly, the TIGER vanishes and ABLOGIN stands triumphantly in its place. The audience gasps and then rises to its feet applauding the extraordinary illusion.

BERIA has had enough. He steps into the aisle and walks toward the exit. As he nears the lobby door, he nods, and suddenly the auditorium is inundated with his AGENTS. ABLOGIN is dragged from the stage as the audience watches in stunned and passive silence. An AGENT motions for the band to play. The music blares.

INT. – BARREN ROOM – NIGHT.

A door opens. ABLOGIN, sitting on the floor, looks up. Standing above him is BERIA. The two men stare at one another, both radiating enormous power. They do not speak. The silence between them is highly charged. Finally BERIA steps forward.

                        BERIA
            I have a mission for a man of special
            abilities. If he succeeds, he will become a
            man of great power in the Soviet Union. But
            if he refuses, or if he fails – he will die.

                        ABLOGIN
                (Staring confidently at Beria.)
            There can be no failure. I am destined for
            power.

EXT. – STALIN'S SUMMER DACHA – DAY.

JOSEPH STALIN is frolicking with a group of CHILDREN on the vast lawn of his summer retreat. Security GUARDS blanket the grounds, armed with heavy weapons.

Several OFFICERS convene on the huge porch surrounding the dacha. There is a sense of urgency in their gestures. After a moment, they break up and head toward STALIN, walking quickly but in unison.

One of the OFFICERS approaches STALIN and whispers something to him. STALIN'S playful manner turns grave. He stands abruptly, surprising the CHILDREN, and hurries back to the dacha. A covey of NANNIES scurries to retrieve the CHILDREN.

INT. – GUARD HOUSE – DAY.

GUARDS assemble hurriedly as OFFICERS circulate photographs. They are photographs of ABLOGIN.

>
> OFFICER
> (*Addressing the men.*)
> We have reason to suspect that an attempt will be made on the life of Comrade Stalin. If you see the man in this photograph, he is to be shot on sight.

EXT. – WOODED AREA – DAY.

A huge boulder on the edge of a dense forest suddenly begins to move. It pivots effortlessly. ABLOGIN and two of BERIA'S AGENTS emerge from behind it. They are in a wooded area just yards from the massive lawn of STALIN'S dacha. GUARDS can be seen everywhere patrolling the grounds.

One of the AGENTS, carrying a metal box, opens it carefully. A black revolver sits inside. He holds the box out to ABLOGIN.

The second AGENT points his own gun at ABLOGIN'S head, holding it steadily as ABLOGIN reaches into the box and removes the revolver.

>
> AGENT
> (*His voice just above a whisper.*)
> If you fail, expect no mercy. You will be killed within moments of your arrest.

ABLOGIN nods. Several beads of sweat appear on his forehead. He stands quietly for a moment – then closes his eyes. As they open it is obvious he has entered a trance.

ABLOGIN steps cautiously toward the break in the trees. The two AGENTS withdraw. The boulder swivels shut. ABLOGIN steps onto the edge of the huge lawn.

A PACK OF ATTACK DOGS – suddenly alert. In an instant they erupt into a frenzy of barking, straining on their leashes.

Startled GUARDS jump and scan the perimeter of the lawn. One of them spots ABLOGIN emerging just yards away. His finger jerks for the trigger of his gun as he aims it at ABLOGIN. Then, unexpectedly, a look of confusion flushes over his face. The gun trembles in his hand.

In seconds, other GUARDS converge on the scene and stop suddenly in their tracks. One of them drops his gun as his face turns red with fear. The first GUARD, bewildered, tries to speak.

> GUARD
> Our apologies, sir. We didn't… We didn't…
> mean to interrupt your stroll. Please…
> excuse us.

Other GUARDS mumble and back away, clearing a path for ABLOGIN. He steps between them and continues walking.

In broad daylight ABLOGIN crosses the main lawn as more perplexed GUARDS snap to attention. Suddenly we observe ABLOGIN as viewed through their eyes. It is BERIA they see.

INT. – STALIN'S DACHA – DAY.

ABLOGIN, following his own psychic radar, makes his way through the complex of corridors into:

INT. – STALIN'S STUDY – DAY.

STALIN is sitting upright, asleep. His mouth is open. His head hangs back on the chair. A large desk spreads out before him, teeming with papers and mementos.

ABLOGIN crosses the ornate room and stops just inches from the desk. He stares at STALIN a moment and then raises his gun, but doesn't shoot.

Angle on STALIN as his right eye cracks open and stares at ABLOGIN. ABLOGIN notices and freezes.

> STALIN
> Shoot. (*Ablogin doesn't move.*) Shoot me!

ABLOGIN holds his position. Suddenly STALIN lurches forward and grabs hold of the gun. He aims it at ABLOGIN and smiles. ABLOGIN doesn't flinch. STALIN presses the trigger. The gun clicks. There is no bullet.

STALIN breaks out in a roar of sudden laughter, drops the gun, and loudly applauds a startled ABLOGIN.

Instantly, the room is overrun with GUARDS. BERIA is leading them. He is smiling and joins STALIN in applause.

> BERIA
> (*To Stalin.*)
> What did I tell you? He is remarkable. He fooled them all. No one challenged him. They thought he was me.

> STALIN
> Astounding.

> BERIA
> I knew when I saw him we had found something extraordinary. His gifts can be of great service to us. I have plans for him.

STALIN
You would use him as an agent?

BERIA
No. (*He looks directly at Stalin.*) As a weapon!

STALIN smiles, but his eyes are like daggers. He motions for BERIA and a short, portly MAN to follow him into the next room. He is NIKITA KHRUSHCHEV.

INT. – ANTECHAMBER – DAY.

An extreme close-up of Stalin's face as it contorts with rage.

STALIN
(*Roaring at Beria.*)
WHO DO YOU THINK YOU ARE?! WHAT INSANITY IS THIS?! HOW DARE YOU BRING THAT MAN INTO MY CHAMBERS!! HOW DARE YOU RISK MY LIFE, THE LIFE OF THIS NATION!!!

FOCUS ON BERIA as the color drains from his face. KHRUSCHEV begins to sweat.

BERIA
But you approved...

STALIN
I APPROVED NOTHING!!!

BERIA
But... but... you understood...

STALIN
I UNDERSTOOD? I UNDERSTOOD ONLY THAT MY GUARDS WOULD LAY DOWN THEIR LIVES TO PROTECT ME! HE WAS IN MY STUDY!!!

BERIA
But I told you...

STALIN
...THAT HE WOULD ATTEMPT TO ENTER – NOT THAT HE WOULD SUCCEED.

BERIA
He has great powers. You were informed.

STALIN
THEY ARE DARK POWERS... DANGEROUS POWERS.

BERIA
Yes. And they can serve us. He will be a valuable friend.

STALIN glares at him.

STALIN
(*Quieting down.*)
A dangerous friend. I want him eliminated.

BERIA
(*Caught offguard.*)
But I have great plans for him.

STALIN
You would do well to examine them.

STALIN turns toward KHRUSHCHEV, who snaps to attention.

STALIN
Khrushchev! See that it is done... quickly!

INT. – PADDED ROOM – NIGHT.

A dark figure with a bag draped over his head is dragged into a corner. The GUARDS unhand him and back away quickly. The CHIEF GUARD turns toward KHRUSHCHEV standing in the shadows.

>   GUARD
>   We are ready, Comrade.

KHRUSHCHEV nods his head. The GUARD motions to a group of MEN in dark coats. They raise their handguns and fire. KHRUSHCHEV pulls the bag from the dead man's head. It is not ABLOGIN.

>   KHRUSHCHEV
>   (*Turning toward the guard.*)
>   Tell Comrade Stalin that it is done.

EXT. – TRAIN DEPOT – NIGHT.

A sealed railroad car pulls out of a freight yard into the darkness. SOLDIERS, posted at both ends of the train, are heavily armed.

DISSOLVE TO:
EXT. – MOONLIT LANDSCAPE – NIGHT.

THE TRAIN speeds through backwater villages and on toward the Russian Steppes. The landscape grows barren and foreboding.

DISSOLVE TO:
EXT. – DESOLATE LANDSCAPE – DAY.

NOMADIC TRIBESMEN tend their herds as the train hurls by.

DISSOLVE TO:
INT. – TRAIN ENGINE ROOM – DAY.

A MAN, shoveling coal into the furnace, freezes in terror. Looking out at him from the roaring flames is ABLOGIN'S face, burning. His charred lips move, silently mouthing, "Help me!"

DISSOLVE TO:
EXT. – VAST WILDERNESS – NIGHT.

THE TRAIN chugging through the moonlit night.

DISSOLVE TO:
EXT. – TRAIN ROOF – NIGHT.

THREE SOLDIERS man a machine gun station on top of ABLOGIN'S car. They are huddling together against the cold summer air.

Suddenly the train's whistle blows. The SOLDIERS tense and grab their ears. The whistle mysteriously increases in pitch until it is a piercing scream. In moments it has become a cacophony of wailing voices crying, "Help me! Help me!"

DISSOLVE TO:
EXT. – FROZEN TUNDRA – DAWN.

THE TRAIN speeds toward the rising sun. As the camera pulls far back, the train nearly disappears in the vastness of the Siberian wasteland.

EXT. – FREIGHT YARD – DAY.

Groups of SLAVE LABORERS load coal by hand into huge freight cars.

A LINE OF GUARDS not far away turn to see ABLOGIN'S train pulling into the yard. The train slows alongside them and stops. An OFFICER disembarks. His MEN look pale and weary. He marches up to the DIRECTOR of the prison camp and salutes.

                    OFFICER
            We have your prisoner.

                    DIRECTOR
            He is still alive?

                    OFFICER
            We have reason to believe so.

                    DIRECTOR
              (*Turning to his guards.*)
              Lieutenant, take two men...

                    OFFICER
              You'll need more.

                    DIRECTOR
              More?

                    OFFICER
              You'll need them all.

                    DIRECTOR
                    (*Smirking.*)
              For one prisoner?

                    OFFICER
              Has Khrushchev not informed you?

                    DIRECTOR
              Only that he must be kept alive.

                    OFFICER
              Send them all.

The DIRECTOR shakes his head and nods to his MEN. Six GUARDS mount the ramp. The huge metal doors slide open. A few MEN grab their noses. Slowly they enter the darkness.

INT. – ABLOGIN'S SEALED CAR – DAY.

ABLOGIN is huddling in a corner under a woollen blanket. The GUARDS laugh as they see him.

                    GUARD
              They sent six of us for him?

One of the GUARDS reaches out roughly to grab ABLOGIN. Instantly ABLOGIN explodes before their eyes into a raging BEAR. The

GUARDS yell and fall all over one another trying to back away. One runs screaming from the train.

EXT. – FREIGHT YARD – DAY.

The DIRECTOR, shocked by his men, signals to additional GUARDS. They grab special rifles and rush in.

INT. – ABLOGIN'S CAR – DAY.

THE BEAR is towering on its hind legs. It growls menacingly and lunges at the MEN.

A shot rings out. The BEAR staggers, then crumbles to the ground. The GUARDS watch in amazement as its bulky form suddenly evaporates. Lying in its place is ABLOGIN trembling on the floor. The tremors continue for an instant and then subside as his body grows limp and motionless.

The GUARDS with special rifles approach ABLOGIN and examine an array of tranquilizer darts that have pierced his skin.

INT. – ABLOGIN'S CELL – DAY.

ABLOGIN, empty-eyed and powerless, is carried into a solitary cell and deposited on the floor. The heavy door slams, leaving him in darkness. The locks tumble shut.

NEWSREEL FILM.

MARTIAL MUSIC blares from the screen as the Soviet "Kino Pravada" unspools in black and white. The images are a condensation of WWII footage: HITLER'S invasion of Russia, the massive Soviet defense, the Allies winning the war, ROOSEVELT and CHURCHILL meeting with STALIN at Yalta.

INT. – ABLOGIN'S CELL – NIGHT.

Years have passed. ABLOGIN'S eyes are hollow. He has grown a long black beard and appears fearsome. He sits motionless in the center of his cell, a sullen, pathetic figure. Through a small observation hole in the cell door, we see an eye peering in.

INT. – PRISON CORRIDOR – NIGHT.

Several GUARDS are taking turns staring at ABLOGIN. One of them turns to a comrade.

>   GUARD 1
> He hasn't moved in three days.

>   GUARD 2
> Like a sitting corpse.

>   GUARD 3
> He scares me, that one.

CUT BACK TO:
INT. – ABLOGIN'S CELL – NIGHT.

The camera moves slowly into a close-up of ABLOGIN'S face. For all the deadness of his features, his eyes are strangely determined and alive.

CUT BACK TO:
NEWSREEL FILM.

Images of STALIN'S funeral and KHRUSCHEV'S rise to power.

INT. – ABLOGIN'S CELL – NIGHT.

ABLOGIN appears wilder than before, his eyes more sinister, more focused. He is sitting cross-legged on the floor, his back supported by the wall. A metal tray bearing stale black bread and a thin porridge sits before him, untouched.

ABLOGIN'S eyes are fixed on the bread. They do not waver or blink. Suddenly a beam of energy seems to emit from his forehead and move toward the bread. It is an almost invisible force, only vaguely noticeable as it penetrates the physical space around it.

The bread suddenly seems to move. ABLOGIN intensifies his concentration. The veins throb in his head. The energy beam begins to glow with a greenish haze. Slowly, as if by magic, the bread begins to rise off the tray. For a moment it hovers unnaturally in the air and then it falls – like a bomb – and splatters on the floor.

NEWSREEL FILM.

An atomic explosion bursts across the screen.

INT. – KREMLIN – DAY.

KHRUSHCHEV is meeting with his top advisors in a mahogany paneled conference room. The MEN are all silent. KHRUSHCHEV seems deeply disturbed.

> KHRUSHCHEV
> How large was the American blast?

> ADVISOR
> We are awaiting word.

> KHRUSHCHEV
> They were testing in the Pacific again?

> ADVISOR
> Bikini.

> KHRUSHCHEV
> Can we speed up our program?

> ADVISOR
> The bomb is not yet ready. Another two months.

KHRUSHCHEV grinds his teeth for a moment, looking distractedly at the ceiling. Suddenly one of his MINISTERS interrupts the silence.

                          MINISTER
            I can't help but wonder if there isn't another
            power greater than the atom.

KHRUSHCHEV glances at the MINISTER as he speaks and then looks back at the ceiling. The others observe his silence. Suddenly his eyes drop and he sits forward in his chair. He seems to have thought of something.

                          KHRUSCHEV
                          (*Whispering.*)
            Ablogin.

INT. – ABLOGIN'S CELL – DAY.

ABLOGIN is sitting. An aura of growing power surrounds him.

He is poised in a state of supreme concentration, staring at his cell door. Suddenly the energy beam emerges from his forehead. The greenish glow zeros in on the heavy metal lock. Gears can be heard shifting, and then slowly, the lock clicks open. The huge door begins to move, revealing the corridor beyond. The hallway light enters the darkness of the cell, exposing a look of intense satisfaction on ABLOGIN'S face.

The light is blinding. He squints to get a glimpse of a world he has not seen in many years. ABLOGIN makes no effort to get up or leave the confines of his imprisonment. He seems content simply to observe the freedom beyond the doorway. After several moments the beam from his forehead guides the door and it begins to close. The energy recedes gradually into ABLOGIN'S head. The cell grows dark once more and the heavy lock clicks shut.

STARS appearing in the blackness of the cell as a sudden panorama of outer space emerges on the screen. The words "Thirty Years Later" fade in over the image of space and then fade out.

Slowly the earth rises from the bottom of the frame, a massive blue globe overwhelming the screen. Soon afterward an earth-orbiting satellite comes into view. It is a huge, complex, technological marvel. The camera holds on it as the earth rotates silently four hundred miles below.

Suddenly tiny pinpoints of light begin flashing at various coordinates across the surface of the earth. In seconds, a scattering of energy beams are shooting toward the satellite from many locations around the planet. They emit the same greenish glow observed coming from ABLOGIN'S head. Like so many cosmic searchlights, the beams begin to converge on the satellite and envelope it. In moments, the satellite begins to rotate. Outer appendages, tiny robot arms and metal dishes, shift into new positions.

After a number of subtle operations, the full array of beams focus onto one of the satellite's mirrors, and merge into one intense and powerful ray shooting back down to the earth. The transmission lasts only a few seconds and the beam withdraws back into the satellite.

Suddenly, delicate gears begin to click. Then, with a tiny explosive blast, the satellite is propelled from the frame.

INT. – TELEVISION STUDIO – DAY.

A bank of television monitors flickers to life in a control room at the ABC news Washington headquarters. The name WASHINGTON D.C. appears over the image.

The CAMERA pulls back from the monitors, revealing a room abuzz with TECHNICIANS and STAFF PEOPLE waiting for a satellite feed from China.

Angle on PETER SOLOMON, 22, a jovial young man with an endearing sweetness and inner brightness about him. He is being led into the control room by KEVIN O'CONNOR, 38, a film editor with the network. They stand toward the back of the room as additional PRODUCTION PEOPLE squeeze past them.

         KEVIN
        (*To Peter.*)
This is the control room for the evening news.

         PETER
      (*Surveying the premises.*)
Very nice. Impressive.

KEVIN
(*Greeting a cohort.*)
How ya doin' Elliot?

ELLIOT
(*Not stopping.*)
What ya say, Kevin?

KEVIN
Hey, I'd like you to meet Peter Solomon.
He's starting with us today.

ELLIOT
Great. Look, I'll catch ya later.

KEVIN
(*To Peter.*)
They're getting ready for a satellite feed.
(*Hearing a commotion near the doorway.*)
Hey, you'd better step back.

A PRODUCER charges into the room, talking to STAFF PEOPLE rushing in behind him.

PRODUCER
Do they know if he's dead?

WRITER
(*Trying to keep up.*)
They don't think so.

PRODUCER
(*Calling out to a technician.*)
When's it coming?

TECHNICIAN
We're getting it now.

PRODUCER
Quiet down everybody!

Monitors fill with technical data, then cut to a CORRESPONDENT in the Beijing studio.

> **CORRESPONDENT**
> Hello Washington. Mac wants me to apologize that this stuff's on film but we couldn't get a video unit fast enough. Stanley just grabbed a movie camera from one of the locals and started shooting. (*Turning to someone off camera.*) How's my hair Charlie?

> **CHARLIE (V.O.)**
> Perfect. You ready?

The CORRESPONDENT nods and assumes a more formal pose.

> **CHARLIE**
> Okay. Rolling.

> **CORRESPONDENT**
> Chinese Premiere Xo Ping collapsed just moments ago in the lobby of the Imperial Hotel. Several deputies rushed to his aid and began immediate cardiopulmonary resuscitation. Ambulances have already arrived and we are told that the Premiere will be taken momentarily to Zhou Enlai Memorial Hospital. The following footage was shot just seconds after...

The transmission suddenly goes dead.

> **PRODUCER**
> What the hell happened?

> **TECHNICIAN**
> We're checking.

PRODUCER
Well, hurry up. What a place to cut!

TECHNICIAN
We've lost the feed.

PRODUCER
What do you mean, "lost it?"

TECHNICIAN
It's dead.

PRODUCER
Well, get it back!

TECHNICIAN
There's nothing getting through. No signal at all.

PRODUCER
What is that supposed to mean?

The TECHNICIAN shrugs his shoulders.

PRODUCER
Damn it to hell! I've got a show to produce here. Get me Beijing!

ASSISTANT
(*Cradling a phone.*)
I'm already on it, sir.

PETER and KEVIN are hanging near the back door.

KEVIN
Welcome to *ABC Evening News*.

PETER
Is it always like this?

                    KEVIN
                  (*Smiling.*)
            Just wait. This is the calm part.

                   ASSISTANT
            No go with Beijing. Nothing's getting
            across. They think it's the satellite.

                    PRODUCER
            Phones too?

                   ASSISTANT
            That's what it sounds like.

                    PRODUCER
            JESUS H. CHRIST! Find out what the hell
            we're dealing with here. And tell George
            that if that feed can't be transmitted in the
            next half hour I want them to put the film
            on the Concorde. Arrange a motorcycle
            pickup at Dulles and alert the writers to be
            ready for a possible rush job.

The PRODUCER turns and hurries out the door, followed by a near stampede of PRODUCTION PEOPLE. PETER and KEVIN are left standing in their wake.

                    KEVIN
            It may get busy around here this afternoon.
            I hope you catch on fast.

PETER smiles impishly. It is an endearing smile but not one to inspire confidence.

INT. – STUDIO FILM CHAIN – DAY.

PETER and KEVIN are standing in a room filled with movie projectors aimed directly at television monitors.

KEVIN
This is the film chain. Now it's important
you remember how you got here, okay? It'll
be your job to run the film down here just
before airtime.

PETER
Run? You mean "run"?

KEVIN
Just down the hall. It's not like a marathon
or anything. Just a fifty-yard dash.

PETER
That's a little primitive, isn't it? You
would think with the miracles of modern
technology they'd have come up with a
more efficient system.

KEVIN
Something wrong with your legs?

INT. – STUDIO HALLWAY – DAY.

PETER is standing next to an elevator as KEVIN pushes the button.

KEVIN
Look, don't sweat it. This is a cushy job.
The elevator drops you off here and you just
jog to the room down there. It's the most
energy you'll expend all day. Trust me.

Angle on the elevator door opening, exposing an elevator stuck between floors.

A REPAIRMAN, kneeling on top of the cab, peers out.

REPAIR MAN
Sorry, out of order.

KEVIN
Well, you could have fooled me.

INT. – ABC CAFETERIA – DAY.

PETER and KEVIN are sitting at a small table in a busy dining room. KEVIN is chomping into an oversize hamburger oozing mustard and catsup onto his plate. PETER is eating cooked vegetables.

KEVIN
When was the last time you ate meat?

PETER
About two years ago… in Namibia.

KEVIN
That was in the Peace Corps?

PETER
(*He nods yes.*)
We ate wild boar till it was coming out of our ears. Wendy and I even helped with the slaughtering.

KEVIN
Wendy? Your girlfriend?

PETER
Ex. (*Kevin nods understandingly.*) She was wonderful. She used to do things you wouldn't believe. Stuffing the intestines, cleaning the eyeballs. You ever eat eyeballs? (*Kevin nearly chokes.*) They're terrible.

KEVIN
And that's when you stopped eating meat?

PETER
Oh, no. Not until I entered the monastery.

                        KEVIN
            Monastery?

                        PETER
            A Zen monastery. In Japan.

                        KEVIN
                    (*Rolling his eyes.*)
            And what were you doing there?

                        PETER
            Sitting mostly. Meditating. I stayed for
            about six months... but it didn't work out.

                        KEVIN.
            You flunked sitting, huh?

                        PETER
                    (*Smiling.*)
            Something like that.

He pauses, as though about to say more, but then simply grins and continues eating. KEVIN stares at him curiously and then reaches for his Coke.

EXT. – DULLES INTERNATIONAL AIRPORT.

THE CONCORDE is landing. An ABC COURIER is waiting for it and grabs a specially marked can of film the instant it comes off the plane.

EXT. – WASHINGTON STREETS – EVENING

THE COURIER, on his motorcycle, weaves through heavy traffic.

INT. – EDITING ROOM – EVENING.

PETER is fumbling with a film splicer as KEVIN watches.

                        KEVIN
            I see you're a real mechanic.

> PETER
> Well, I'm pretty good with the simpler things.

> KEVIN
> "Simpler" things. Such as...

> PETER
> Oh, you know, opening doors, turning on the TV, things like that.

PETER smiles his impish smile. KEVIN stares at him for a moment and then smiles back.

With a loud crash the editing room door slams open as the PRODUCER comes barging in. He is followed by several WRITERS and STAFF PEOPLE.

> PRODUCER
> Drop what you're doing. (*He holds out a can of film.*) Get this on the machine.

INT. – *ABC EVENING NEWS* TV STUDIO. – EVENING.

TECHNICIANS are positioning cameras for the show. The room is bustling with activity.

INT. – CONTROL ROOM – EVENING.

> DIRECTOR
> Five minutes everybody. John, fix your glasses. I'm picking up a glare. (*He pushes a switch and speaks into a mike.*) You boys got the film down there?

> VOICE
> Not yet.

> DIRECTOR
> Why the hell not? (*He turns to an associate.*) Harry, see what's happening.

                    HARRY
Righto!

INT. – EDITING ROOM – EVENING.

HARRY rushes into KEVIN'S tiny room. KEVIN is sweating. It is a madhouse. Everyone is yelling. The PRODUCER is pacing nervously.

                    HARRY
Two minutes, guys. You gonna make it?

                    PRODUCER
WE'LL MAKE IT!

                    HARRY
Can you give me an estimate?

                    WRITER
One more minute.

                    KEVIN
                 (*To the writer.*)
How's this shot?

                    WRITER
Terrible. What's that greenish glow?

                    PRODUCER
SHUT UP AND JUST USE IT! Jesus, I hate film. (*He turns and notices Peter sitting cross-legged on one of the editing tables.*) What the hell do you think you're doing? Meditating? (*Peter smiles.*) Who is this guy? Where d'you think you are? Tibet? He's meditating and I'm about to have a heart attack. Now, either you stand here and show some involvement or you get the hell out. (*Peter jumps off the table and tries to look concerned.*) Hey, who's gonna run the film? (*Kevin nods sheepishly at Peter.*) God help us!

                    HARRY
          One minute to airtime!

                   PRODUCER
          Jesus Christ! (*He grabs hold of one of his
          staff.*) Scott, grab an elevator. Tell 'em to
          hold it.

SCOTT tears out of the room.

                   PRODUCER
          Come on Kevin, I'm dyin' here.

KEVIN quickly rewinds the film and shoves it at PETER.

                    KEVIN
          RUN!

PETER surges out of the room.

                   PRODUCER
              (*Yelling out the door.*)
          GET THAT FILM ON THE AIR OR I'LL
          CUT YOUR BALLS OFF!

INT. – ABC ELEVATORS – EVENING.

SCOTT holding an elevator and talking distractedly with its pretty young OPERATOR.

PETER charges breathlessly down the corridor. As he rounds the corner a "down bell" flashes on an elevator closer by.

He speeds toward it full speed as the door opens.

Angle on an empty shaft..

                    PETER
          OH SHIT!

Unable to stop his momentum, PETER lunges for the door as the film flies out of his hands and crashes three stories below. PETER'S fingernails dig into a thin strip of aluminum moulding as his body hovers over the shaft. His feet, poorly positioned, begin to slip.

                     PETER
      OH GOD!

INT. – EDITING ROOM – EVENING.

The opening music for *ABC Evening News* is heard. KEVIN, the PRODUCER, and a few WRITERS are watching a monitor suspended from the ceiling.

                 ANCHORMAN
      Good evening. Two top stories are
      unfolding at this moment. An AMX
      satellite, responsible for much of our
      international communication network, has
      mysteriously failed high in Earth orbit. And
      in China, a nearly fatal brain seizure has
      struck Chinese Premiere Xo Ping. Reports
      on his condition are still trickling in since
      the satellite failure has made it impossible
      to maintain our normal communication
      linkage. Now here with a filmed report on
      the China story shot earlier today is our
      Beijing Correspondent, Donald Taylor.

The ANCHORMAN waits anxiously as nothing appears on the screen. The PRODUCER, watching, looks up anxiously and then explodes.

                 PRODUCER
      WHERE IS THAT KID? I'M GONNA
      KILL HIM!

In a flash he shoots out the door with KEVIN and the WRITERS in hot pursuit.

INT. – ELEVATOR SHAFT – EVENING.

PETER, his fingers cramping, is barely holding on. His face is red. His eyes are bulging. Suddenly his fingers begin to give.

KEVIN surges past the PRODUCER and is the first to round the corner. He spots PETER dangling precariously and gasps.

PETER'S fingers are sliding across the moulding.

KEVIN lurches for PETER'S wrist. PETER, in a desperate gamble, reaches out. Their hands nearly touch – but miss – and PETER tumbles screaming into the shaft.

KEVIN stares at PETER'S body disappearing into the darkness. There is a loud thud and the screen goes black.

A SIREN BLARES.

EXT. – WASHINGTON STREETS – NIGHT.

A bird's eye view of an ambulance racing through the streets of Washington. The helicopter shot travels above the ambulance, peering straight down. It is a frenetic and dizzying perspective.

EXT. – HOSPITAL – NIGHT.

The elevated camera persists as PETER'S body is wheeled from the ambulance into the

INT. – EMERGENCY ROOM – NIGHT.

It is as though PETER'S own consciousness is observing the proceedings. Physicians rush into the room and begin a frantic race to save his life. The camera, positioned near the ceiling, observes the flurry of activity below.

Suddenly a loud buzzing sound goes off in the room. One of the DOCTORS grabs emergency electrodes and places them over PETER'S heart. High voltage electricity slams through them.

PHYSICIAN
            Come on! Come on! Don't give up now!

THE CAMERA holds near the ceiling for a moment and then rockets on a collision course toward PETER'S body. It is as though his spirit is flying back into its mortal frame. At the instant of their collision PETER'S heart begins beating again and the buzzing sound stops. The PHYSICIANS can be heard cheering far in the distance as the screen goes black.

INT. – INTENSIVE CARE UNIT – DAY.

PETER'S eyes flash open. He is lying in a hospital bed. His skull is bandaged and his rib cage is encased in a plaster cast. Tubes move in and out of every orifice. His eyes roam the ceiling and then gaze around the room. Early morning sunlight is shining in the window and a bird is singing on the ledge. He looks at it with loving eyes and then drifts off to sleep.

INT. – HOSPITAL ROOM – DAY.

There is a commotion in the corridor outside PETER'S room. He is no longer in intensive care. The shadows on the wall indicate that many hours, or perhaps many days, have passed. PETER is lying quietly staring into space. Gradually he looks to the hallway and sees a group of matronly CANDY STRIPERS staring at him. They smile awkwardly and one of them waves.

                    CANDY STRIPER 1
            Hi. We saw your picture in the paper.

                    CANDY STRIPER 2
            And on TV.

                    CANDY STRIPER 3
            Keep fighting. You're gonna make it.

A NURSE bustles into the room, shooing the CANDY STRIPERS away. She approaches PETER'S bed and reaches for his chart. PETER watches her curiously. After a moment she notices him looking.

NURSE
Hi there. How's the miracle boy today?
Head okay?

PETER
(*Speaking softly.*)
Still screwed on.

NURSE
Any dizziness?

PETER
Only when I breathe.

He smiles. The NURSE does too. PETER'S eyes gravitate to a WOMAN waking up in a chair near the bed. It is his mother, MILDRED SOLOMON, a frumpy Washington socialite. He seems surprised and happy to see her.

PETER
Hi, Mom. (*He looks sympathetically on her disheveled state.*) How are you? How you feeling?

MILDRED
Awful. These chairs. I have such a headache.

PETER
Want some aspirin? We should be able to arrange that around here. (*He looks at the nurse.*)

MILDRED
No. I'll be all right. (*She instinctively pulls a compact from her purse to check her hair and makeup.*) Oh my God. (*She shuts the compact, holds it closed for a second, then furtively opens it again.*) What did I ever do to deserve this? (*She pinches her puffy face.*)

PETER
You look beautiful to me.

MILDRED
Right. You just had a brain concussion.

PETER
(*Smiling.*)
I hear I've been in all the papers.

MILDRED
Not all. Just the *Enquirer*.

PETER
Aha! Since when do you read the *Enquirer*?

MILDRED
When my family's in it.

PETER
(*Rolling his eyes.*)
My apologies. I hope I didn't embarrass you.

MILDRED
Who? Me? Listen, after living with you all these years I am beyond embarrassment.

PETER smiles impishly at his mother. She smiles back warmly and gently strokes his hand.

PETER
Has Wendy called?

MILDRED
Peter, do bears shit in the woods? Of course she called. (*Peter grins.*) Don't worry. She'll be here. As long as someone points her in the right direction.

EXT. – GEORGETOWN UNIVERSITY CAMPUS – DAY.

WENDY RAPPAPORT, 23, exits the law building. She is an attractive young woman with strong features and frizzy hair. There is something dynamic about her, highly charged and determined. But at the same time she is slightly dizzy and out of touch. The combination is charming. TOM, a handsome but conceited young law student, approaches her as she struggles with a load of books.

       TOM
Hi... Wendy? Right? (*She nods coolly.*) Can I give you a hand?

       WENDY
Thanks – I can manage.

       TOM
You sure? Those law books are a bitch. (*She keeps walking.*) Where you headed?

       WENDY
Hospital.

       TOM
What's a matter? Sick of school?

       WENDY
I'm going to see a friend.

       TOM
A friend, huh? Wanna lift?

       WENDY
It's all the way across town.

       TOM
I don't mind.

       WENDY
I was going to take a cab.

                    TOM
        My meter's running.

He smiles seductively and reaches for her books. She relents. They head toward his car.

                    TOM
        So tell me about this friend. A boyfriend?

                    WENDY
        Ex. (*Tom's eyes brighten.*) You really want to know?

INT. – TOM'S CAR – DAY.

TOM and WENDY are driving in a spiffy Jaguar. The Watergate apartments pass by. WENDY is rambling non-stop. TOM, it seems, is not sure what he's gotten himself into. His eyes are glazing over.

                    WENDY
        It was in Namibia where things went sour. It all started when the tribal chief decided Peter was a great soul and should be initiated into the tribal mysteries.

                    TOM
        Heavy duty.

                    WENDY
        Awful. They kept him in this tent for three days, stark naked, covered in cow dung. And they started feeding him this brew, fermented urine and God knows what else. (*She makes a face.*) He was never the same after that.

                    TOM
        I'll bet.

                        WENDY
He claimed he had a mystic vision. He was
so out of it. It was a terrible time for us. We
tried to keep it together. We stuck it out
through the Peace Corps. But when he got
involved with the commune I had to call it
quits.

                        TOM
Commune?

                        WENDY
I told you it was complicated.

The car pulls up in front of the hospital. WENDY is still talking.

                        WENDY
The thing is, he's a wonderful person. I've
never known anyone quite like him.

                        TOM
I'm not surprised. Well, here we are.

WENDY smiles and gathers her books. TOM seems relieved as she gets out.

INT. – PETER'S ROOM – DAY.

A TOM AND JERRY CARTOON fills the screen. Suddenly WENDY'S head obscures it.

                        WENDY
Can I come in?

                        PETER
           (*His face bright with surprise.*)
Are you kidding? Sure. (*He flicks off the
TV.*)

WENDY
(*Holding out some flowers.*)
I brought these. A little ragweed, to liven things up.

PETER
Thanks.

WENDY
I'm sorry it's taken so long to get here but… law school, you know.

PETER
Don't worry about it. (*He makes a sign of the cross.*) You're absolved.

WENDY
Thanks. (*She smiles.*) How are you?

PETER
You want the truth?

WENDY
(*Laughing.*)
No. (*They both smile.*)

PETER
It's really good to see you Wendy.

WENDY
Ditto. (*She nods and they embrace with deep affection.*)

PETER
Wow! I should fall down elevator shafts more often.

WENDY
I was really happy to hear about your job. Surprised in fact. It seemed so out

of character, your getting paid to do something.

                PETER
Maybe I'll make it to adulthood yet.

                WENDY
That might be a bit optimistic.

                PETER
Well, you know me. (*He eyes her longingly.*) Do me a favor? One more hug. (*She strokes his forehead and obliges. He looks at her tenderly.*) I'm glad you came.

CUT ON A LOUD BUZZING SOUND TO:
INT. – A NURSE'S STATION – NIGHT.

                NURSE 1
        (*Looking up at a clock. It is 4 a.m.*)
It's Solomon again. You wanna handle it this time?

                NURSE 2
Do I have a choice?

INT. – PETER'S ROOM – NIGHT.

The NURSE enters PETER'S room. He is still pressing the buzzer.

                NURSE
What's up?

                PETER
I've got this ringing sound in my ears.

                NURSE
Oh. (*She removes Peter's thumb from the buzzer and takes it from his hand.*) That should help.

                                PETER
Don't joke. This is serious. I feel like my
head's splitting open. (*She looks at him
unsympathetically.*) Really. The pain is
awful. I'd be climbing the walls if I could get
out of this cast.

                                NURSE
                        (*Looking at her watch.*)
Mr. Solomon. We are authorized to give you
your pain medication once every four hours,
not every twenty minutes. We're nurses, not
dope dealers. Now, you can buzz all you
like but there is nothing we can do. You'll
get your pills at 6 a.m.

The NURSE turns and leaves the room. PETER stares distractedly at the ceiling for a moment and then allows his eyes to close.

Suddenly a barely audible but high-pitched ringing sound begins vibrating in PETER'S head. He grabs his temples. It grows louder. His eyes dart wildly around the room. The sound grows in volume and intensity. It becomes shrill and powerful.

PETER'S eyes widen. His mouth opens, as if to yell, but nothing comes out.

The ringing sound surges suddenly into a upward spiral of ever increasing pitch. It is a ferocious sound that appears to be rushing toward a furious and unimaginable climax. PETER'S face turns a ghostly white.

The sounds builds to an unbelievable intensity and then shatters in a terrible explosive roar.

PETER'S body seems propelled upward by the explosive sound and he is shocked to find himself standing on his feet in the middle of the room. The sound is gone.

PETER moves hesitantly around the room as though trying to figure out what has happened, but he sees no sign of any disturbance. Suddenly his hand reaches for his chest. He feels it carefully and notes with amazement that his cast isn't there. He looks down for confirmation and his eyes widen. The cast is gone.

Perplexed, PETER sits down and it is several moments before he realizes that there is no chair beneath him and that he is sitting suspended in mid-air. The shock of this awareness sends him bolt upright and running madly toward the door.

PETER lurches for the doorknob but his hand passes right through it. In fact, his momentum propels his entire body right through the molecules of the wood and he finds himself, much to his astonishment, standing on the other side.

INT. – HOSPITAL CORRIDOR – NIGHT.

Awed and confused, PETER stands motionless in the middle of the hallway. Suddenly he sees a NURSE approaching and he runs to express his astonishment to her.

                    PETER
     Excuse me! Excuse me!

But the NURSE does not stop. In fact, she doesn't even realize that he is there.

                    PETER
     Hey!

An ORDERLY turns the corner wheeling a cart. He aims straight at PETER and makes no effort to avoid him. PETER stares in disbelief. Then, just as they are about to collide, PETER yells and instinctively jumps back, passing right through the wall. He is shocked to find himself back in his room.

INT. – PETER'S ROOM – NIGHT.

PETER stands frozen in the center of the room, his mind whirling. Suddenly his attention drifts toward the bed and he notices, to his continuing confusion, that someone is sleeping in it.

PETER draws closer to the bed to take a look and then stops dead. His hair raises straight up in the air.

PETER'S P.O.V., as he stares at his own body, still in bandages and a cast, lying there.

PETER screams. The shock of it jolts him right out of the air and, in an instant, he is back in his physical body, locked in his plaster cast. There is an expression of profound dislocation on his face as his hand gropes wildly for the buzzer.

CUT ON THE SOUND OF THE BUZZER TO:
INT. – THE NURSE'S STATION – NIGHT.

           NURSE 1
  Peter Solomon again.

           NURSE 2
    (*Looking at the clock.*)
  Let him ring.

INT. – PETER'S ROOM – DAY.

DR. THEODORE ROSENBLOOM is sitting quietly next to PETER'S bed. PETER finishes a cup of water and then continues with a story he is in the process of telling.

           PETER
  The tribal chief used to call it "Oolacchi,"
  which means, loosely interpreted, soul
  travel, or astral travel. The idea was that
  our spirit, or something in us, can leave our
  bodies and return at will. We can travel in
  the astral plane.

          ROSENBLOOM
  (*Yawning and covering his mouth.*)
  Excuse me.

> PETER
> I know it sounds odd, but that's what I
> experienced. I think the accident must have
> jarred something in my head.

DR. ROSENBLOOM stares at PETER blankly for several seconds before speaking.

> ROSENBLOOM
> Look, Peter, I don't know what you're
> talking about. Astral Planes... TWA. Don't
> worry about it. My advice is, just relax.
> Given time this'll all fade away.

> PETER
> Fade away? (*Peter smiles impishly.*) Who
> wants it to fade away?

DR. ROSENBLOOM gives PETER a curious look and shakes his head.

INT. – PETER'S ROOM – NEXT MORNING.

A ray of early morning sunlight bursts through the window and falls directly on PETER'S face. He opens his eyes, squinting, and stares at the dust particles floating in the air. Suddenly the particles waft upward, as the high-pitched ringing sound erupts unexpectedly in his head. PETER tenses. The sound begins to rise.

> PETER
> (*With fear and excitement.*)
> Relax, Peter!

Angle on PETER'S face as the tension in it subsides. The sound, which has been shrill and abrasive, becomes suddenly bearable, almost pleasant.

> PETER
> Go with it, Peter!

PETER closes his eyes. Momentary spasms shoot across his arms and legs but gradually his body becomes perfectly still. The SOUND begins to rise quickly and, although its power increases dramatically, it is no longer threatening.

All of a sudden, PETER'S astral form begins to rise from his physical body. It is a simple separation, with none of the violence of his first experience.

The astral body hovers a foot above the bed, then levitates to a standing position. PETER steps off the mattress and floats gently to the floor.

PETER'S astral body looks much like his physical one but is more luminescent. It radiates an inner light which makes him seem brighter and shinier than everything else around him.

PETER stands quietly in the middle of the room, slowly exploring his new terrain. The panic of the first encounter is replaced by a childlike wonder and exhilaration. He begins by looking at the glow of his own hands.

       PETER
  Wow!

PETER walks to the bathroom to see himself in the mirror. There is no reflection. He likes that and smiles.

PETER approaches his own body lying on the bed and stands alongside it staring at himself. When he tries to touch his face his astral hand passes right through it. The sensation shocks PETER and he jumps back, tripping. But he does not fall. His body simply assumes a horizontal position and floats in mid-air. PETER'S mouth drops open.

       PETER
  WOW!

Show a montage of PETER discovering the power of astral flight. At first he seems content to glide around the room, bounding from wall to wall. He looks like an astronaut experiencing weightlessness for the first time. Soon he is skimming the room in circular movements, like a dolphin in a tank.

Gradually PETER advances to more complex flights culminating in a display of special grace.

We see PETER rising gently toward the ceiling. He holds there for a few seconds and then, diving like a bird, he glides beneath the bed, sails across the floor and then skims back up the wall to the light fixture on the ceiling. It is a beautiful, ballet-like flight, and PETER seems immeasurably pleased.

PETER returns to his physical body. He lies calmly on the bed, a beatific smile on his face. A male NURSE enters to take his pulse. After a few seconds holding PETER'S wrist the NURSE looks into PETER'S eyes.

>   NURSE
> Hey dude, whatchya doin'?

>   PETER
> What do you mean?

>   NURSE
> You've barely got a pulse here.

>   PETER
> You're kidding!

>   NURSE
> No, I'm not kidding. (*He takes a whiff of the air.*) You smokin' dope or somethin'?

>   PETER
> Who? Me? In here? No. I was... mediatating. Hey, did I really lower my pulse?

>   NURSE
> Lower it? I thought you were dead.

PETER is intrigued. He smiles with a special gleam in his eyes. The NURSE observes him and shakes his head.

INT. – PETER'S ROOM – LATER THAT DAY.

PETER, back in his astral body, pauses before the door in his room. He takes a breath and like a swimmer jumping into a pool, dives through it.

INT. – HOSPITAL CORRIDOR – DAY.

PETER soars down the hallway with dreamlike ease. His freedom of movement is sensual and satisfying to watch. Occasionally he lands on his feet to walk but then spontaneously takes to the air again. His eyes beam with childlike pleasure.

Suddenly PETER spots an attractive NURSE working down the hall. He flies toward her and finds her even more beautiful up close. With gentle ease he soars around her and peers advantageously into her lovely cleavage. A great big smile breaks out across his face. The promise of astral flight explodes inside him.

                              PETER
               YEOW!!!

He bursts into rapid somersaults in the air.

INT. – LARGE PICTURE WINDOW – DAY.

PETER is on an upper floor of the hospital gazing out on a Washington vista many stories below. With sudden bravado he steps through the molecules of the glass and stands on the ledge outside.

The view down is dizzying. PETER instinctively reaches for the window moulding to hold on but his hand passes right though it. He laughs.

It takes PETER a moment to screw up his courage, but then, in a gesture of sudden daring, he grabs his nose and jumps. Hs body moves several feet off the ledge of the building and stays there.

PETER gazes down at his feet hovering in the air and screams for joy. Then, aiming himself at the far horizon, he soars into the afternoon sky.

EXT. – WASHINGTON D.C. – DAY.

PETER flies like a bird over trees and rooftops and soon all of Washington spreads out beneath him. He soars around the Lincoln Memorial and encircles the Washington Monument. His face beams as he delights in the ecstasy of free flight.

INT. – WENDY'S BEDROOM – EARLY EVENING.

WENDY is sitting at a desk writing. Suddenly PETER comes flying in through the huge bay windows open to the evening air. He is delighted to see her and begins speaking excitedly.

>   PETER
> WENDY! IT'S ME! I CAN FLY! (*He soars energetically around the room.*) LOOK! LOOK! CAN YOU BELIEVE IT?

WENDY neither hears nor sees him. Her eyes are glued to her paper.

PETER lands on her desk and sits beside her.

>   PETER
> I know it must sound crazy, but it's true. I'm really here.

He reaches out to caress her soft skin but his hand passes through the middle of her face. The lack of touch is disturbing to him. He stares closely into WENDY'S eyes.

>   PETER
> God, you're beautiful. (*Leaning close and whispering.*) I love you, Wendy. (*Using all the air in his lungs.*) I LOVE YOU!!!

Suddenly WENDY looks up as though she hears something. PETER is surprised. He yells again.

>   PETER
> I LOVE YOU WENDY!!!!

Again she looks up – her eyes scanning the room. There is a curious and confused expression on her face.

>PETER
>WENDY! DO YOU HEAR ME? IT'S PETER! NEXT TO YOU! I LOVE YOU!!!

Perplexed, WENDY gets up and crosses to the window. PETER flies after her, somersaulting and swirling around her. He looks, literally, head over heels in love. WENDY peers out the window into the yard below. There is no one there. Shrugging her shoulders she sits back down at her desk and distractedly sips from a cup of cold coffee. PETER perches beside her.

>PETER
>You know, I've been thinking. I've got a job. I'll be making decent money. We could move in together again. We could live at my parents till I build up a little reserve and then get a place of our own. What do you think? Huh, Wendy? (*He leans in close and yells.*) DO YOU HEAR ME?

Startled, WENDY jumps. Her hand knocks into the coffee and spills it all over her notes and plaid skirt.

>WENDY
>SHIT!

>PETER
>YOU HEARD ME!

PETER flies off the desk, guilty but happy with the effect he has had. WENDY grabs tissues to wipe up the mess. She is angry and cursing. PETER tiptoes to the window.

>PETER
>Sorry about that. (*Wendy snarls.*) Look, I'll catch you later, okay?

He jumps up to the window ledge, throws a kiss, and then soars into the darkening sky.

EXT. – WASHINGTON D.C. – NIGHT.

PETER flies joyfully over the city. It is night and the city sparkles below him. Suddenly, in the distance, he sees a strange beam of energy piercing the heavens and shooting down toward the earth. The greenish glow intrigues him and he flies in its direction.

PETER grows curious as he approaches the beam and flies around it several times. It is about three feet in diameter and very subtle in appearance. A strange energy is emitting from it unlike anything he has ever seen before. It is hard to get a fix on. The beam is both there and not there at the same time.

With great caution PETER reaches out to feel the beam. Instantly it explodes into a much wider arc, encompassing him. Frightened, and in sudden pain, PETER shoots back out.

Suddenly the beam divides into many separate beams. PETER tries to fly away but the rays seem to follow in pursuit. Appearing to be highly intelligent and intuitive the beams converge on PETER'S astral body and lock him in their power. PETER is frozen with terror. He opens his mouth as though about to yell when suddenly his body disappears.

INT. – PETER'S HOSPITAL ROOM – NIGHT.

PETER'S physical body sits up in his bed screaming. A NURSE runs to his bedside. PETER stares at her – his face filled with confusion.

> NURSE
> What's wrong? Are you all right?

> PETER
> (*Deeply disoriented.*)
> Okay. I'm okay. A dream. It was a dream.

The NURSE looks at him strangely, nods her head, and leaves. PETER clutches for the cast on his chest to make certain he is really there. After a moment he exhales deeply, but the look of fear and confusion stays in his eyes.

INT. – HOSPITAL ROOM – DAY.

AN ELECTRIC SAW is cutting into PETER'S cast. PETER seems more and more relieved as each section is taken off.

>   DOCTOR ROSENBLOOM
> Bet you're glad to get this off, huh?

PETER smiles.

INT. – ENTRANCE TO PETER'S HOME – DAY.

A DOORBELL IS RINGING. A MAID rushes to answer it. PETER is standing there. She takes one look and carefully throws her arms around him.

>   DELL
> Peter. Peter.

>   PETER
> Hiya Dell.

>   DELL
> Oh, I'm so happy. So happy.

A small DOG comes charging down the stairs, yelping and jumping.

>   PETER
> Hiya Whiskers. How you doin' old girl?

>   DELL
> She's happy to see you.

MILDRED SOLOMON emerges from a spacious living room. She kicks the dog aside and hugs her son.

                    MILDRED
Welcome home. (*She turns to the chauffeur entering with Peter's bags.*) Just take those upstairs and then come help us with Peter. (*He nods.*) I spoke with the doctor this morning. Did you know he wants you in bed for two weeks? I had no idea.

                    PETER
Don't worry, Mom. You'll hardly know I'm around.

MILDRED gives PETER a disbelieving look. She knows her son.

INT. – SOLOMON LIVING ROOM – DAY.

The room is crowded with well-dressed women attending an afternoon tea. PETER, in torn pajamas, passes quietly through the gathering. He is carrying a huge sandwich and a beer. WHISKERS trails behind him, stopping every so often to sniff at the crotches of several WOMEN there.

PETER spies his MOTHER across the room and smiles. She nods politely and waves them both along.

INT. – PETER'S ROOM – DAY.

PETER'S space is eclectically furnished with African and Japanese artifacts. His bed, a futon, is on the floor. WHISKERS hurries to a corner of the room with her own little futon. PETER joins her, pouring half his beer into her dish and putting half his sandwich into her bowl.

                    PETER
            (*Lifting his beer can and
              proposing a toast.*)
To life.

WHISKERS rises to the occasion and slurps up every drop.

INT. – SOLOMON FAMILY ROOM – NIGHT.

WENDY is sitting in a huge sofa across from PETER staring at him with her mouth open. He is sitting on a hassock, leaning toward her.

                PETER
Look, I know how it sounds but you have to believe me. I can fly. I'm mastering the art of astral flight. Just like the Malam in Namibia.

                WENDY
Peter. Peter. It's me you're talking to. This fantasy stuff doesn't work on me anymore, remember? It's lost its charm.

                PETER
It's not fantasy. It's the most wonderful thing that's ever happened to me. I've been all over Washington, to the movies, to the ball game, right on the pitcher's mound. I've been to parties at the Watergate. I've been everywhere. (*He hesitates and then blurts out.*) I was in your bedroom last Wednesday. (*Wendy's mouth drops open.*)

                WENDY
You were what?

                PETER
I couldn't keep myself away.

                WENDY
What are you talking about? What do you mean?

                PETER
I flew in through the window. You were writing.

                    WENDY
               (*Shaking her head*)
          Peter. Do you have any idea how this
          sounds?

                    PETER
          I saw you spill the coffee. All over your
          notes and your plaid skirt.

WENDY'S face turns white. She stares at PETER incredulously.

                    PETER
          I'm telling you, I was there. I was sitting on
          your desk. I was right next to you.

WENDY, suddenly very uncomfortable, begins to stand. She stares at PETER angrily and uncomprehendingly.

                    WENDY
          Goddamn it! This isn't cute anymore. It's
          pathological. It's deranged. You're out of
          your mind, Peter. You need help.

                    PETER
          Wait, let me talk...

                    WENDY
          No! I've had it. I put up with your craziness
          in Africa. I stuck it out with you in Japan.
          But that's it, Peter. I mean it. You go flying
          all you want. I'm keeping my feet on the
          ground.

She turns and heads out of the room. PETER jumps up quickly, wrenching his back.

                    PETER
          WENDY! (*He grabs his side.*)

INT – ABC NEWS STUDIO – DAY.

THE LOGO for ABC'S *GOOD MORNING AMERICA* SHOW fills the screen. The voice of JORDAN PINE, a film editor, is heard.

> JORDAN (O.S.)
> The boys upstairs decided to put you on the morning show. Not much work. It won't strain your back.

As JORDAN talks the camera pulls back to show him walking with PETER through the *Good Morning America* set. It is unlit and deserted.

> JORDAN
> I realize that the hours may be a problem for you. We start at midnight and go through eight the next morning. But then if you want to be in the news business, you have to surrender the nine to five mentality.

> PETER
> No problem for me.

> JORDAN
> Great. Most of your work won't really hit till four, unless there's something breaking. So if things are quiet I have no problem with you relaxing. Sometimes I nap in one of the projection rooms. It's dark and quiet. As long as I know where you are.

> PETER
> Sounds great.

INT. – PROJECTION ROOM – NIGHT.

PETER is sleeping beside a projector. The high-pitched sound can be heard faintly in the atmosphere.

INT. – WENDY'S BATHROOM – NIGHT.

PETER is sitting on the bathroom sink staring longingly at WENDY as she smothers her face in cold cream. A dab of the cream gets in her eye and she blindly reaches for a tissue. Her hand misses the box and hits the cold cream jar. It falls on her big toe.

INT. – WENDY'S KITCHEN – DAY.

A telephone is ringing. WENDY'S MOTHER answers it. WENDY is at the breakfast table – eating.

> MOTHER
> For you. It's Peter.

> WENDY
> Not interested.

> MOTHER
> (*Hesitating and apologetic.*)
> Peter, I'm sorry. (*She pauses to listen.*) He says he's sorry about the cold cream jar and hopes you can still walk.

Wendy's spoon falls from her hand as the camera pans to her bandaged foot. There is a disturbed expression on her face as she glances uncomfortably around the room.

INT. – WENDY'S KITCHEN – NIGHT.

The clock on the wall says 2:18 a.m. as WENDY opens the refrigerator and takes a container of Häagen-Dazs chocolate ice cream from the freezer. She eats half of it in one sitting. A low angle shot reveals PETER on top of the refrigerator – watching.

INT. – WENDY'S KITCHEN – DAY.

A TELEPHONE IS RINGING. WENDY, still dressing for school, answers it.

                    WENDY
          Hello.

                    PETER (V.O.)
          Häagen-Dazs, chocolate, 2:18 a.m., half a
          carton. I love you and you're gonna get fat.

WENDY slams down the phone. Again she gazes uneasily at the wall around her.

INT. – WASHINGTON BUS – DAY.

WENDY is sitting on a crowded Washington bus, a satchel of books at her side. Suddenly PETER walks literally through the PASSENGERS and stands in front of her.

                    PETER
          Hi, Wendy.

WENDY'S eyes flash up and see PETER standing there.

                    TOM
          Well, guess I'll see you in class.

She smiles awkwardly. PETER keeps walking.

                    WENDY
          (*Turning toward Peter and muttering.*)
          You son of a bitch! (*Tom turns around.
          Wendy blushes.*) Oh, not you. I don't mean
          you.

TOM stares at WENDY curiously, nods, and continues on his way. WENDY slams her hand against her forehead and follows along behind him. PETER smiles.

INT. – WENDY'S BATHROOM – NIGHT.

WENDY steps out of a shower, dries herself, and wraps a towel around her.

INT. – WENDY'S BEDROOM – NIGHT.

WENDY steps into her room and sees PETER sitting on the chair. The sight of him startles her and she screams.

> PETER
> (*Excitedly.*)
> I knew you were starting to see me. I knew it on the bus. You're the only one Wendy. No one else.

> WENDY
> How did you get in here?

> PETER
> I'm not... in here.

> WENDY
> GET OUT! GET OUT!

She charges at PETER and swings out to slap him, but her hand slices right through his face and leaves her teetering. She stares at PETER and at her hand for a long and difficult moment, then runs screaming hysterically from the room.

INT. – UPSTAIRS HALLWAY – NIGHT.

PETER flies after WENDY and finds her huddling in a corner. Her MOTHER comes rushing from the kitchen and hurries to her aid. WENDY is crying and shaking.

> MOTHER
> Wendy, darling, what's wrong? What's wrong?

WENDY is unable to answer. PETER looks on with sudden compassion and guilt. He withdraws shamefaced, and in an instant is gone.

INT. – PETER'S BEDROOM – NIGHT.

PETER is lying on his futon next to WHISKERS. He is stroking her and seems deeply upset. The doorbell can be heard ringing downstairs. After a moment there is a knock on PETER'S door. PETER doesn't answer. Slowly the door opens and WENDY comes in. PETER jumps to a seated position as he sees her. WHISKERS rushes to her side.

WENDY walks slowly toward PETER and sits down beside him. She stares at him quietly without saying a word. He gazes back. It is a long and pregnant silence. Then WENDY reaches out and gently touches his knee. She seems relieved that it is solid. He puts his hand on hers.

> WENDY
> You scared me before. It was like touching a ghost.

> PETER
> I know. I'm sorry. I realized afterward how frightening it must have been.

> WENDY
> It's not one of your everyday occurrences.

> PETER
> I know. I'm sorry. It's taken me weeks to get used to it myself. (*He pauses.*) I'm really sorry for what I did. It was childish. I didn't mean to scare you.

They sit quietly.

> WENDY
> It's all quite amazing, you know.

> PETER
> I know.

> WENDY
> It must be quite distracting.

PETER
Quite.

WENDY
And exciting. (*Peter smiles and nods his head.*) Am I really the only one who can see you? (*He nods again.*) Isn't that strange? I wonder why?

PETER
We're like one soul.

WENDY smiles tenderly and leans over to embrace PETER. He lowers her to the futon and they kiss. WHISKERS watches excitedly.

PETER
I'm awfully glad you came.

WENDY
Ditto.

WHISKERS jumps on top of them – excitedly. PETER shoos her off and shakes his head.

PETER
I guess that makes it unanimous.

WENDY laughs. They embrace once more.

INT. – ABC EDITING ROOM – NIGHT.

PETER is rewinding some film and whistling at his job. JORDAN comes over to him and hands him another reel.

JORDAN
This is the background film for the President's news conference tomorrow morning. Bob said he won't get to it till around three. Just put it on the machine and then you can rest till he gets here.

INT. – PROJECTION ROOM – NIGHT.

PETER is lying on the projection room floor. His eyes are rolled up into his head and he seems far away.

EXT. – WASHINGTON – NIGHT.

PETER is cavorting in the sky high above the Washington Mall when suddenly he sees the greenish energy beam shooting down from the sky. He observes it from far away and notices, to his astonishment and concern, that it is aimed at the White House. PETER flies toward it.

EXT. – WHITE HOUSE – NIGHT.

PETER approaches the beam and observes with sudden fear that it is penetrating into the President's private quarters. PETER is within ten yards of the beam when it mysteriously disappears, vanishing back into the night sky.

PETER cautiously approaches the Presidential balcony. He seems amazed by his easy access to so powerful a spot. Slowly he moves over to the window and sticks his head through it. The PRESIDENT is inside, with his WIFE, his STAFF MEMBERS, and a number of PHYSICIANS. The PRESIDENT is holding his head and moaning in great pain.

>   PRESIDENT
> It's just a migraine.

>   FIRST LADY
> He's had it for two weeks. This is the worst
> it's been.

>   PHYSICIAN 1
> We should have been informed, Mr. President.

>   PRESIDENT
>   (*Angrily.*)
> ABOUT A HEADACHE? What am I
> supposed to do, call you every time I stub
> my toe?

                    AIDE
          I think we should cancel the news
          conference.

                  PRESIDENT
          NO! I'm fine... I...

He does not finish the sentence but grabs his head. The FIRST LADY puts her arms around him and looks toward the AIDE.

                  FIRST LADY
          Cancel.

Suddenly PETER is aware of the high-pitched ringing sound arising out of nowhere. It drowns out the conversation in the room and seems to exert a physical pull on him. All at once he feels a powerful tug and his body jerks back out of the window. He looks around quickly to see what is happening but there is no one there.

The high-pitched ringing sound intensifies and PETER suddenly finds his astral body catapulting backwards through the air. He can't control it.

EXT. – WASHINGTON – NIGHT.

Washington rushes by below and in seconds PETER is rocketing over Baltimore. His eyes are wide and frightened. He can barely breathe. A large complex of buildings rushes toward him from below.

INT. – APARTMENT – NIGHT.

PETER is hovering near the ceiling of a small apartment. Sitting below him is an elderly, articulate, feisty WOMAN in a black dress. After a moment of observing her visitor, she addresses his astral form. She has a Russian accent.

                    BEULAH
          Good evening. Thank you for coming. My
          name is Beulah Fish. We have a lot to talk about,
          you and I, but this is so inconvenient. Why
          don't you come and visit me at ten tomorrow

morning, in the flesh, if you will? My address is 29 Burton Street, Apt. 12A, Baltimore. I think it's important that we speak.

PETER is speechless. Suddenly he feels his body beginning to shake violently.

INT. – PROJECTION ROOM – NIGHT.

PETER is lying on the floor. JORDAN is shaking him. PETER is stunned and disoriented.

                JORDAN
Where have you been? Jesus, you're hard to wake. Come on, hurry. Bob is waiting to cut that stuff for the news conference.

                PETER
         (*Coming back to himself.*)
News conference? (*Pause.*) There won't be any news conference.

JORDAN gives PETER a strange look.

INT. – EDITING ROOM – NIGHT.

BOB is waiting for JORDAN as he and PETER enter.

                JORDAN
Hey Bob, sorry we're late.

                BOB
No matter. The piece has been scratched.

                JORDAN
You're kidding?

                BOB
       (*Waving a teletype message.*)
They cancelled the news conference.

                    JORDAN
                (*His jaw drops.*)
            How did you know that?

                    PETER
                (*An impish grin on his face.*)
            Psychic.

INT. – BEULAH'S HALLWAY – DAY.

PETER, wearing a suit and tie, walks down a dimly lit corridor in a large apartment complex. He approaches apartment 12A and rings the bell. The door opens and BEULAH is standing there. She is larger than PETER realized, nearly six feet.

                    BEULAH
            Come in. I'm glad you could come. (*She
            reaches out to shake his hand.*) Peter, isn't it?
            Like the fisherman? (*Peter nods, amazed.*)
            And Solomon, like the king. (*Peter is
            dumbfounded.*) Please call me Beulah.

INT. – BEULAH'S APARTMENT – DAY.

PETER AND BEULAH enter a modestly furnished flat that has an old-world flavor. It is homey and comfortable. PETER glances around the room taking everything in. BEULAH sits behind a desk and motions for PETER to sit on a chair across from her.

                    BEULAH
            Well now, I'm sure you're wondering
            why you are here. Let me begin by saying
            that you are one of the most gifted astral
            travelers I have ever observed, and I have a
            great sensitivity to these matters – although
            I'm not a traveler myself. I am more of a
            seer. I've been aware of you for some time,
            since your first flights. You are an audacious
            flyer.

PETER
(*Stunned by her revelations.*)
How did you get me here last night?
Something pulled me through the air.

BEULAH
There are forces, my young friend, beyond your comprehension. Attracting you here was child's play (*She stares at him with a serious gaze.*) You have a weak mind, loose and uncontrolled, like diarrhea. Given time, however, I can form you into something firm.

PETER
A solid turd!

BEULAH
(*Smiling.*)
Ahh, a man of insight. (*She reaches out and takes his hand.*) I'm glad you've come. These are momentous times. There are immense and terrible powers at loose in the world. They will easily devour you.

PETER
I don't understand.

BEULAH
Understanding is not important. I need your trust. I want to train you. I want you to come to me every day, during your sleep, so that I can teach you what I know. There is little time and so much to learn if you are to master the secrets of the astral plane.

PETER is nearly mesmerized by BEULAH'S words and strange power. He stares deeply into her eyes as she speaks and then nods in agreement when she is done.

EXT. – CIA HEADQUARTERS – DAY.

COLONEL FOSTER WARD, 54, steps out of a chauffeured limousine in front of the CIA BUILDING in McClean, Virginia. He is a portly man, whose crew cut suggests a military background, despite his pinstripe suit.

INT. – CIA HEADQUARTERS – DAY.

COLONEL WARD enters the building and passes a long array of security clearances before being admitted to a room deep in the interior of the building.

INT. – SECURITY ROOM – DAY.

Eight MEN are sitting around a conference table. A media wall occupies the far end of the sanctum. The others are bare. COLONEL WARD is directed to a seat by one of several MARINES serving as attendants.

      COLONEL WARD
    (*Leaning over to the man next to him.*)
  Unusual security precautions this morning.

      MAN
  Wilson's coming. Top level stuff.

HERBERT WILSON, director of the CIA, enters the room. All of the MEN stand to greet him. He motions for them to sit. The MARINES leave the room. A huge door is closed behind them. WILSON takes his place at the head of the table and sits in a large leather chair. He acknowledges COLONEL WARD.

      WILSON
  Obviously you are all aware of the Code
  Green nature of this meeting.

Heads nod. WILSON pushes a button on the table before him. A hissing sound, like a vacuum seal, surges through the room. A light in the table flashes "SECURE" and WILSON begins.

                    WILSON
          I'd like to introduce Colonel Foster Ward.
          He was formerly with the Pentagon and,
          a few years ago, spearheaded a special task
          force there. I've asked him to join us this
          morning and to give you a brief account of
          his work. Colonel Ward.

                  COLONEL WARD
          Right. (*He stands and clears his throat.*)
          Back in 1965 our intelligence confirmed
          that the Soviet Union established a major
          center devoted to psychic research. My
          job was to initiate a similar program here.
          After several years we had isolated a few
          "gifted" subjects, people who could "see"
          numbers or objects in other people's minds.
          It was interesting, but their skills were not
          sufficiently evolved to be of any real covert
          use. It seems the Soviets had the same
          problems and all indications are that they
          abandoned their unit just shortly after us.
          (*He looks at Wilson.*) Is that brief enough?

WILSON nods appreciatively.

EXT. – BUS STATION – DAY.

BEULAH FISH steps off a bus in the Greyhound Bus Station in downtown Washington. She makes her way to a crowded taxi stand where people are jockeying for cabs. With astonishing ease she walks through the crowd that actually seems to part to let her pass. A cab door opens as she reaches the curb and she gets in.

INT. – CIA SECURITY ROOM – DAY.

                    WILSON
          Colonel Ward, I regret to say that high-level
          reports surfacing in the last two months
          reveal that the USSR did not abandon its

psychic research unit. It appears, in fact, that they may have been surprisingly successful. The indications are that we may already be engaged in some form of psychic warfare.

EXT. – WASHINGTON, D.C. – DAY.

BEULAH is sitting in a taxi crossing the Potomac and heading toward Virginia. The DRIVER peers back at her in his rearview mirror and, for an instant, thinks he sees an army general sitting there. He blinks and looks again and sees BEULAH, her eyes rolled up in a semi-trance. He shakes his head and doesn't look back again for the rest of the trip.

INT. – CIA SECURITY ROOM – DAY.

WILSON is standing in front of a projection screen showing a diagram of the White House and surrounding area. Concentric circles emanate from the White House for two hundred yards.

                    WILSON
Our surveillance systems have detected a blanket of microwave-type radiation periodically enveloping the White House. You may remember that we had a similar situation at our Moscow Embassy some years back. (*Heads nod.*) Tests over the years have failed to identify any source for that radiation. Now, new radical theories are being presented, theories of psychic radiations spreading from the Soviet Union. This is a theory you and I would like to ignore, but gentlemen, such ignorance may be a luxury we can no longer afford. (*Pause.*) For the past several months the President, and a number of other world leaders, have been complaining of intense and disabling head pains that are growing more and more severe.

                    MAN
Premiere Xo Ping?

                  WILSON
            (*Nodding "yes."*)
The problem is growing more serious by the
hour.

EXT. – CIA HEADQUARTERS – DAY.

BEULAH'S cab pulls up in front of the CIA BUILDING. She pays her bill and heads through the main doors.

INT. – CIA HEADQUARTERS – DAY.

BEULAH approaches a RECEPTIONIST at the main desk.

                  BEULAH
I would like to see the Director of the CIA.

               RECEPTIONIST
What?

                  BEULAH
          (*Speaking forcefully.*)
I would like to see the Director of the CIA.

The RECEPTIONIST stares at BEULAH in disbelief but after several seconds her amazement seems to evaporate and the expression on her face shifts from one of humor to a look of sudden seriousness.

               RECEPTIONIST
Is he expecting you?

                  BEULAH
             (*Her eyes closing.*)
He is talking about me now.

INT. – CIA SECURITY ROOM – DAY.

WILSON is standing before the projection screen. On it is the image of a handwritten letter.

> WILSON
> I want to share with you parts of a letter I recently received. It is from a Baltimore woman claiming to be a clairvoyant. Her name is Beulah Fish. It is one of a series of letters that our computers retrieved from the crank file. All of them, you might be interested to know, predict imminent world destruction if her predictions are not heeded.

Several of the MEN roll their eyes. Others smile.

> WILSON
> "Dear Mr. Wilson, I am deeply disturbed to have discovered a field of powerful psychic energies converging on the White House. It concerns me that these energies may lead to severe mental disorders in the President and others operating in or near the White House."

He looks up from the letter to a room full of eyes widened by the shock of what she has written.

INT. – INTERIOR OF THE CIA BUILDING – DAY.

BEULAH is being escorted by a MARINE GUARD toward the first of several checkpoints leading into the interior of the building. The first checkpoint GUARD stops her but grows suddenly flustered.

Suddenly we see the image of a uniformed general standing in BEULAH'S place. The GUARD snaps to attention. BEULAH, showing the hint of a smile, walks past him.

INT. – CIA SECURITY ROOM – DAY.

WILSON is sitting at the head of the table.

> **WILSON**
> A dossier on Miss Fish reveals several interesting facts. She is 69 years old, a Russian émigré who arrived in the U.S. during the Stalinist purges. She is unmarried, has worked as a translator, but supports herself primarily as a psychic reader and advisor.

A buzzer suddenly interrupts WILSON's meeting. WILSON, surprised, pulls out a set of keys and inserts one into a slot on the table. The guard station flashes onto the screen behind him.

> **GUARD**
> I'm sorry for interrupting, sir, but there is a woman here who claims that you are waiting to see her. Her name is Beulah Fish.

WILSON sits up suddenly in his chair. It is apparent from the shock on his face that she was not expected. The men all stare at one another.

> **COLONEL WARD**
> You didn't know she was coming?

WILSON shakes his head "no," then speaks into a microphone.

> **WILSON**
> Show her in.

The hissing sound escapes from the room and the door slowly opens. BEULAH is standing there. The MEN rise. She walks boldly into the room.

> **BEULAH**
> Good afternoon gentlemen. I realize I was not invited to your meeting but I

felt it important to be here. You would
have sent for me sooner or later anyway.
Unfortunately we don't have time for
formalities. Please sit down.

The MEN all sit. BEULAH reaches into her purse and unfolds a world map marked with colored stickers.

                    BEULAH
If you don't mind I'd like to get right down
to business. It saddens me to tell you that
we are all in grave danger. The psychic force
fields I wrote to you about are spreading
like a cancer over the surface of the globe.

BEULAH points to her map. There are markings on every continent with a grid of interconnecting lines.

                    BEULAH
These centers are forming a kind of
planetary nervous system, each working
like relay stations, transmitting and focusing
their power. One need only look at the
President to know their effectiveness. His
mind will not withstand this assault.

                    WILSON
An assault by whom?

                    BEULAH
Look to the map if you have any doubt.
The lines converge on the Kremlin itself.
We are dealing with an insidious power of
increasing strength. If we do not attack it
soon, it will become too massive to destroy.
It is already too late for your missiles. (*The
generals look suddenly vulnerable, exposed.*)
I know what is happening in your silos. I
know the power of this force.

WILSON
(*Looking at her nervously.*)
We have other weapons.

BEULAH
There is no material barrier to psychic power. The President's mind will collapse. The Chinese leader too.

There is a stunned silence in the room.

WILSON
And how would you stop this?

BEULAH
I have thought about this for many days, but I have no more answers than you. I only know that we must discover the source of this disturbance before we can devise an attack. If we could infiltrate one of their centers, one of their weaker outposts, I believe that would lead us to a key, a clue to their power.

WILSON
And how would you propose to do that?

BEULAH
With a few gifted persons, who I would have to choose myself. Your men are powerless in the face of what I see. I would have to create a team, small but diversified, a kind of tiny psychic organism capable of penetrating Soviet defenses unnoticed and unseen.

WILSON
And where would you find these people?

                    BEULAH
You have lists of American psychics and
occultists. I know many, but I want access to
yours. I want the most invisible and obscure
of our psychic resources. And I want him.
(*She points at Colonel Ward.*) He knows what
I'm talking about. He will be able to help.
Your name is? No, don't tell me. (*She closes
her eves and begins to sing.*) "Way down
upon the Swanee river, far, far away." (*She
stops.*) Stephen Foster. Your name is Foster.

                COLONEL WARD
Colonel Foster Ward.

                    BEULAH
Oh good, we're on a first name basis. Call
me Beulah.

The MEN around the table are sitting with their mouths open, staring first at BEULAH and then at Wilson.

                    BEULAH
So, when can we start?

INT. – PENTAGON OFFICE – DAY

A FLURRY OF FACES appears on a television monitor. BEULAH is sitting in a darkened room watching them. COLONEL WARD is with her. Suddenly she calls out.

                    BEULAH
Stop. Go back one.

The image backs up to a face of a young woman. COLONEL WARD reads from a computer terminal.

                COLONEL WARD
Merribelle Johnson, 35, teaches art in
an elementary school in Chevy Chase,

Maryland. A divorcee, claims she's a medium.

BEULAH
Ah, yes. I know her. Go on. A tea-time dabbler.

The images flash forward, one after another, as BEULAH watches them intently. An image of two elderly twin men appears on the screen.

BEULAH
Stop.

COLONEL WARD
Robert and Raymond Barelli, 68, twins, telepathic. They describe themselves as one person in two bodies.

BEULAH
Hmmm... Interesting, but not for us. Go on.

COLONEL WARD seems impatient as he sends the images rushing forward again. The image of a middle-aged black MAN appears.

BEULAH
That one. I want him.

COLONEL WARD
But you don't even know anything about him.

BEULAH
His face tells me all I need to know.

COLONEL WARD
Henry Stryker, 34, Alderman from Chicago's south side. He has helped the police department in finding lost objects, persons and criminals.

                    BEULAH
          Perfect. See what you can do.

                    COLONEL WARD
                    (*Exasperated.*)
          Six hours and we now have a team of one. If
          he'll join us.

                    BEULAH
          He'll join. Continue please. I sense another
          member coming up soon.

Once again the images pass by. A young BOY appears. BEULAH calls out.

                    BEULAH
          Stop! That's our other one. We'll be done
          soon. See, I told you.

COLONEL WARD reads the BOYS' file with great concern.

                    COLONEL WARD
          Joseph North, 10, currently residing in the
          Wollman Juvenile Detention Center in Terre
          Haute, Indiana. An orphan, he has lived in
          twelve foster homes and two institutions
          since he was born. His uncontrolled anger
          erupts in displays of psychokinetic powers.
          It is claimed that he has tossed guards
          and beds across the room with his mind.
          (*Looking up.*) Oh come on now, you don't
          really believe this, do you? None of these
          claims have been authenticated.

                    BEULAH
          His face is the only proof I need. The truth
          is there, like a road map. He's had a long
          journey for such a young boy. I suspect he
          needs us as much as we need him. Well, that
          should wrap it up for us. We're done?

                    COLONEL WARD
Two members.

                    BEULAH
No. I have another one at home. Peter
Solomon. An astral flyer. You'll like him.
We've been working on speed flight. He can
do Washington – L.A. now in under three
minutes. That's slow, actually. The speed still
scares him. But he's learning.

COLONEL WARD stares at BEULAH with total incredulity. It is obvious that he is not completely at home in the realm of the occult.

INT. – PETER'S BEDROOM – DAY.

PETER is sitting on his futon. WENDY, pacing the floor, is fuming. She storms around the room for a moment and then pauses to regain her composure.

                    WENDY
Now let me get this straight. You've quit
your job? The first honest paycheck you
have ever earned and you've quit – after 41
days.

                    PETER
                (*Interrupting.*)
It's a leave of absence.

                    WENDY
            (*Holding up her hand.*)
And now you've gone to work for the FBI.

                    PETER
The CIA.

                    WENDY
Oh, excuse me, the CIA.

PETER
The Central Intelligence Agency.

WENDY
I KNOW WHAT THE CIA IS! (*She controls her temper.*) But you can't tell me what you're doing for the CIA because it is a highly classified, covert operation that could affect the very existence of life on this planet as we've known it.

PETER
Right.

WENDY
(*Screaming at the top of her lungs.*) AAAAHHHHHHHHH! (*Again she controls her temper.*) Okay. Let me consider this calmly. You're asking me to believe that we have to postpone moving into our own apartment until the history of the free world is once again safe and secure?

PETER
Yes, in a way, but not the way you make it sound. Wendy, these are perilous times. More than you could ever imagine.

WENDY
Well, I'm sure I couldn't imagine. My imagination has never equalled yours.

PETER
Are you implying that I'm making this up?

WENDY
Who? Me? Do I think you would resort to some kind of underhanded manipulative bullshit just to back out of moving in with me?

PETER
Why the hell would I do that?

WENDY
I DON'T KNOW WHY!

PETER
I want to live with you. But not now.

WENDY
Not yet.

PETER
It's only temporary. As soon as this is over…

WENDY storms angrily out of the room. PETER runs after her.

INT. – SOLOMON LIVING ROOM – DAY.

WENDY rushes through one of MRS. SOLOMON'S afternoon gatherings. The WOMEN look up as PETER grabs her. WENDY pulls away and hurries from the room. PETER stands angrily in the midst of the white-haired ladies as the front door slams.

MILDRED
(*Standing stoically.*)
I believe you all know my son Peter.

The LADIES attempt to smile politely. PETER, suddenly aware of their presence, smiles back and quickly steps out of the room.

INT. – BEULAH'S APARTMENT – DAY.

BEULAH is carrying a tray into her living room. It is loaded with vodka and some soft drinks. She passes it around, starting with PETER. He is sulking on the sofa.

PETER
No thanks.

                    BEULAH
          Don't brood. She'll come back. You'll see.

PETER is shocked that BEULAH knows. She gives him a compassionate look and moves over to HENRY STRYKER. He is a good-looking young black man, nattily dressed.

                    STRYKER
          How 'bout a scotch?

                    BEULAH
          This isn't a nightclub.

She hands him the vodka. BEULAH moves over to JOEY NORTH, a streetwise ten-year-old with a tough, aggressive manner. She pours him a soft drink.

                    JOEY
          I'll take the hard stuff.

                    COLONEL WARD
                    (*Butting in.*)
          Like hell you will.

                    JOEY
          Up yours.

                    COLONEL WARD
          Watch it buster.

                    JOEY
                    (*To Beulah.*)
          Where'd you find this asshole?

COLONEL WARD starts to grab JOEY but BEULAH holds him back.

                    BEULAH
          Ahh, already like family. (*She raises a glass.*)
          To our success!

PETER raises an empty hand. The others all belt down their drinks, except for JOEY, who disdainfully raises his glass and tosses its contents over his shoulder – onto COLONEL WARD. The COLONEL turns angrily and grabs JOEY by the collar.

> COLONEL WARD
> You little son of a...

Before he can finish his sentence the COLONEL flips into the air and lands on the couch. He sits up stunned and stares at JOEY.

> JOEY
> You're playin' with fire, mister.

The COLONEL doesn't say a word. There is an uncomfortable silence in the room.

BEULAH takes charge of the situation.

> BEULAH
> Well, Joey, if you can't control your energies better than that you might as well go back home.

JOEY doesn't like that. He begins to fume. His eyes lock on COLONEL WARD and suddenly the COLONEL is beginning to levitate over the couch.

> COLONEL WARD
> God Almighty, let me down. LET ME DOWN.

Instead of coming down he rises higher toward the ceiling.

> COLONEL WARD
> Do something. Someone do something. Please.

PETER and STRYKER position themselves to catch the COLONEL. BEULAH looks to JOEY. Slowly he lets the COLONEL down.

                    JOEY
          Was that more controlled?

BEULAH doesn't answer. JOEY smiles.

INT. – BEULAH'S BEDROOM – DAY.

COLONEL WARD is lying on BEULAH'S bed. He is disoriented.

                COLONEL WARD
          In all our studies at the Pentagon, I never
          saw anything like it. I saw one man bend a
          spoon once, but it was nothing like this.

                    BEULAH
          You were dealing with the wrong people,
          academic lightweights, psychic dilettantes.
          The really gifted ones are rarely recognized.
          Life hides them from us.

                COLONEL WARD
          I'm not sure I can handle this.

                    BUELAH
          You have no choice. The President's mind
          won't last ten days. I couldn't tell the CIA
          that. But the force fields are growing.
          Something terrible is going to happen if we
          don't work quickly. We have to train our
          boys. We have to get them to work together,
          to be sensitive to one another.

                COLONEL WARD
          It will never happen.

                    BEULAH
          It has to.

EXT. – DOWNTOWN WASHINGTON – DAY.

STRYKER and COLONEL WARD are walking down Pennsylvania Avenue. STRYKER is following a kind of psychic radar, stopping, turning, backtracking, but constantly on the move. He stops suddenly when he notices a SENATOR stepping out of a car.

> STRYKER
> Hey, that's Senator Millman. Excuse me Colonel, but I gotta say hello.

> COLONEL WARD
> Do you know him?

> STRYKER
> Not yet.

> COLONEL WARD
> (*Holding his arm.*)
> Hey, let's set our priorities here. We're in the middle of a test run. We have no time to waste.

> STRYKER
> It won't take a minute.

He runs over to the SENATOR who is heading into a restaurant

> STRYKER
> Senator Millman, Henry Stryker, Alderman, fifth ward, Chicago. I just wanted to say hello.

> SENATOR
> (*Curtly, without stopping.*)
> Hello.

STRYKER watches as the SENATOR disappears into the restaurant doorway and then returns to COLONEL WARD.

                    STRYKER
                (*Smiling proudly.*)
            Nice guy. (*Colonel Ward nods.*) A good man
            to know.

Then, without missing a beat, STRYKER'S radar is functioning again and he continues down the street. He follows a winding path that ends up in the lobby of the Shoreham Hotel.

INT. – HOTEL LOBBY – DAY.

STRYKER follows his nose to a bank of phone booths, studies them individually, and then enters one. After sitting in it for a moment, he reaches underneath the seat and smiles.

An envelope is taped to the bottom of the seat as STRYKER pulls it out. Inside is half of a $20 bill. COLONEL WARD is speechless as he pulls the other half out of his wallet. STRYKER matches them, smiles proudly, and carefully slips both halves into his pocket.

                COLONEL WARD
            Astounding!

INT. – BEULAH'S BEDROOM – DAY.

PETER and BEULAH are in her bedroom. His physical body is lying on the bed while his astral body is floating just above it. BEULAH, sitting in a trance, watches him.

                    BEULAH
            The whole trick to materializing is in your
            concentration. You must begin with your
            extremities and work back toward your
            heart. First your hands and feet will become
            visible, and then slowly, the rest of you.
            Begin to concentrate on your hands. The
            more mental energy you can put into them
            the more visible they will become. Try.

The fingers on PETER'S right hand begin to appear dense and molecularly solid.

                    PETER
          It's hard.

                    BEULAH
          Concentrate.

                    PETER
          Am I doing it?

                    BEULAH
          Just a little. Your fingers.

                    PETER
          It feels weird.

                    BEULAH
          Don't talk.

PETER keeps trying. Soon his whole hand and wrist materialize. BEULAH approaches it and tries to place a pencil in his hand. It falls right through.

                    PETER
          What did you do?

                    BEULAH
          The great masters were known to
          materialize so completely that they could
          grasp solid matter in their astral form.

                    PETER
          I've got a ways to go, huh?

                    BEULAH
          Just keep trying.

INT. – BEULAH'S LIVING ROOM – DAY.

FOCUS ON BEULAH'S bedroom door as PETER'S disembodied arm begins to pass through it. It is a bizarre sight. COLONEL WARD looks up and gasps.

The arm emerges from the door and floats into the center of the living room. The COLONEL lurches back on the couch. STRYKER looks up to see an unattached arm moving in his direction. He smiles and waves.

                STRYKER
         Hey, man, give me five!

PETER obliges and slaps right through his hand. STRYKER laughs.

                STRYKER
        Far out!

INT. – BEULAH'S DINING ROOM – DAY.

A row of Coke bottles lines BEULAH'S dining room table. JOEY is sitting across from them. Suddenly the neck of one of the bottles shatters and the Coke comes fizzing out.

                BEULAH
        No good. Try again.

                JOEY
        This sucks.

                BEULAH
        Just get the top off. You need precision.

                JOEY
        It's boring.

                BEULAH
        It's important.

Once again JOEY concentrates his energies on one of the bottles. COLONEL WARD and PETER stand in the background, watching. Suddenly one of the bottles shoots off the table like a rocket ship and lodges in the ceiling. It hangs there for a second and then comes crashing to the floor – minus the top, which remains embedded overhead.

>   JOEY
>   You want the top off? It's off.

>   BEULAH
>   Very clever. Now do it the right way.

JOEY stares angrily at BEULAH and then suddenly erupts. In seconds the bottles are flying off the table and crashing all over the room. BEULAH ducks. PETER and COLONEL WARD hit the floor. STRYKER peers in from the bedroom.

All of a sudden PETER jumps up furiously, grabs JOEY, and throws him to the carpet. COLONEL WARD tenses. Even BEULAH looks frightened. JOEY and PETER eye each other angrily in a kind of psychic stand-off. Then, unexpectedly, PETER pulls JOEY over his knees and spanks him.

The expression on JOEY'S face is hard to read. He looks like he is about to explode PETER into a million parts. But then, to everyone's astonishment, he begins to cry. It's not a simple cry, but a deep and affecting one, ten years in the making. PETER, amazed by the unexpected outburst, holds JOEY closely, stroking his head with tenderness and affection.

BEULAH and COLONEL WARD look at one another with surprise and relief.

INT. – BEULAH'S DINING ROOM – LATER.

A row of beer bottles is now on the table, replacing the Coke bottles that had been there before. Joey is sitting opposite them, with PETER.

>   PETER
>   Now remember, every one you open, you
>   can drink.

                    JOEY
          Every one?

JOEY smiles. He stares at the bottles for a second and then pops the lids with the utmost ease. They fly off with an almost rhythmic humor – pop poppity pop pop pop pop. JOEY turns and smiles at PETER.

                    PETER
          So, you could do it all the time, huh?

JOEY shrugs. PETER grabs one of the bottles and hands it to him, motioning to drink up. JOEY takes the bottle and, with real beer commercial gusto, downs a slug. He holds it in his mouth for several seconds and then, unexpectedly, spits it across the room.

                    JOEY
          Yukk! That stuff's awful.

                    PETER
                 (*Smiling.*)
          I never liked it much when I was your age,
          either. (*He musses Joey's hair.*) How 'bout a
          Coke?

                    JOEY
          Sure. Anything.

PETER gets up and heads toward the kitchen. He passes BEULAH sitting in the living room. She looks up at him and smiles.

                    BEULAH
          Something is about to happen. A break.
          Somewhere far away. I can feel it.

PETER smiles and nods politely.

EXT. – INDIA – DAY.

The camera tracks down a crowded market street in the city of Benares. An INDIAN MAN is walking nervously carrying a can of 16mm film.

AN AMERICAN MAN is standing in the distance. The two MEN see one another. They pass casually. The film can, almost unnoticeably, changes hands.

Suddenly a beam of psychic energy shoots down from the sky and divides into many rays moving rapidly through the streets. They seem invisible to PEOPLE walking by although many touch their heads in sudden pain as the rays pass through them.

One of the beams hits the INDIAN MAN who delivered the film. Almost instantly the other beams converge on him. His face contorts in sudden and terrible pain as he falls writhing on the ground. Several PEOPLE run up to him but they are too late. He is dead. The beam is gone.

INT. – CIA SCREENING ROOM – DAY.

A black and white movie is flickering on a screen. Its subject matter is both fascinating and bizarre. We are inside a Hindu temple. Several RUSSIAN AGENTS in dark suits are placing a futuristic electronic helmet over the head of a nearly naked Indian SADHU.

A butterfly is in a bamboo cage, being carried by one of the AGENTS. Unexpectedly he opens the cage and sets it free. The SADHU follows it with his eyes. After a few seconds its wings stop fluttering as it hovers motionless in mid-air. The helmet emits a barely visible energy beam and the tiny insect explodes into a fireball many times its size. The RUSSIAN AGENTS smile at the camera as the film ends.

BEULAH is watching the film with CIA and MILITARY OFFICIALS. They are all staring at the screen with their mouths open. WILSON is the first to speak.

       WILSON
  That's it. It was shot somewhere in or near
  Benares, India about two months ago. That's
  all we know.

       GENERAL
  Computerized voodoo.

                        BEULAH
            In a sense, you're right. (*All eyes turn to
            Beulah.*) They are using technology to
            amplify weak psychic forces. I knew it in
            my bones. There are very few true psychics
            in this world, very few. Technology... They
            will rise and fall by it.

The camera moves in for a close-up.

                        BEULAH
            We must go to India.

INT. – BEULAH'S LIVING ROOM – DAY.

PETER is sitting on BEULAH'S couch.

                        PETER
            India? You're kidding. That's halfway
            around the world. How am I supposed to
            find it? I can't even find my toothbrush.
            Besides, I've never flown that far. I'm not
            ready.

                        BEULAH
            If people always waited till they were ready,
            we'd still be in caves. Let's give it a try,
            Peter, huh?

INT. – BEULAH'S BEDROOM – DAY.

PETER'S astral body is separating from his physical form. It hovers for a moment in the air. BEULAH is holding a globe and focusing on India.

                        BEULAH
            You are looking for a Hindu temple near
            Benares. You should know it when you see
            it. Just head due East. See what can find.

PETER nods. The camera zooms into the globe.

A rush of high-speed imagery as PETER rockets across the ocean and flies over Europe. Clouds, water, landmasses appear with breathtaking velocity.

Zoom in on PETER coming in over Japan. He realizes he has overshot his mark.

      PETER
  Whoops!

He turns and within seconds zeros in on the Indian subcontinent. He murmurs to himself.

      PETER
  A small temple.

Zoom in on India. It is teeming with temples. It is also bursting with people, elephants, cows, camels, cars, and trucks. It is an overwhelming sight and PETER is paralyzed by it. He flies into the dense mass of humanity with no hint of where to find his quarry. After a short and futile search, he stops and sighs.

INT. – BEULAH'S BEDROOM – DAY.

PETER is back on BEULAH'S bed. BEULAH eyes him anxiously as he settles back into his body.

      PETER
  Nothing. It was just too big. I told you I'm
  no good at finding things. I'm sorry.

      BEULAH
   (*Shrugging her shoulders.*)
  It was a good experience. You'll learn.

      PETER
  What do we do now?

An Air India jet landing in Benares. Exotic Indian music is heard as we cut to:

EXT. – INDIAN STREETS – DAY.

A bicycle rickshaw carries PETER and STRYKER through the bustling streets of Benares. It stops in front of a small Indian tourist hotel.

INT. – INDIAN HOTEL – DAY.

AN INDIAN PORTER shows PETER and STRYKER to a spartan room.

> PORTER
> This is sink. Water every morning. Toilet at end of hall.

He holds out his hand for a tip which STRYKER gives him.

> STRYKER
> Hey brother, what's the nightlife like in this town?

> PORTER
> Very good. Temple chanting every night.

He bows and leaves. STRYKER doesn't seem excited.

EXT. – INDIAN STREETS – DAY.

PETER and STRYKER stroll through the crowded streets of the city posing as tourists. STRYKER, carrying several cameras, takes photos of everything.

The TWO MEN walk along the banks of the Ganges, watching as thousands of Hindu worshippers perform their ritual baths. As they continue walking, they approach the burning ghats. Huge flames shoot into the afternoon sky.

> STRYKER
> Hmm! Bar-B-Q. Smell those ribs. He smacks his lips.

                    PETER
You wouldn't want to eat 'em. Not those
ribs.

                    STRYKER
Come on! They smell great!

They approach the ancient funeral pyres and see a glimpse of human
bodies roasting. STRYKER takes one look and nearly throws up.

                    STRYKER
I just lost my appetite. What the hell are
they doin'?

                    PETER
This is the cremation ground. People come
from all over India to die here. It promises
them a higher birth in the next life.

                    STRYKER
Higher than what? Come on. We're heading
in the wrong direction.

Following STRYKER'S psychic radar the two MEN move through the winding streets. They pass a VENDOR selling food. STRYKER reaches out to buy some, handing the man some coins.

                    PETER
Don't. You shouldn't eat anything, except in
the hotel.

                    STRYKER
Don't worry about me. (*He rubs his
stomach.*) Cast iron.

INT. – TOILET STALLS – DAY.

PETER is listening to STRYKER moaning inside.

                    PETER
            You all right?

                    STRYKER (V.O.)
                    (*Not sounding very well.*)
            Just a couple more minutes.

                    PETER
            That's what you said half an hour ago.

                    STRYKER (V.O.)
            Well, there can't be much left now.

PETER rolls his eyes, knowingly.

EXT. – STREETS – DAY.

PETER and STRYKER walking slowly down the street. STRYKER looks weak but he is trying manfully to stay on course.

                    STRYKER
            We're getting hot.

They walk a short way and emerge into a crowded bazaar.

EXT. – HINDU TEMPLE – DAY.

On the far side of the many shops is the golden facade of a Hindu temple.

                    STRYKER
                    (*Excited.*)
            That's it.

                    PETER
            How do you know?

STRYKER leads PETER slowly around the temple and up the stairs to the balcony of a building across the street. From their vantage point they can see the shiny gleam of a dish antenna. They both smile, excitedly. STRYKER takes photos.

A HINDU MONK sitting near the temple looks up at PETER and STRYKER with a disturbed expression on his face. He signals to two RUSSIAN MEN in a cafe across the bazaar and directs their attention to the MEN on the balcony. The MONK closes his eyes and enters a trance.

A close-up of the balcony railing that STRYKER is leaning on. Suddenly the metal mysteriously snaps. PETER grabs hold of STRYKER just as it collapses and tumbles to the ground.

STRYKER
Jesus Christ! (*He catches his breath*.) They don't make 'em like they used to.

STRYKER leans over the balcony edge and sees several PEOPLE below shaking their fists at him.

STRYKER
We better split!

FOCUS ON THE MONK watching as PETER and STRYKER hurry down the stairs. The TWO RUSSIAN MEN stand and follow from a distance.

INT. – HOTEL ROOM – DAY.

PETER is lying on his hotel bed.

PETER
Don't leave this room! I don't want anyone disturbing my body.

STRYKER
I'll guard it with my life.

PETER closes his eyes. THE HIGH-PITCHED RINGING SOUND is heard.

INT. – HINDU TEMPLE – DAY.

PETER's astral body zeros in on the temple and flies inside it. The corridors are dimly lit and full of shadows.

PETER traces his way deep into the temple's interior. Suddenly he hears Russian voices coming from the other side of the wall. He steps through and emerges in the same room seen in the 16mm film. The SADHU is there along with the RUSSIAN AGENTS. The futuristic helmet is on his head. PETER sees a part of the room he had not seen before. Positioned opposite the SADHU is a massive computer console and a large video monitor.

INT. – HOTEL ROOM – DAY.

STRYKER is holding his stomach and rocking on his bed. He is in obvious discomfort. Suddenly he jumps up, drapes PETER'S body with a sheet, and races quickly down the hall.

EXT. – HOTEL – DAY.

THE TWO RUSSIAN MEN who followed PETER and STRYKER are standing outside the hotel along with TWO INDIANS. The RUSSIANS speaks to them.

                    RUSSIAN
    We must do this quickly. They must
    disappear without a trace.

The INDIANS nod.

INT. – HINDU TEMPLE – DAY.

The computer console inside the temple comes alive. A series of instructions appear on the screen in Russian. The AGENTS make subtle mechanical adjustments.

An image emerges on the screen. It is a powerful face with dark eyes and long dark hair. It takes a moment to recognize it as VLADIMIR ABLOGIN.

ABLOGIN, looking many years older, stares from the screen with a mesmerizing gaze. The SADHU stares into ABLOGIN'S eyes.

An energy beam emits from ABLOGIN'S forehead and shoots toward the screen. Simultaneously a beam from the SADHU'S helmet reaches toward it. When both beams interlock on the screen, a new beam, infinitely more powerful, blasts out of a special aperture on top of the SADHU'S headgear.

EXT. – EARTH – DAY.

We see Earth from four hundred miles away. The AMX communication satellite comes into view. Suddenly a multitude of tiny lights flash below. In less than a second, a vast array of psychic beams are converging on it. An outer relay dish catches the beams and focuses them back onto Earth.

INT. – HINDU TEMPLE – DAY.

A computerized image of the earth appears on the SADHU'S screen. There is remarkable detail in its imagery as first continents, then countries, cities, buildings and even pedestrians come into view with vivid clarity. The image represents an era of satellite spying far more advanced than anything the American public has seen before.

PETER watches with horror and fascination as Washington, D.C. appears on the screen. The image of the city computes down to a view of the White House. Inside a window the PRESIDENT can just barely be seen sitting at his desk. The psychic beam penetrates the building and surrounds him. The SADHU focuses on his image with malevolent concentration. The PRESIDENT grabs his head.

INT. – HOTEL LOBBY – DAY.

THE RUSSIAN MEN and their INDIAN ACCOMPLICES enter PETER'S hotel lobby. The INDIANS approach the MANAGER and converse with him. The MANAGER nods and points to the stairs.

INT. – PETER'S ROOM – DAY.

The door flies open in PETER'S room. The RUSSIANS and INDIANS rush inside, guns cocked and ready to shoot. They are shocked to find PETER lying motionless underneath the sheet.

The INDIANS approach the bed cautiously, guns aimed at PETER'S head. Slowly the sheet is pulled back exposing a pale and seemingly lifeless body. The MEN are confused. One of them grabs PETER'S wrist and feels his pulse.

>   INDIAN
> Nothing.

>   RUSSIAN 1
>   *(Perplexed.)*
> Where is the other one?

>   RUSSIAN 2
> We're not waiting to find out. *(Turning to
> the Indians.)* Get rid of him.

The INDIANS nod as the RUSSIANS gather stray clothes and other belongings into a suitcase and hurry from the room.

INT. – HOTEL LOBBY – DAY.

THE RUSSIANS approach the registration book and tear out the top two pages. The MANAGER watches quietly. Suddenly he looks up and sees PETER'S body, wrapped in bedsheets, being carried through the lobby. He carefully averts his eyes.

EXT. – INDIAN STREETS – DAY.

A funeral procession moves through the streets of Benares. A line of MOURNERS follows several linen-clad bodies on their way to the burning ghats. At the end of the line are the two INDIANS carrying PETER.

INT. – HOTEL ROOM – DAY.

STRYKER returns to his room. He appears tired and severely weakened. He enters an empty chamber and starts to leave, thinking he's in the wrong room. But then he stops and stares at the empty bed, minus its bedsheet. Suddenly a shock seems to surge through his body.

EXT. – HOTEL LOBBY – DAY.

Instantly STRYKER charges out of the room and nearly flies down the stairs. He hurries to the MANAGER and grabs him.

>   STRYKER
> WHERE'S PETER? WHERE'S MY
> FRIEND?

The MANAGER shrugs his shoulder. STRYKER glares at him furiously and shoves him against the wall.

EXT. – INDIAN STREETS – DAY.

In near panic STRYKER bolts into the crowded streets. He dashes around wildly for a moment and then stops. He takes a deep breath and closes his eyes. His psychic radar switches on. He looks down a narrow road with a sense of sudden assurance and then rushes toward it at full speed.

INT. – HINDU TEMPLE – DAY.

PETER'S astral body watches as the transmission with ABLOGIN is completed. The SADHU seems strangely vacant and depleted as the RUSSIAN AGENTS remove his helmet and help him to lie down on a nearby bed.

EXT. – GANGES – DAY.

PETER'S sheet-wrapped body is being carried to a funeral pyre along the banks of the Ganges. Slowly it is hoisted up toward the flames by the caretakers of the fire. Other bodies are burning nearby and hundreds of MOURNERS are gathered to observe the ongoing ritual.

EXT. – INDIAN STREETS – DAY.

STRYKER runs madly through the streets, jumping over sleeping cows and other obstacles that appear in his way.

EXT. – GANGES – DAY.

PETER'S body is being lowered to the flames.

INT. – HINDU TEMPLE – DAY.

A strange and frightening look comes over PETER'S face. His mouth opens as though about to scream. Suddenly, without warning, his body catapults through the temple walls and shoots into the afternoon sky, aiming for the Ganges.

EXT. – GANGES – DAY.

PETER'S body is lying on top of the funeral pyre. All at once, to the terror and disbelief of those watching, it begins to sit up. PETER, looking dazed and confused, takes one look at the flames shooting up around him and screams.

Hundreds of MOURNERS gasp as PETER'S body shoots straight up, dancing wildly on the burning wood. The PEOPLE howl in amazement, as though a god has emerged from the flames.

PETER jumps from the pyre. Hordes of MOURNERS bow to kiss his feet and throngs of BATHERS surge forward to see the miracle. The two INDIANS, stunned by what they have seen, try to get PETER but are cut off by the growing crowds. PETER is nearly crushed by the attention. The situation looks ominous. STRYKER, who appears on the edge of the crowd, can't get near him.

Suddenly PETER'S wits return. Standing absolutely still he motions for the crowds to step back. To his amazement, they obey. Like Moses parting the Red Sea, he walks between them, right into the Ganges.

Mimicking the ritual bathing he had observed during his walk with STRYKER, PETER dunks himself two times as the masses watch. On the third time he does not come up. The crowd waits expectantly for a few moments and then dives in after him. Miraculously, he is gone.

PETER reappears moments later floating alongside a wooden dinghy a short distance downstream. He quickly discards his clothing, tying his shirt around his waist like an Indian dhoti, and then re-emerges as one of the crowd. The faithful are chanting and prostrating themselves before the river as he makes his way, unnoticed, back into the street.

We trail Peter from behind. Someone is gaining on him. A hand reaches out and grabs his shoulder. PETER gasps and spins around. It is STRYKER. They embrace.

>   PETER
> What the hell is going on here?

>   STRYKER
> Don't ask. All I know is that they're on to
> us and we're in big danger. I suggest we get
> out of this place asap.

>   PETER
> You don't have to convince me. Let's move
> it.

EXT. – AIRPLANE – NIGHT.

An Air India jet shoots into the dark sky.

EXT. – PETER'S HOUSE – NIGHT.

A cab pulls up to PETER'S door. He walks up the front stairs and quietly enters the house.

INT. – PETER'S HOUSE – NIGHT.

WHISKERS charges down the stairs. Peter motions for her to be quiet but it is too late. MILDRED SOLOMON appears on the upstairs landing.

                    MILDRED
          Do you have any idea what time it is?

                    PETER
          Not really. (*Carrying Whiskers up the stairs.*)

                    MILDRED
          You know, I don't understand why you
          can't get a job with decent hours.

                    PETER
          Me either. (*He kisses her cheek.*) Don't wake
          me. Night.

MILDRED watches exasperated as her son heads down the hall and quietly closes his door.

INT. – CIA SECURITY ROOM – DAY.

COLONEL WARD and CIA DIRECTOR WILSON are meeting behind locked doors. They are speaking intimately.

                    COLONEL WARD
          The boys arrived home late last night. We'll
          be debriefing them at 10 a.m.

                    WILSON
          I pray they've learned something.

                    COLONEL WARD
          We all do.

                    WILSON
          We don't have much time, Colonel. The
          situation is deteriorating rapidly.

                    COLONEL WARD
          The President?

                    WILSON
He is exhibiting periods of total irrationality
and refuses to acknowledge that it is
happening. His staff is at a loss. There is talk
of hospitalization, but no one knows how to
proceed. Too much is at stake.

WILSON stops and looks intently into COLONEL WARD'S eyes to
make sure the severity of his message is getting through to him.

                    WILSON
We've been transferring many of his duties
to the Vice President but are being stopped
at every turn. The President is in a constant
uproar. Yet we can't hold him back without
alerting the world to what is happening. These
are dangerous times, Colonel. (*His forehead
tightens.*) We have a great deal invested in
Beulah Fish.

                COLONEL WARD
She's doing everything she can.

                    WILSON
Time is running out. I'm fighting for every
minute.

                COLONEL WARD
I'm sure she knows that, sir. She's an odd
duck, this woman, but an amazing one. I've
seen things you wouldn't believe. I trust her,
sir. She'll do it.

INT. – BEULAH'S LIVING ROOM – DAY.

PETER and STRYKER are debriefing everyone on their Indian journey.
BEULAH sits quietly for a moment absorbing it all. Finally she speaks.

                    BEULAH
         Tell me more about the man on the screen –
         the Russian.

                    PETER
         Did you ever see pictures of Rasputin? He
         looked like that, only worse. I've never seen
         such eyes.

                    BEULAH
         Do you have a picture of him in your mind?
         (Peter nods "yes.") Good. I want you to
         clear out everything else and focus on that
         picture. Foster, give me that pad over there,
         and a pencil. *(Foster obeys.)* Everyone else,
         keep quiet.

BEULAH enters a trance and suddenly her hand begins moving over the large pad. Like scan lines forming a computer graph, the image begins to take shape. With amazing graphic detail the picture emerges. It is ABLOGIN.

BEULAH lay down her pencil and comes out of trance. She looks down at the picture on her lap and her body tenses. Her skin turns white. PETER notices.

                    PETER
         What's wrong?

                    BEULAH
              (Almost too emotional to talk.)
         I know him. He was the Great Ablogin – a
         gifted psychic – known all over Russia. *(She
         pauses, obviously quite disturbed.)* For many
         years it was feared he was dead. Now I fear
         he is alive.

BEULAH stands up suddenly and begins pacing the room. PETER notices tears in her eyes. She blows her nose. After a few moments she sits back down with the group.

BEULAH
We are in terrible danger. They have discovered us. (*Looking at Peter and Stryker.*) They knew you in India. We must move fast now and strike at the heart if we are to succeed. We must go to Russia.

COLONEL WARD
But… their defenses. You said yourself they were nearly impenetrable. Are we sufficiently prepared?

BEULAH
We have to be. We have no choice.

COLONEL WARD
But how will we get in?

BEULAH
I don't know.

COLONEL WARD
Do you have any ideas, any schemes?

BEULAH
To trust providence. It will guide us.

COLONEL WARD
But no plan?

BEULAH
Just faith. No plan, Foster.

COLONEL WARD stares at her with his mouth open.

PETER
Let me go, Beulah. I can try an astral reconnaissance flight, check out the Kremlin, or whatever you want. Maybe that will suggest a plan.

> BEULAH
> (*Smiling at Peter and then looking at Colonel Ward.*)
> You see, Foster. Providence never fails me. Thank you Peter.

> COLONEL WARD
> What are you talking about? He couldn't find India.

> PETER
> It was just the temple I couldn't find. There were thousands of 'em.

> BEULAH
> And there's only one Kremlin. You must fly there Peter. You must search for a control center.

> COLONEL WARD
> And how will he find his way around? It's a massive place.

> BEULAH
> Do you have any suggestions?

> COLONEL WARD
> I have access to Kremlin maps. I can have them here in twenty minutes. He should study them.

> BEULAH
> Ahh, providence is bountiful today. Thank you Foster.

INT. – BEULAH'S BEDROOM – DAY.

PETER is lying on BEULAH's bed.

BEULAH
Be swift Peter, and be wary. Do not linger in
any spot for long. There are dangers there.
Stay on the move. Take in all you can and
hurry back. We will be waiting.

She leans over and gives PETER a kiss on his cheek. He smiles and closes his eyes. The high-pitched SOUND arises. BEULAH watches as his astral body rises and takes to the air. COLONEL WARD peers into the room.

                 COLONEL WARD
         Has he left?

                    BEULAH
Shh! (*Motioning for him to come closer.*)
Yes. (*She stands up and offers him her chair.*)
I want you to stay with him. I need to lie
down for a while. Call me when he gets
back. I'll be in my office.

INT. – BEULAH'S OFFICE – DAY.

BEULAH pulls a yellowing scrapbook from her desk drawer. On the cover are portraits of MARX and LENIN. She opens the book carefully. It is filled with old photographs. She files through them for a moment, surveying images of old Russia. She stops suddenly on one photograph and pulls it out. It is a picture of ABLOGIN and his young blonde ASSISTANT holding hands beneath a tree. She stares at it in deep and loving silence.

INT. – BEULAH'S BEDROOM – DAY.

COLONEL WARD is reading. His eyes are growing heavy and starting to close.

INT. – BEULAH'S OFFICE – DAY.

BEULAH lies down on the couch in her office. She pulls an old afghan up around her shoulders and dozes off. The photo of ABLOGIN is resting beside her.

EXT. – EARTH – DAY.

An extraordinary rush of clouds speeds by as PETER rockets over Europe and comes in over Russia. He homes in on Moscow with no apparent difficulty and easily recognizes the Kremlin and Red Square. The sight of the huge domed towers of Saint Basil's excites him and he smiles, pleased with himself.

INT. – KREMLIN – DAY.

PETER penetrates one of the large Kremlin buildings, an old eighteenth-century structure. The halls are paneled with dark mahogany and still lit by chandeliers. He flies through them observing a constant bustle of bureaucratic activity. A massive door at one end of the corridor is heavily guarded. PETER passes through it.

INT. – PRESIDIUM – DAY.

The leaders of the Soviet Presidium are gathered in an ornate room that exudes power and authority. The three most powerful MEN sit at the far end of a long thick table.

An OLD MAN is delivering a loud tirade. Suddenly, in the middle of his harangue, PETER sees the psychic beam breaking though the ceiling and surrounding the speaker. No one else in the room seems to see it. All at once the OLD MAN grabs his head and collapses to the floor. Everyone in the room tenses. The beam withdraws.

The face of KGB CHIEF YURI KARMALE, at the far end of the table. He is wearing an eye patch. His good eye focuses on the OLD MAN, viewing his plight without surprise.

SIRENS BLARE as medical teams rush through the corridor and pour into the room. Batteries of sophisticated medical equipment are rushed in. The OLD MAN is quickly attached to the machinery, placed on a stretcher, and wheeled away.

FOCUS ON the remaining MEN in the room. No one is speaking but their silence expresses a communal fear. PETER watches them all for a moment and then flies from the room.

INT. – KREMLIN CORRIDORS – DAY.

PETER is gliding down new corridors when he sees a group of MEN pushing a cart stacked with unmarked cartons. SIX GUARDS, fully armed, accompany the cart. PETER is intrigued. He follows them to a bank of elevators in a far corner of the building which are guarded by their own security FORCES. They examine the cartons. One of them is opened. PETER is stunned to see one of the same psychic helmets worn by the Indian SADHU in Benares. The helmet is shoved back into the carton and an elevator door opens.

INT. – KREMLIN ELEVATOR – DAY.

PETER enters the elevator along with the helmets. A button is pushed and they begin a long descent into the bowels of the Kremlin. The doors open.

INT. – KREMLIN BASEMENT – DAY.

A futuristic hallway appears. It is strikingly different from the eighteenth-century architecture on the floors above. The cart is wheeled through a series of holding chambers and then enters the main control center. PETER is awed by what he sees.

INT. – CONTROL ROOM – DAY.

We are in a vast room of striking power and complexity. In the middle of the enormous space is a huge chair with its back to the camera. It overlooks a wall of a hundred television monitors, bright with faces of many nationalities. All are wearing the psychic helmets.

FOCUS ON the central chair as it begins to pivot toward us. Slowly VLADIMIR ABLOGIN comes into view. Powerful beams of psychic energy are radiating from his forehead, directed to each of the many monitors. It is an extraordinary, otherworldly sight.

The camera zooms into one of the faces, the INDIAN SADHU, and for the first time PETER witnesses the full magnitude of ABLOGIN'S psychic network.

A large screen is mounted at an angle in front of ABLOGIN's chair. On it appears the image of the OLD MAN who collapsed during the Presidium meeting minutes before. Suddenly sirens blare in the room, disrupting the collective consciousness of ABLOGIN'S network. An army of HELMETED MEN burst into the chamber and begin scanning every corner of the room with beams emitting from their headgear.

The large screen in front of ABLOGIN registers a fuzzy but recognizable image of PETER'S ASTRAL BODY hovering in the air. PETER gasps as he sees it. Fifty HELMETED MEN have turned their beams toward him.

The huge chair pivots slowly as ABLOGIN rises and stares at PETER'S floating presence. After a moment he begins speaking. Surprisingly, his lips are not moving.

>ABLOGIN
>So, you have come. I have been expecting your visit for many days. (*He stares angrily at Peter.*) What a shame it will be so short. (*Peter can hardly move.*) The pain you feel will not last long. Do not struggle. Your life is over. No matter how quickly you return to your body, you will find it no longer your home. That is the price you must pay for interfering with the destiny of this planet.

PETER stares at ABLOGIN, overwhelmed by the power radiating from him. It takes him a moment to register what ABLOGIN has said – and then it is too late.

EXT. – EARTH – DAY.

PETER, in a wild panic, flashes over Europe and the Atlantic as they blur into a solid streak beneath him.

INT. – BEULAH'S BEDROOM – DAY.

PETER'S BODY is surrounded by dark forms as an assembly of DEAD SPIRITS converge on BEULAH'S bedroom. They are hungering for his body, to possess his flesh. PETER screams hysterically as one of them slips into his physical form, jumps up, and runs swiftly from the room. COLONEL WARD wakes up dazed.

> COLONEL WARD
> Peter. PETER!

> PETER
> OH MY GOD!

INT. – APARTMENT CORRIDOR TO LOBBY – DAY.

PETER flies after his own BODY as it surges out of the apartment and into the elevator. He is delirious. He slashes and kicks at his own flesh, climbing his shoulders, smashing into his face. But he is powerless. His astral body has no effect. The BODY rushes out into the street.

> PETER
> GET OUT OF MY BODY! GIVE IT BACK!

INT. – APARTMENT CORRIDOR – DAY.

BEULAH, COLONEL WARD, STRYKER and JOEY charge at the elevator but it is too late. They run to the stairs.

EXT. – STREET – DAY.

PETER'S battle continues into the Baltimore streets. He fights in a state of white terror. Cars and buses swerve screeching as his BODY lunges uncomprehendingly through rapidly moving traffic.

> PETER
> MY GOD! WATCH OUT! THOSE ARE CARS, YOU IDIOT. DON'T YOU KNOW CARS? OH GOD! BEULAH!

INT. – BEULAH'S APARTMENT – DAY

PETER rockets back into BEULAH'S apartment. He flies wildly from room to room. There is no one there. It is empty.

> PETER
> BEULAH! BEULAH! WHERE ARE
> YOU? YOU'VE GOT TO HELP ME!
> BEULAH! ISN'T THERE ANYONE
> WHO CAN HEAR ME?

Suddenly PETER stops dead as something strikes his mind.

INT. – UNIVERSITY CLASSROOM – DAY.

PETER flies into an amphitheater-style classroom on the campus of Georgetown University. There are hundreds of students in attendance. A PROFESSOR is lecturing on corporate law.

PETER anxiously scans the rows of STUDENTS. Suddenly his face brightens as he zooms toward the center of the room.

> PETER
> WENDY!

WENDY looks up, and then, realizing who she has heard, drops her head. PETER flies to her side. He speaks urgently.

> PETER
> Wendy! It's me! I'm sorry to bother you
> here but it's important. I'm in terrible
> trouble.

WENDY tries inconspicuously to shoo PETER away. STUDENTS behind her watch curiously, including TOM.

> PETER
> Someone's taken over my body. Another
> spirit.

WENDY doesn't respond. Suddenly PETER gets a desperate idea. Crouching beside her he concentrates on his right arm. Within seconds it has begun to materialize.

WENDY is seen from the PROFESSOR'S P.O.V. For an instant it looks like she has three arms. His lecture stops dead for moment as he sees her. She turns and sees PETER'S unattached arm resting on her shoulder. She gasps. Then, in an act of sudden inventiveness, she shoves her armpit over it, hiding her own arm behind her back. Now it appears that she has two arms again, but that one of them is out of control. PETER'S hand begins reaching across WENDY'S face, down her blouse, and over to her other hand.

>PETER
>You're coming with me if I have to drag you out of here!

PETER yanks at WENDY'S hand. It jerks into the air. He is stunned.

>PETER
>IT MOVED! MY GOD! I MOVED IT!

PETER pulls WENDY'S hand again. WENDY fights to pull it back down. The sight of one hand flying into the air while the other tries to hold it back is so compelling that the PROFESSOR abandons his lecture to watch. In moments the entire class has turned to see what he is staring at. Mortified, WENDY stands and tries to appear as dignified as possible as she leaves the hall.

EXT. – UNIVERSITY STEPS – DAY.

WENDY rushes outside. PASSERSBY cut a wide arc around her as she rants and raves at an invisible PETER.

>WENDY
>You son of a bitch! Who the hell do you think you are? What gives you the right to inflict your insanity on my life!? I don't deserve this. You're insane, Peter. You know that? You're mad!

						PETER
			ME? I'M MAD? AND WHAT ARE YOU?
			MISS NORMAL? LOOK AROUND YOU!

WENDY suddenly realizes that everyone is staring at her. Blushing like a fire engine and hurling epithets under her breath, she sits down on the school steps and cries.

PETER'S arm instantly materializes to comfort her and stroke her neck. WENDY slaps it.

						WENDY
			STOP THAT! Don't you realize what
			people must think?

PETER'S arm disappears. He sits down next to her and begins to cry too.

						PETER
			Wendy. What am I supposed to do? I didn't
			ask for this to happen. I need you. I'm in
			terrible trouble. Wendy. Oh God. Please
			help me.

WENDY is unexpectedly moved by PETER'S tears and the depth of his despair. She reaches out to comfort him but her hand passes right through his body. She smiles and looks at PETER'S astral form. After a moment she nods her head.

						WENDY
			Okay. What do I do?

INT. – BALTIMORE CAB – DAY.

WENDY is sitting in the back seat of a taxi, apparently talking to herself. The DRIVER watches her uncomfortably through his rearview mirror.

						WENDY
					(*To Peter.*)
			I don't know the first thing about Baltimore,
			so don't say Hopkins Park and expect me to

understand what you're talking about. This could be Outer Mongolia for all I know.

                    DRIVER
It's okay lady. I know where it is.

                    WENDY
I'm not talking to you.

The DRIVER nods his head and shuts up.

A little later.

THE CAB cruises up and down the streets near BEULAH'S apartment.

                    DRIVER
It might help if I knew what you were looking for.

                    WENDY
The body of a friend. About 5'10" (*She looks at Peter.*) 150 lbs right?

                    PETER
148.

                    WENDY
Excuse me, 148.

The DRIVER'S eyes cross.

                    WENDY
Dusty hair.

                    DRIVER
Living or dead?

                    WENDY
            (*Caught up short.*)
What do you mean?

                    DRIVER
          Well, um, huh...

                    WENDY
          Look, I know this must sound crazy...

                    DRIVER
                 (*Trying to act nonplussed.*)
          No, no.

                    PETER
                    (*Screaming.*)
          BEULAH! STOP THE CAR!

                    WENDY
          STOP! WHERE?

                    DRIVER
          WHAT? WHO?

                    PETER
          THERE! ON THE CORNER! STOP!

                    WENDY
          THERE! STOP!

WENDY grabs for the door. The DRIVER pulls nervously to a halt.

EXT. – BALTIMORE STREET – DAY.

WENDY and PETER jump out. The DRIVER watches as the GROUP begins an animated discussion (much of it addressed to an invisible presence). Suddenly they turn en masse and rush back to his cab. In an instant BEULAH, STRYKER, JOEY, WENDY, COLONEL WARD and PETER pile inside.

INT. – BALTIMORE CAB – DAY.

                    DRIVER
          I can't take this many! It's not allowed.

BEULAH glares at him. Almost instantly the DRIVER recants.

> DRIVER
> Like I said, where we headed?

> STRYKER
> Just head north.

> DRIVER
> Where to?

> STRYKER
> I'll tell you when I know.

The DRIVER gives him a strange look and takes off. STRYKER turns to BEULAH.

> STRYKER
> No wonder I couldn't find him. He wasn't in his body.

> BEULAH
> Do you think you can still do it?

> STRYKER
> I'm already tuned in. He's not far.

> BEULAH
> So you're Wendy? It's a pleasure to meet you. I wish we had had you with us before.

> STRYKER
> STOP! (*He points to a man walking down the street.*) THERE HE IS!

The GROUP jumps out of the cab.

EXT. – BALTIMORE STREETS – DAY.

THE GROUP charges down the street. PETER'S BODY sees them and begins to run. Just as they are closing in on him the BODY jumps into a car waiting at a stoplight, yanking out the WOMAN DRIVER and leaving her on the street. In a split second the car is hurling into the intersection and speeding down the street. The GROUP stares in amazement. PETER, horrified, flies after it.

INT. – BALTIMORE TAXI – DAY.

The GROUP jumps back inside the cab. JOEY pops up front.

>   STRYKER
>   Follow that car!

>   DRIVER
>   Come on. What's this? The movies?

BEULAH stares at him. He takes off.

INT. – SPEEDING CAR – DAY.

PETER flies into the speeding car, yelling insanely at his own BODY.

>   PETER
>   STOP THIS CAR! YOU'RE GONNA
>   KILL US! SLOW DOWN!

His BODY, an inexperienced driver, pushes and pulls at the buttons on the dashboard. The windshield wipers begin wiping, water spritzes, and the radio blares a religious sermon at full volume.

EXT. – SPEEDING CAR – DAY.

The car swerves through the streets with the taxi close behind it. PEOPLE scurry out of the way, but one WOMAN stands frozen as the car bears down on her. PETER screams. Just as the car is about to hit her the WOMAN mysteriously rises over the car and floats back down after the taxi has passed.

INT. – BALTIMORE TAXI – DAY.

JOEY, who has just engineered the feat, is bouncing up and down. The DRIVER is wide-eyed. BEULAH glances at the WOMAN through the rear window. She is standing on the curb, stupefied.

INT. – SPEEDING CAR – DAY.

The face on PETER'S BODY appears terror-stricken as cars and buses skid out of their way. PETER tries madly to materialize his arm as the radio sermon blasts loudly.

> PREACHER (V.O.)
> And I say to you sinners, the wages of sin
> are death. Repent now, or beware the Hand
> of God.

At that exact instant PETER'S hand appears, gripping the steering wheel. His BODY takes one look at it and screams. The car shoots out of control. PETER'S hand swerves it away from an oncoming truck and aims it at a streetlamp. They crash.

EXT. – STREET CORNER – DAY.

The collision knocks PETER'S BODY unconscious and the invading spirit flies out of it. PETER howls greedily and jumps back into his own skin.

The cab rushes to the collision site and everyone jumps out. They are just in time to see PETER limping from the wreck. He looks up and a great big grin breaks across his face.

> PETER
> IT'S MEI! IT'S ME! I'M BACK!

He jumps and dances excitedly for a moment and then collapses to the ground.

INT. – BEULAH'S BEDROOM – DAY.

STRYKER and COLONEL WARD are lowering PETER into BEULAH's bed. BEULAH and WENDY are beside them. BEULAH motions for everyone but WENDY to leave.

PETER looks up at BEULAH. His body is beginning to shake. BEULAH places her hand on his forehead.

>PETER
> There are beings out there, Beulah. Ghosts. Spirits. You never said a word. They could have killed me.

>BEULAH
> The spiritual domain is much vaster than our world, Peter. I have never denied its danger. Few people have the courage to travel in these realms. Now you know why.

>PETER
> I don't want to do it again. Ever. I've seen enough.

>BEULAH
> (*With compassion.*)
> You are a gifted soul, Peter. You are being made strong.

>PETER
> I'm afraid.

>BEULAH
> There's nothing wrong with being afraid. "Yea though I walk through the valley of the shadow of death, I shall fear no evil…" Well, no one ever said you wouldn't be shitting in your pants every step of the way. You have to face your fears, Peter. You have to keep walking.

                    PETER
I don't mind walking. I just don't want to
fly. I can't. Not again, Beulah. (*He pauses
and gazes into her eyes.*) I can't.

BEULAH nods her head understandingly and strokes his forehead once more.

                    BEULAH
        Rest.

BEULAH motions for WENDY to stay with PETER and leaves the room. WENDY sits on the bed and takes PETER'S head in her lap. He curls up like a small child.

INT. – BEULAH'S LIVING ROOM – DAY.

BEULAH returns to the others and sits next to COLONEL WARD.

                COLONEL WARD
        Will he be all right?

                    BEULAH
        It's hard to say. His gift has been like a toy
        to him. Now he must use it like a man.

                COLONEL WARD
        What do we do now?

                    BEULAH
        Wait. Providence will guide us.

                COLONEL WARD
        What if it guides the Russians too?

                    BEULAH
        Providence guides us all, Foster. But not
        everyone listens.

INT. – PETER'S BEDROOM – DAY.

PETER is lying on the futon on his own floor. WHISKERS is licking his face.

Suddenly there is a knock at the door.

> DELL (V.O.)
> Telephone, Peter. It's Beulah.

> PETER
> Tell her I'll call back.

> DELL (V.O.)
> I told her that an hour ago.

> PETER
> Well, tell her again, okay?

DELL's footsteps can be heard as she walks away. PETER does not move. Light jazz is playing in the background. Suddenly the music stops.

> RADIO ANNOUNCER
> We interrupt this program to bring you an important news bulletin from ABC. The White House has just announced that the President has suffered a massive brain stroke. Ambulances are now rushing him to St. Luke Memorial Hospital.

PETER hears the bulletin and jumps up instantly.

> PETER
> Oh shit! Oh shit!

INT. – ENTRANCE WAY – DAY.

PETER shoots out of the room and blasts down the stairs. His MOTHER, who is standing in the vestibule, calls out to him.

                    MILDRED
            Peter. Slow down. Don't you ever stop
            running?

                     PETER
            They got the President! I'm taking your car.

                    MILDRED
            They what? Where are you going?

He doesn't stop to answer.

EXT. – PETER'S HOUSE – DAY.

PETER backs his mother's green Mercedes out of the driveway and pulls into the street.

He doesn't notice a black sedan pulling out behind him.

EXT. – WASHINGTON STREET – DAY.

PETER stops at a red light. He is tense and upset. Two black sedans pull up alongside him. PETER nervously glances at the light and then at his watch. Suddenly, in a blur of dark suits, his car door is pulled open and he is dragged out of it.

In an instant PETER is stuffed into one of the sedans and a dark-suited MAN is driving his car. The light turns green and the cars speed off. The exchange has taken place so quickly that even PEOPLE standing on the street corner aren't aware of what has happened.

INT. – AIRLINE TERMINAL – DAY.

At the Aeroflot check-in counter in Dulles International Airport, a large trunk is being wheeled up to the baggage x-ray station.

                  OFFICIAL VOICE
            You don't have to x-ray this one. It's a
            diplomatic parcel.

The ATTENDANT nods and a flurry of red stamps are put on the trunk.

INT. – BEULAH'S APARTMENT – DAY.

WENDY rings the bell at BEULAH's front door. COLONEL WARD answers it.

> WENDY
> (*Bursting into the room.*)
> No one has seen him! No one! His mother's distraught. He's just disappeared.

> COLONEL WARD
> (*Trying to comfort her.*)
> Come sit down. Stryker will find him.

> WENDY
> Is there anything we can do?

> COLONEL WARD
> Just relax. It's out of our league.

INT. – PRISON CELL – DAY.

PETER, dressed only in his jockey shorts, is lying strapped to a table. Groggy and blurry eyed, he gradually begins to focus on a strange room. Suddenly his body stiffens as his eyes meet ABLOGIN'S. ABLOGIN is staring at him. After a moment PETER experiences ABLOGIN'S words entering his mind.

> ABLOGIN
> You have failed. You are too late. Your President will be dead within forty-eight hours. (*Ablogin smiles.*) But only you and I will know that he died. You see, to everyone else, he will seem to have recovered, miraculously. Everyone will remark on the renewal of his inner spirit. (*Ablogin laughs.*) But only you and I will know just how new his spirit really is.

PETER
You bastard!

ABLOGIN
Did you really think I could let you interfere with my plans? Did you? (*Peter doesn't answer.*) You are a fool. But a fool with friends. I want their names. I want them fast. Either you can give them to me or we can dig them out. Your President's mind is not the only territory I can invade.

PETER
If you're so powerful, why do you need me? (*Ablogin stares at him angrily but does not answer.*) I have nothing to tell you.

ABLOGIN sneers, turns away from PETER, and walks out the door. Three large MEN come in as he leaves. A cart bearing three psychic helmets is wheeled in behind them. PETER looks at it and tenses.

The three MEN remove the helmets from the cart and slowly lower them over their heads. PETER struggles to get free but cannot move.

The MEN position themselves around the table. Suddenly an intensely focused energy beam emerges from their helmets. PETER grits his teeth. The beams focus on his forehead.

One of the MEN appears over PETER'S head, looking down at him. His face is upside down. PETER squirms.

MAN
Now tell us, please, the names of your friends... or we will extract them from your brain, one by one.

PETER looks frightened, but does not respond. The psychic beams begin to penetrate his skull. PETER'S face contorts and turns a bright red.

> PETER
> (*Screaming.*)
> NO!

Suddenly PETER reaches inside and trips the astral lever. In an instant he is free, flying out of his body, which collapses beneath him.

INT. – BEULAH'S APARTMENT – NIGHT.

PETER appears, almost instantly, hovering near BEULAH'S ceiling.

> PETER
> BEULAH!

> BEULAH AND WENDY
> (*Hearing him simultaneously.*)
> PETER!

They both look up and see him. Everyone else cheers. BEULAH motions to be quiet.

> PETER
> I'm in Russia. Moscow, I think. I've been kidnapped. Ablogin is trying to kill the President and take over his body. We have to stop him – fast!

PETER is about to say more when his astral form suddenly disappears from the room.

> BEULAH
> PETER!

INT. – PRISON CELL – DAY.

PETER, strapped to the interrogation table, howls in a surge of unbearable pain and passes out, unconscious. The three helmeted MEN stand up and slowly remove their helmets.

INT. – AIRPORT TERMINAL – DAY.

CROWDS OF PEOPLE surge through the bustling international terminal at Dulles International Airport. An AIRLINE HOSTESS for Aeroflot is addressing a crowded Moscow bound waiting room.

> HOSTESS
> Will the members of the Wild Flower
> Association of Greater Baltimore please
> have your tickets and boarding passes ready.

A group of about twenty middle-aged and elderly TOURISTS line up at the boarding gate. Clustered among them is the GROUP. BEULAH is dressed in a loud floral print dress. It is the first time we have seen her in something other than black. COLONEL WARD is wearing a polyester leisure suit. WENDY, looking matronly, holds JOEY by the hand. STRYKER, sporting wire-rimmed glasses, appears professorial. JOEY pulls WENDY toward the head of the line.

> JOEY
> Hurry up, Mom!

WENDY takes a deep breath and scurries after him. BEULAH smiles.

INT. – PRISON CELL – DAY.

PETER is lying weak and exhausted in his cell. His eyes roam around the sterile environment. He notices a small window in the cell door and drags himself toward it. Outside the door he spies a GUARD sitting in a small antechamber, a revolver resting on the table beside him.

INT. – ANTECHAMBER – DAY.

FOCUS ON THE GUARD as PETER'S smiling astral body comes floating through the door. Suddenly the GUARD looks up and sees a severed arm holding his gun, hovering in the air in front of him. He gasps loudly as his body tumbles backwards off the chair.

The GUARD'S face is white as he stares mesmerized at his own gun pointing at his head. Then he watches with astonishment as PETER flips the revolver and grabs hold of the barrel. Covering his eyes and wincing, PETER raises the gun high into the air and then brings it down with all his might over the GUARD'S skull.

INT. – PRISON CELL – LATER.

THE GUARD, stripped to his long underwear lying in a corner of PETER'S cell. PETER is wearing the GUARD'S uniform. It is about five sizes too big.

PETER steps cautiously from the cell and struggles for a moment trying to lock the door. As he turns to leave he is stunned to find his three INTERROGATORS standing behind him. Before he can react a cloth bag is forced over his head and he is dragged from the room.

INT. – AEROFLOT – DAY.

BEULAH and her TEAM are sitting on the airplane. A HOSTESS reaches for the microphone near the bulkhead.

> HOSTESS
> Please fasten your seatbelts. We will be
> arriving at Moscow's International Terminal
> in approximately twenty minutes. Your
> Intourist Guides will be waiting there to
> greet you and to help you through customs.

INT. – KREMLIN ROOM – DAY.

The cloth sack is pulled from PETER'S head. He is disoriented to find himself on the upper floors of the Kremlin, in a dark mahogany room. Sitting opposite him is KGB CHIEF YURI KARMALEV. He is the man with a patch over one eye who PETER saw during his first astral reconnaissance flight. PETER tries to move but finds he is strapped to his chair. ABLOGIN'S INTERROGATORS are standing behind him.

                    KARMALEV
        You cannot escape from the Kremlin. It
        is an ancient fortress. (*He grins at Peter.*)
        Your brain has been most cooperative. (*He
        holds up a piece of paper and reads from it.*)
        Beulah Fish, Colonel Foster Ward, Wendy
        Rappaport... Should I go on?

PETER is enraged by his involuntary disclosures and pulls at his restraints.

                    KARMALEV
        Don't try to leave us. We have need of your
        skills.

KARMALEV smiles, his lips curling into an uncontrollable sneer.

INT. – MOSCOW HOTEL LOBBY – NIGHT.

MEMBERS of the Wild Flower Association of Greater Baltimore arrive at their hotel along with their officious INTOURIST GUIDE. As most of the members are checking in, BEULAH and her TASK FORCE slip quietly out, only to be met on the hotel steps by their GUIDE.

                    GUIDE
        Sightseeing will begin tomorrow morning,
        not tonight!

BEULAH stares at the GUIDE who becomes suddenly distracted.

                    GUIDE
        Excuse me, I think I'm needed at the desk. I
        apologize. Excuse me.

BEULAH smiles and nods politely as the GUIDE leaves them to their own designs.

EXT. – RUSSIAN STREETS – NIGHT.

BEULAH and her COHORTS hurry into the Moscow streets. It is twilight and the boulevards are crowded, but hardly anyone notices the black sedan following them from a distance.

      STRYKER
  He's not far. Follow me.

The GROUP follows STRYKER'S psychic instincts and within minutes is standing in Red Square, outside the Kremlin walls. STRYKER looks up at the imposing structure.

      STRYKER
  He's in there.

      BEULAH
  The Kremlin!

INT. – BEULAH'S HOTEL ROOM – NIGHT.

BEULAH and COLONEL WARD sit in two straight back chairs while the others sprawl over the two beds. JOEY is holding WENDY'S hand.

BEULAH pulls out a tape recorder and turns it on. JOEY is surprised and delighted to hear hard rock blasting from the machine.

      BEULAH
  They have devices everywhere. (*She looks at everyone seriously.*) I have to enter Ablogin's presence. It is our only hope. I must get inside the Kremlin.

      COLONEL WARD
  And how do you propose to do that?

      BEULAH
  I will walk in. How else?

COLONEL WARD
Ah! And what makes you think you can get in?

BEULAH
Foster, I penetrated the CIA. You think the Kremlin can stop me?

COLONEL WARD
You can't go alone.

BEULAH
I can't take you with me.

COLONEL WARD
But it's dangerous.

BEULAH
Yes. All life is dangerous.

COLONEL WARD
There must be a better plan.

BEULAH
I have been waiting for providence to suggest something, but time is short.

COLONEL WARD
Don't lose faith now. Ask again. We've come too far for you to go alone. There must be a reason that we're all here. We can't just drop it in your lap now.

BEULAH
(*She smiles warmly.*)
All right. I'll try again. We'll find a plan. Too much is at stake to let us fail.

BEULAH closes her eyes and enters a trance. Everyone else in the room seems to enter it too. Even COLONEL WARD seems to be imploring the Fates with real fervor. Several moments pass before BEULAH opens her eyes. Everyone looks at her hopefully but she does not appear to have gotten her response.

>   BEULAH
> Let us wait a few moments. I feel as though
> our answer is about to come.

At that exact moment there is a knock at the door. STRYKER goes to answer it. BEULAH turns off the tape recorder.

>   STRYKER
> Who's there?

>   BEULAH
> Providence!

STRYKER opens the door. His face freezes in sudden shock. WENDY'S eyes widen.

>   WENDY
> PETER!

PETER is standing there in the doorway. Behind him is an army of KGB AGENTS, armed with submachine guns. They barge into the room. Everyone jumps to their feet. JOEY tenses, preparing to attack. BEULAH holds him back.

>   BEULAH
> NO! Not now.

INT. – LOCKED ROOM – NIGHT.

THE GROUP is imprisoned in a large dark room. They are surrounded by SOLDIERS with heavy artillery. Suddenly a door opens and KGB Chief KARMALEV enters. He stares at the group with his one good eye and then greets them.

KARMALEV
Good evening. I am Yuri Karmalev. I
apologize for your rude treatment but it
was important that we secure your safety as
quickly as possible.

The GROUP MEMBERS are shocked, eyeing each other and KARMALEV with amazement.

KARMALEV
We are not your jailers. We are your friends,
united by a common enemy.

BEULAH
Vladimir Ablogin.

KARMALEV
We need your help. We have no weapons left
to fight him. You are our only hope.

He stares at BEULAH imploringly. BEULAH fixes her gaze on him. She seems to be penetrating his very soul. After a moment she nods her head in agreement and smiles. KARMALEV'S face blossoms with relief.

KARMALEV
My people are ready. We have a special
forces team waiting to invade. But we must
move quickly. Tomorrow morning we will
strike.

BEULAH
And we will be with you. But one thing, and
this you must swear – you must not kill him.

KARMALEV looks at BEULAH curiously, but knows he is in no position to argue. He nods his head.

KARMALEV
Done.

INT. – WASHINGTON D.C, HOSPITAL – DAY.

A HUGE PRESS CORPS is assembled in a makeshift auditorium in St. Luke's Memorial Hospital. An OFFICIAL steps up to the podium.

> OFFICIAL
> Ladies and gentlemen, can I have your attention please. The Vice President of the United States.

Looking weary, the VICE PRESIDENT stares quietly into the television cameras as REPORTERS yell random questions. He holds up his hands and everyone grows silent.

> VICE PRESIDENT
> The President is not doing well. I know this is unorthodox, but I have come here to ask for your love and prayers. Medical science has done all it can. We must all pray for a miracle.

He closes his eyes. The room is hushed.

INT. – KREMLIN – DAY.

BEULAH and her GROUP are in a Kremlin corridor. As the camera tracks in we see they are dressed as heroes of the Soviet State, wearing drab clothes decorated with bright ribbons and medals. KARMALEV is with them and appears to be leading a tour, stopping to point out artwork and fixtures. The GROUP pretends to be interested as he rattles off facts and historical data in Russian.

EXT. – MOSCOW STREET – DAY.

A convoy of military trucks is rolling down a street outside the Kremlin walls. It is a stop-and-go movement.

INT. – MILITARY TRUCK – DAY.

Forty SOLDIERS are packed inside a canvas covered truck. As it stops several SOLDIERS remove a circular lid from the floor and begin to slide into the hole beneath it. In seconds all forty MEN are gone.

The truck rolls forward, revealing a large steam duct grate in the middle of the street. Another truck rolls over it and stops.

INT. – KREMLIN – DAY.

KARMALEV and his group of Soviet HEROES approach the elevators that lead to ABLOGIN'S power center. Many GUARDS surround the elevators. They salute when KARMALEV appears. KARMALEV addresses them in Russian but is disturbed to find that they will not let his group pass.

KARMALEV argues with the GUARDS but to no avail. BEULAH steps forward and speaks in her native tongue. The GUARDS are obstinate but eventually step aside. The elevator door opens and they get on.

INT. – ELEVATOR – DAY.

PETER, frightened of elevators, closes his eyes. WENDY holds his hand as the elevator descends into the earth. Gradually it comes to a stop and the doors open. WENDY takes one look and shrieks. A mass of ABLOGIN'S helmeted SOLDIERS is waiting for them.

> PETER
> Oops, wrong floor. (*He reaches for the buttons.*) Going up?

The doors begin to close. Several helmeted SOLDIERS glare at the closing doors. Beams of energy melt them into a puddle of molten metal. KARMALEV watches, terror-stricken.

INT. – KREMLIN BASEMENT – DAY.

The SOLDIERS lead the GROUP from the elevator and begin marching them down the twisting corridors that lead to ABLOGIN'S inner sanctum. BEULAH holds onto JOEY to restrain him.

          BEULAH
Don't do anything to provoke them. We must get to Ablogin.

          STRYKER
Don't worry about me. I'm not gonna do nothin'.

WENDY grabs hold of PETER.

          WENDY
I should have stayed in school. I've got finals next week.

          PETER
Just stay close to me.

          KARMALEV
       (*Whispering to Beulah.*)
Be ready.

Suddenly steam grates fly off the walls on both sides of the corridors leading to ABLOGIN. The helmeted SOLDIERS are startled as waves of KARMALEV'S MEN drop into their midst with machine guns firing.

          KARMALEV
       (*Grabbing Beulah.*)
DOWN!

BEULAH and the GROUP fall to the floor and begin crawling back toward the elevator.

The attack takes ABLOGIN'S MEN by surprise and many are killed in the first seconds. But the tide turns quickly. The helmeted SOLDIERS turn on KARMALEV'S MEN, using the helmets' power to literally liquidate their adversaries. Bodies crumble. Some explode. The fighting is fierce.

BEULAH shoves her group back into the elevator. PETER looks out on the carnage, appalled by what he sees. A SOLDIER explodes just feet away. PETER backs into a corner of the elevator and closes his eyes. BEULAH looks at his withdrawal with sudden concern.

RETURN TO the battle. Suddenly WENDY sees a disembodied arm floating heroically through the air. She cheers. BEULAH jumps up. JOEY yells. The arm rushes at ABLOGIN'S MEN and begins punching them in the face. The blows seem to hurt PETER more than the MEN who are simply stunned to see a hand flying at them from out of nowhere.

Suddenly PETER reaches for one MAN'S helmet and yanks it from his head. The MAN nearly crumbles without its power and KARMALEV'S MEN blow him away. PETER grins and begins flying from MAN to MAN ripping off their helmets. JOEY'S eyes widen with excitement. He focuses his energies onto the battlefield and suddenly helmets are flying all over the place. ABLOGIN'S MEN begin to falter.

The doors leading to ABLOGIN'S control room slide open and hordes of helmeted REINFORCEMENTS surge into the fray. The battle intensifies.

Occasional de-helmeted MEN fall into the elevator. STRYKER uses kung fu footwork to knock them back into the fighting arena. WENDY acknowledges his prowess. He nods back like it's no big thing. KARMALEV cowers in the corner awaiting the outcome.

JOEY has turned helmets into missiles and they fly across the room like radar guided rockets. He plays with them like so many blips on a fast paced video game. He is having a great time.

ABLOGIN'S MEN weaken. Without their helmets they are pitifully vulnerable. KARMALEV'S MEN begin to prevail with nothing but their conventional weapons to carry them to victory. Within minutes they are triumphant.

ABLOGIN'S MEN are taken prisoner and herded into captured elevators where more of KARMALEV'S MEN are waiting to take them away.

INT. – CONTROL ROOM – DAY.

ABLOGIN is sitting in the central chair of his massive room. The hundreds of video monitors are on, each filled with the helmeted representative of his worldwide network. Beams of psychic energy bind them to ABLOGIN. All of a sudden the full intensity of their collective power sends a massive beam penetrating through the ceiling. The beam splinters into many parts, each ray scanning rapidly through the whole of ABLOGIN'S underground sanctuary.

Large formations of KARMALEV'S MEN are pressing toward the control room as the beams appear. MEN scream and collapse as the rays pass through their bodies. Many of them explode with terrifying force. Within seconds much of KARMALEV'S army is decimated. Only those huddling in the elevator near BEULAH seem somehow protected.

Suddenly PETER'S ASTRAL FORM flies over the dying MEN. He dodges the beams like a warplane dodging searchlights and flack and zeroes in on ABLOGIN'S control room.

ABLOGIN is aware of PETER'S arrival but cannot pull his gaze away from his network. The beam from his forehead continues to energize all the others.

PETER invades the inner workings of ABLOGIN'S complex machinery. Heroically he begins pulling at the wiring and dislodging the circuitry. The result is immediate. Monitors begin to flash and explode.

ABLOGIN feeds all of his strength into his psychic network. The beam from his forehead throbs with power. Suddenly the random rays begin to reassemble, converging with the full force of a single beam on PETER'S astral body. The impact seems devastating to PETER, his whole body contorting under the magnitude of the pain. And yet he endures it, refusing to give up.

FOCUS ON ABLOGIN'S face sweating with anger.

> ABLOGIN
> DESTROY HIS BODY!

INT. – KREMLIN BASEMENT – DAY.

The beam breaks again into many parts searching the sanctuary. In seconds they are closing in on PETER'S body, cradled in BEULAH'S lap. They converge on it with a vengeance. WENDY screams as she sees them descending on the GROUP. BEULAH, in a deep trance, hovers over PETER. The beams attempt to enter her space but seem unable to do so. They crisscross in a broad arc around her and the others, but don't come close.

The beams, unable to find their quarry, move on, searching wildly. BEULAH emerges from her trance. WENDY turns to her.

> WENDY
> They stay away from you. Why?

> BEULAH
> (*Beginning to understand.*)
> Vladimir cannot see me.

> WENDY
> Vladimir? (*Pause.*) Ablogin?

> BEULAH
> (*Nodding her head.*)
> I am a blind spot in the corner of his heart.
> He cannot see me. He sees only what he hates.

> WENDY
> (*Looking at Beulah
> with wide eyes.*)
> You knew him. (*Understanding.*) You were... lovers.

> BEULAH
> A long time ago. (*Pause.*) It is our protection now. Pray that it endures.

WENDY looks closely. There are tears in BEULAH'S eyes.

INT. – CONTROL ROOM – DAY.

PETER is wreaking havoc on ABLOGIN'S psychic network. The faces on the monitors try escaping from their helmets as the machinery fails. Their faces are contorting in terrible psychic pain. Soon the beam is fluctuating wildly, its energy dissipating.

INT. – KREMLIN BASEMENT – DAY.

KARMALEV and a small contingent of his MEN are cowering near BEULAH. They feel the beam weakening and begin to get up.

INT. – CONTROL ROOM – DAY.

ABLOGIN watches his global empire crumbling before him. Suddenly KARMALEV'S MEN burst into his control room, their guns drawn. BEULAH rushes after them, yelling.

              BEULAH
STOP!

But she is too late. Bullets rip into the walls and tear into ABLOGIN. Shards of computers and exploded monitors hurl like missiles in every direction. They slash into ABLOGIN, ripping through his body. And yet, mysteriously, he continues to stand, seemingly impervious to the all-out assault. It is an awesome and terrifying image, the figure of ABLOGIN, unwilling to die, standing in the center of his own holocaust.

Gradually ABLOGIN'S body begins to weaken as KARMALEV enters the room. BEULAH rushes toward his collapsing form as it sinks slowly to the floor. A look of victory shines in KARMALEV'S eyes as ABLOGIN'S eyes close.

BEULAH stares at KARMALEV, a sense of betrayal visible on her face. KARMALEV sees it and responds.

              KARMALEV
    I couldn't stop them.

Secrets of the Astral Plane   465

The GROUP gathers around their fallen enemy. BEULAH bends down and kneels beside ABLOGIN.

A close-up on Beulah's fingers as they reach for ABLOGIN'S hand, to clasp it in her own. The moment she takes hold of it a shattering laugh breaks out of ABLOGIN's mouth and his body disappears. BEULAH and the others back away stunned. All eyes turn to BEULAH for an explanation.

                BEULAH
      We have failed. We have attacked his astral
      form. (*She pauses.*) I have always perceived
      a vacuum in this place. His body has never
      been here.

INT. – PRISON CELL, SIBERIA – DAY.

ABLOGIN, a frail old man, is sitting in his cell. His eyes are wide open and motionless, as though watching the whole world in his mind. The camera tracks in to a tight close-up of his eyes.

INT. – KARMALEV'S OFFICE – DAY.

BEULAH'S GROUP sitting with KARMALEV. They listen intently.

              KARMALEV
      In 1953, Nikita Khrushchev brought
      Ablogin out of Siberian exile and established
      him here, in the depths of the Kremlin. I
      have never seen him leave this place. He has
      never been observed above ground. Ablogin
      was a secretive man. Few if any knew him.
      Yet he exerted a terrible influence on us all.

                BEULAH
      It was only his mind, materialized, that was
      housed in the Kremlin. His body is still
      in Siberia. I must tell you that he is more
      dangerous now than ever before, and we
      must find him if we are to prevail. (*She looks*

at *Karmalev*.) Do you know the camp he was in? Can you help us?

KARMALEV nods.

INT. – SOVIET JET – DAY.

A SOVIET TRANSPORT PLANE and a squadron of support fighters hurl above the Russian Steppes. BEULAH and the GROUP, dressed in Soviet military fatigues, are sitting inside. KARMALEV and a contingent of top KGB AGENTS are with them.

INT. – ABLOGIN'S CELL – DAY.

A shot of the jet reveals it flying in the center of ABLOGIN'S eyeball. The camera holds on ABLOGIN'S face. He looks angry and determined.

EXT. – SIBERIA – DAY.

THE GROUP is in a convoy of Soviet military vehicles riding at full speed along a barren road in the middle of nowhere.

>   DRIVER
>   (*Calling back*.)
>   There's nothing out there. There's no camp.
>   Nothing!

>   BEULAH
>   It's there. Keep going.

>   DRIVER
>   Well, either I'm blind or you see something
>   I don't see.

BEULAH nods.

>   STRYKER
>   (to BEULAH)
>   He's out there.

BEULAH
I know.

The convoy continues. The landscape is stark. The sky is vast and filled with clouds. Suddenly the lead vehicle stops. The DRIVER yells.

DRIVER
There's something there. I don't know. It looks like a bridge.

KARMALEV
A bridge? Out here?

DRIVER
My God! There's a huge gorge.

The DRIVER jumps out and others follow. They walk up to the edge of the gorge. It is large and deep. Then they stare up at the bridge that goes across it. It is old and rotting. Planks are dangling from the middle of it.

DRIVER
Well, that is the end of our journey. It would be impossible to cross it. We must turn back.

KARMALEV
(*Turning to Beulah.*)
What do we do?

BEULAH
We forge ahead.

DRIVER
Impossible.

BEULAH
Not impossible. There is no bridge. There is no gorge.

                    DRIVER
     What are you telling me? Do you think I'm
     crazy?

                    BEULAH
     It is an illusion. A protective barrier.

The DRIVER storms over to the edge of the gorge.

                    DRIVER
     This is an illusion? *(He gazes down into it.)*

                    BEULAH
     Yes.

                    DRIVER
     Well, you drive your own vehicle over it.
     I'm not going near it.

PETER steps forward.

                    PETER
     I can drive.

                    DRIVER
     These people are mad!

                    PETER
     Get in everyone.

                    DRIVER
     Not on your life.

                    KARMALEV
                 (To Beulah.)
     Why don't we let your young man test it for
     us? Then we can follow.

BEULAH shakes her head at everyone's lack of faith, and then gets in the vehicle with PETER. He starts the engine. The vehicle rolls forward.

                    BEULAH
          You don't need to go over the bridge. Just
          head straight for the gorge.

PETER follows BEULAH'S orders and drives full speed toward the precipice. KARMALEV and his MEN recoil. WENDY grabs JOEY. The vehicle hits the edge of the gorge. COLONEL WARD holds on. The vehicle, poised to plunge, sails over the gorge and keeps going. The illusion fades. The bridge and the gorge disappear. They are on flat land.

KARMALEV and the DRIVER stare in disbelief. WENDY and the GROUP cheer. SOLDIERS and KGB AGENTS watch in wonderment. PEOPLE jump back in their vehicles and the force moves on.

EXT. – FORTRESS – DAY.

A huge fortress looming on the horizon. Its sheer massiveness is staggering. PETER stops. BEULAH motions him onward. All eyes are glued on the gigantic structure rising out of nowhere. Some of the SOLDIERS tremble.

Suddenly the ground begins to heave around the vehicles. Huge boulders rise out of the earth and deep chasms drop suddenly before the approaching convoy. Although PETER knows that these are illusions it is still difficult driving. Sudden walls jut up in the center of the road. PETER instinctively brakes, the wheels screeching.

                    PETER
          Sorry.

He crashes through the illusion of the wall. The DRIVERS behind him do not share his courage. The convoy stops and SOLDIERS run from their vehicles.

The very earth appears to be quaking beneath them. The sky suddenly grows dark and ominous. Clouds rush toward the GROUP at terrifying speed. The SOLDIERS look up and see the clouds taking on demonic shapes that surge toward them.

Stars rise in the sky and explode and shatter in the heavens. Bolts of lightning crackle through the sky and attack them. SOLDIERS run in all directions, screaming.

KARMALEV falls to the ground, crying like a baby. The air begins to swirl in hundreds of tornado-like formations. KGB AGENTS hug the earth, clutching at it for dear life.

BEULAH screams at her scattering troops.

> BEULAH
> It is all an illusion. Don't accept it and it
> cannot harm you.

Her words fall on deaf ears as they all confront the first stirrings of universal catastrophe. No earthly form obeys its natural laws. The vision is shattering.

WENDY fights desperately to ignore the chaos threatening to overwhelm her, but her mind is not strong enough. A childlike whimper grows into a hysterical scream. PETER grabs her and pulls her to the ground. He seems nearly as frightened as she does. COLONEL WARD is lying on the ground, covering his head with his arms. STRYKER is pressed against the lead vehicle, awed by the display. JOEY, crying, is cradled in BEULAH'S arms.

The very molecules of the air seem to burst into flames and give way to visions of outer space. Meteors seem to shoot through the ground while asteroids collide beneath their feet. The image is totally disorienting. SOLDIERS seem to be falling into the vortex of space, although their bodies are not moving. Still they scream and writhe in terror. PETER sits up and begins to enter a trance. BEULAH sees him and yells.

> BEULAH
> WHAT THE HELL DO YOU THINK
> YOU'RE DOING? DON'T LEAVE
> YOUR BODY! USE IT!

BEULAH'S words spur PETER into action. He runs through a minefield of exploding rocks, grabs STRYKER, and drags him back to WENDY.

                    PETER
            WATCH HER FOR ME!

Summoning all his courage, PETER rises to face the Armageddon. Moving steadfastly, he heads into the center of the maelstrom. Wild forms shoot out at him, evil SPIRITS and alluring WOMEN, attempting to frighten and entrance him.

                    PETER
            Yea, though I walk through the valley of the
            shadow...

He fights to keep walking. Suddenly his bedroom forms around him, complete with WHISKERS. The image is surprising and disorienting but he doesn't stop to think about it. He keeps walking.

Out of nowhere a group of Namibian TRIBESMEN surge around PETER. The TRIBAL CHIEF throws himself at PETER'S feet.

                    CHIEF
            Stop! Stay with us! Go no further!

PETER keeps walking.

Suddenly an ABC elevator shaft materializes before him, looming straight down. PETER stops. The image is dizzying and terrifying to PETER. After a moment he takes a deep breath and steps into the abyss. It vanishes. He sighs and keeps walking.

PETER looks up. Before him appears a hurricane of energy spinning wildly. All the illusions appear to be spinning from it. PETER gazes into the center of the storm and sees, for an instant, an open cell door, and ABLOGIN, the great conjuror, sitting in the middle of it. ABLOGIN sees PETER and a look of panic flashes across his face. The hurricane intensifies but the illusions grow increasingly pathetic.

A huge BEAR rises on its hind legs as PETER approaches. Suddenly it dissolves, revealing a frightened ABLOGIN sitting on the floor. A bengal TIGER roars and growls but PETER is not afraid.

He grows stronger and more assured with every step.

BEULAH and the GROUP. The illusions are subsiding. The walls of the fortress have disappeared and are replaced by a prison camp fence. The ground has settled. The sky has grown quiet. COLONEL WARD gets up and moves toward BEULAH. He helps her up. STRYKER assists him and, together, they support her and head toward the camp. KARMALEV, still shaking, follows behind them. WENDY takes JOEY by the hand and they join the procession.

PETER approaches ABLOGIN'S cell. The illusions have ceased. PETER has penetrated ABLOGIN'S defenses and stands outside his door. Slowly the GROUP gathers behind him.

Cautiously PETER enters ABLOGIN'S cell and stops dead still. He is stunned to see his MOTHER sitting inside. She is huddling in a corner and crying.

MILDRED
Please don't hurt me. Don't hurt me.

WENDY peers into the room and stares into the corner at a tiny baby lying naked, crying. A look of great compassion fills her face.

BEULAH enters the dark cell and sees ABLOGIN, not as he is, but as he was, forty years before. Tears form in her eyes.

BEULAH
Vladimir. Vladimir.

Suddenly ABLOGIN looks up. He blinks and stares as BEULAH approaches.

BEULAH
(*Crying.*)
It's me.

Unexpectedly we see her not as she is, but as she was, a lovely blonde girl, his assistant, leaving him in a dressing room, forty years before. ABLOGIN'S eyes widen.

For an instant ABLOGIN is totally disarmed. There is a moment of tender silence and then a shot explodes in the darkness.

                      BEULAH
NO!

KARMALEV is holding a smoking gun. ALBOGIN'S eyes reach out to BEULAH and then he falls. BEULAH rushes to his side and takes his hand. It holds on to hers tightly. He looks up at her, her face still young, her hair still blonde, and stares with longing and disbelief. They gaze at one another for a long time and then his eyes close. Tears stream down BEULAH'S face.

                      JOEY
    They killed him.

                      BEULAH
    (*Caressing Ablogin's brow.*)
Now he is free.

BEULAH bends down and kisses ABLOGIN'S pale lips as the others look on.

There is a long, deep silence.

EXT. – PENNSYLVANIA AVENUE – DAY.

A DRUMROLL SOUNDS as a Fourth of July parade winds its way down Pennsylvania Avenue in front of the White House. The GROUP, sitting next to a recovered PRESIDENT, is watching from the reviewing stand.

PETER, WENDY and JOEY are sitting together like one happy family. STRYKER is in his element, greeting important SENATORS and CONGRESSMEN. COLONEL WARD is beaming. A great shiny medal is pinned to his uniform. He reaches out and takes BEULAH'S hand. BEULAH looks happy and content, like a mother hen watching over her brood.

A squadron of jets fly in close formation overhead. A sea of American flags flutter as a marching band blares "The Stars and Stripes Forever."

PETER sits joyfully as he watches the bands pass. He closes his eyes and his astral body soars into the air, flying like a free spirit over the parade. WENDY, not realizing that PETER is gone, nudges him to look at a float. With no one inside, his body collapses onto the reviewing stand. Embarrassed, WENDY stoops over and quickly resurrects him. JOEY holds PETER as WENDY scans the sky looking for him. Suddenly, out of the blue, PETER swoops down and sits on the railing in front of WENDY.

>   PETER
>   Watch this!

He flies to the roof of the reviewing stand and perches on the edge. Then, with great dramatic flair, he executes a perfect triple-twisting double somersault dive – straight into his body, which jumps up instantly and takes a bow. It is a remarkable feat. WENDY laughs and hugs him warmly. JOEY wraps his arms around them both.

BEULAH, smiling, her face full of joy.

Drums beat, cannons roar, and the parade marches on.